Beyond Capital and Labor

Originally published in 1995, *Beyond Capital Labor* is a comprehensive empirical study about how and how much technology and regional contextual factors may influence company production and productivity growth. The book constitutes a conceptually consistent and empirically efficient study and provides a consolidated model and an analytical framework to examine the contributions of technology and regional factors to company production and productivity growth. This work goes beyond the current state and brings many scattered theoretical components together to establish an integrated model.

T0382771

Beyond Capital and Labor

The Contributions of Technology and Regional
Milieu to Production and Productivity Growth

Shanzi Ke

Routledge
Taylor & Francis Group

First published in 1995
by Garland Publishing, Inc.

This edition first published in 2018 by Routledge
2 Park Square, Milton Park, Abingdon, Oxon, OX14 4RN
and by Routledge
711 Third Avenue, New York, NY 10017

Routledge is an imprint of the Taylor & Francis Group, an informa business

© 1995 Shanzi Ke

Publisher's Note
The publisher has gone to great lengths to ensure the quality of this reprint but points out that some imperfections in the original copies may be apparent.

Disclaimer
The publisher has made every effort to trace copyright holders and welcomes correspondence from those they have been unable to contact.

A Library of Congress record exists under LCCN: 94043143

ISBN 13: 978-1-138-38504-7 (hbk)
ISBN 13: 978-0-429-42734-3 (ebk)
ISBN 13: 978-1-138-38508-5 (pbk)

BEYOND CAPITAL AND LABOR

THE CONTRIBUTIONS OF TECHNOLOGY
AND REGIONAL MILIEU TO PRODUCTION
AND PRODUCTIVITY GROWTH

SHANZI KE

GARLAND PUBLISHING, INC.
NEW YORK & LONDON / 1995

Library of Congress Cataloging-in-Publication Data

Ke, Shanzi, 1951–
    Beyond capital and labor : the contributions of technology and
regional milieu to production and productivity growth / Shanzi Ke.
        p.   cm. — (Garland studies on industrial productivity)
    Includes bibliographical references and index.
    ISBN 0-8153-1965-7 (alk. paper)
    1. Industrial productivity—United States.   2. Technological innova-
tions—Economic aspects—United States.   3. Industrial efficiency—
United States.   4. Industrial location—United States.   I. Title.
II. Series.
HC110.I52K4   1995
338'.064'0973—dc20   94-43143
                                                            CIP

Printed on acid-free, 250-year-life paper
Manufactured in the United States of America

CONTENTS

v

TABLES

ix

PREFACE

Production and productivity growth concerns most social scientists and practitioners. Collectively, economists, geographers, and many other individuals have made a significant effort to uncover the mechanism of production and productivity growth and the sources of the growth. Their works have resulted in a large volume of literature.

Even a casual review of these studies, however, can tell a reader how much this field is disorganized. Economists emphasize the contribution of technology to production and productivity growth and traditionally ignore spatial aspect of economic growth. Geographers, on the other hand, focus on regional variation of economic activities and normally do not bother to understand the endogenous relationships between relevant variables and the structural forms of the relationships. Many important components in different academic fields do not contradict each other, but, unfortunately, they are not connected to each other either.

My intention in this book is to develop a consolidated model and an analytical framework to examine the contributions of technology and regional factors to company production and productivity growth. Like most academic studies, this work is built upon well established theories and earlier studies. Yet this book shows how we can go beyond the current state when we bring many scattered theoretical components together and establish an integrated model. With the analytical framework, we can place similar studies in perspective and assess the completeness of the studies.

This book also presents a comprehensive empirical study about how and how much technology and regional contextual factors may influence company production and productivity growth. The readers of the book can easily recognize that several seemingly independent parts of the investigation constitute a conceptually consistent and empirically efficient study.

This book evolved from my Ph.D. dissertation. I am afraid that acknowledgements will fail to do justice to the many individuals who gave me help in my years of work on this study. Especially, I wish to thank my dissertation committee members, Edward Bergman, Michael Luger, Harvey Goldstein, Emil Malizia, and John Rees for their advice. I am indebted to my fellow Ph.D. students at UNC Chapel Hill for their critical assistance to my survey. In particular, I would like to thank Daoshan Sun, Lihua Geng, Mei Zhou, Wei Qin, Xuguang Guo, and Zhongqiang Liu. Without their generous help, I never could have completed the large-scale nationwide mail survey in a timely fashion. I would express my special thanks to Rex Clay who read my manuscript and made numerous corrections. Finally, I am extremely grateful to my wife Yunhui Hu and my son Yue Ke for their support and patience. I could not even think about any accomplishment without the support of my wife who shared the burden of the survey with me and supported our family while I was working on this study.

Shanzi Ke

September 1994
Charlotte, North Carolina

Beyond Capital
and Labor

1 Introduction

Technology is frequently reported as a driving force in production growth and as the exclusive contributor to productivity growth at the national aggregate level. Technological progress in a broad sense accounts for about two fifths of national economic growth (Solow 1957, Denison 1962, 1985) and 30-70% of total output growth at the census region and state levels (Hulten and Schwab 1984). It is not surprising that academic and professional researchers, industrial and regional developers, and policy makers are all increasingly interested in technology-based growth.

However, history has witnessed an industrial, especially high-tech industrial, location pattern: technology-driven industrial growth occurs only in certain selected places. This indicates that regional influence on technological progress, technological adoption, and production growth is enormous. There are two fundamental questions, which may interest both theorists and practitioners.

First, how can technological progress and technology-related inputs affect production and productivity growth, and by how much? Although economic agents are individual producers, theoretical and empirical work on technology and growth is dominated by macroeconomic analysis. There is very little, if any, empirical knowledge of how technology affects production and productivity growth of individual producers in different industries.

The ability for a company to employ existing technology and make still another technological progress is determined by technology-oriented inputs, including investment in research and development (R & D) and newer production machinery, inputs of scientific, technical, and professional personnel, and expenditure on training programs. Earlier empirical research (e.g., Griliches 1980, 1984, 1986, Bernsten 1989) shows a positive influence of R & D input on firms' production growth, but the impact on production and productivity growth of many other types of technological inputs has not been systematically investigated. Moreover, industrial variation of the impact has not yet been well examined. We have been ignorant of the extent to which technological efforts have been effective in promoting production and productivity growth of different types of producers.

Second, in seeking a technology-based growth policy or strategy for a particular area, one must answer another fundamental question: to what extent can regional factors contribute to production and productivity growth directly and indirectly? Besides common speculation and a small group of survey studies, no credible answers are readily available.

Regional factors, including regional endowment, economic structure, and regional overhead inputs, contribute to production and productivity growth of individual companies, although regional factors are exogenous to individual producers. Regional factors may influence production and productivity in three different manners as discussed below.

Regional factors such as technological externalities and proximity to market are free or quasi-free goods to a producer as long as the producer is not a dominating force that can alter its regional environment. These locational ingredients can directly contribute to a higher level of production and productivity without imposing internal cost on individual producers. However, it is difficult to examine the relationship between free goods and other inputs and output in traditional production theory.

Regional producer services such as transportation, communication, and maintenance and repair services affect the cost of production. External provision and internal establishment of these services can substitute for each other. External provision usually is more efficient to most small and medial sized producers because of the economies of scale the specialized service firms provide. Adequate regional service sectors are necessary, if not sufficient, condition for production and productivity growth of many companies at a lower producer cost.

Moreover, external conditions, such as improvement of social economic environment and policy incentives, catalyze the process of internal technology-related investment. An economically rationalizing (e.g., profit-maximizing or cost-minimizing) firm must take full advantage of external economies, avoid the disadvantage of external diseconomies incurred by a locality, and adjust all its inputs accordingly. All producer inputs are endogenous variables affected by producer optimization behavior *and* regional factors. It is generally believed that only the developed areas can provide better communication, accessibility to markets, various producer services, a diverse labor pool, and policy incentives. From both theoretical and practical standpoints, it is important to accumulate the knowledge on the contribution of regional contextual factors to production and productivity growth.

This book develops a theoretical framework and a set of operational equations. The framework conceptualizes the interlocked relationships among technological progress, producer technological inputs, regional factors, and production and productivity growth, while the equations specify the functional forms of the relationships. This book further presents a comprehensive empirical study to estimate the contributions of technological progress, technology-related producer inputs, and regional factors to production and productivity growth.

Technological progress consists of many components in different forms, e.g., related to capital goods, labor, production organization, or social environment; embodied and disembodied with respect to physical inputs; exogenous or endogenous to producers. There has not been a universally accepted definition of technological progress. In the literature (e.g., Heertje 1977), a distinction is made between a narrow definition and a broad definition. A narrow definition considers only an invention or an innovation as a technological progress, while a broad definition also takes diffusion of existing knowledge and technique into account. From an economic point of view, technological progress makes sense only if it results in efficiency in economic activities and improvement of the well-being of a society. In this respect, a broad definition is more appropriate. Technological progress in this book is defined as improvements upon quality and uses of factor inputs, organization of production, and general environment, regardless of whether the improvements are due to invention/innovation or adoption of existing knowledge. Innovation or adoption of new technology will inevitably incur costs. An input aimed directly at technological progress is defined as a technological input.

Regional factors in this text are referred to as variables which may be relevant to production, but external to individual producers. Conventionally, a region is considered as a geographical area, like a census region, consisting of many counties and even several states.

However, regional variables in economic research should be measured at such a level that a social economic force can be treated as a constant within the area, but may vary across areas. Thus, a region is a spatial functional economic unit consistent with a local labor market. The study presented in this book measures regional variables at the standard metropolitan area level and at the county level for non metro areas.

It is hard to imagine that any serious study on production and productivity growth could not absorb many elements developed in earlier works. In particular, production theory, aggregate economic growth model, regional science, and economic geography provide an important background for this study.

Theoretical development and empirical verification of economic growth, including the impact of technological progress on the growth, attracted many economists' attention in the 1950s and 1960s. Major progress was made in explaining the contribution of factor inputs, particularly capital and labor, to long-term national economic growth along a steady-state path. The contribution of technological progress was traditionally treated as a residual after the effects on economic growth of capital and labor had been counted (Solow 1956, 1957, 1960, 1962, Nelson and Phelps 1966, Jorgenson 1967, Denison 1966, etc.).

In the 1970s and 1980s, the major motivation to study economic growth was to search for the causes of 'slowdowns' in U.S. productivity growth. Refinements were made to identify and quantify the contributions of major components of technological progress to economic growth at the aggregate level (Hulten 1975, 1989, Jorgenson 1986, 1989, etc.). Empirical research (Denison 1985, Griliches 1986) provided evidence of a positive relationship between technological inputs / technological progress and productivity growth. Technological inputs and progress were considered to include input in R & D, improvement in education, better allocation of resources, and economies of scale, in addition to technology embodied in capital goods. As Solow stressed when he received the Nobel Prize, 'the permanent rate of growth of output per unit of labor input depends entirely on the rate of technological progress in the broadest sense' (Solow 1988). However, technological progress was not treated as the result of an intentional economic behavior. It was also considered that a higher level of conventional inputs, capital and labor, had no effect on the growth rate of productivity in the long term. In this neoclassic tradition, the only driving force of growth is the exogenously determined technological change, largely a by-product of economic activities.

Nelson (1964) developed a somewhat different growth model stressing the importance of complementarity between embodied technological progress and conventional factor inputs. In his model, technological progress is no longer merely considered as a by-product of routine economic activities. Instead, it is both a driving force of growth and a result of intentional investment. Increased educational attainment of employees pushes technological progress and the technological progress in turn leads to higher return to education, thereby inducing more educational input. Similarly, an installation of new equipment amounts to an embodied technological progress and an efficiency gain in production. The technological progress and productivity gain in turn stimulate the next run of new capital investment. The effect of the interaction of embodied technological progress and physical capital and labor inputs on economic growth is considered well beyond the growth of the individual producer's production because new capital and labor inputs are the major means to reallocate the resources in the whole economy. The interaction of technological progress and higher return to the inputs results in a relative movement of resources toward more efficient use of the factor inputs and, hence, a higher productivity for the whole economy.

Nevertheless, not until the mid-1980s did the complementarity between technological progress and conventional inputs and the relationship between endogenous progress of technology and growth of production become a major interest of many growth theorists, giving rise to a new branch of economic growth literature. In principle, the new literature is in line with Nelson's notion of the interaction of embodied technological progress and conventional inputs. The new growth theory emphasizes the internal motives of economic agents in the growth process and assigns a critical role to knowledge and human capital. The new literature also encompasses many more aspects of economic growth and a much larger scope of research in conception and modeling. The investment in human capital is regarded as dependent on individuals' inter-generational utility allocation, which is in turn based on the micro mechanism of optimization behavior (Rosenzweig 1990). Human capital resources are carefully allocated to produce knowledge/ technology. Together, the human capital, technology, and technology induced capital promote production growth. Unlike the neoclassic growth theory, the endogenous growth theory contends that both growth level and growth rate are directly influenced by initial endowment of human capital (Becker et al. 1990, Romer 1990). Externalities of technology can lead to an investment level lower than the social optimum level. Therefore, government intervention is essential to secure growth (Barro 1990). Since the endogenous growth theory is relatively new and less integrated, most studies are purely theoretical, and consistent empirical evidence has not yet appeared.

In spite of the achievement in theoretical and empirical works, with few exceptions (Griliches 1984, 1986, for instance), a variety of growth models, including endogenous growth models, are developed only in a macroeconomic context to explain the 'stylized facts' of the historical growth rates of output level and capital and labor input levels in the U.S. economy. It is obvious that the aggregate growth models are not designed for investigating companies' production and productivity growth because (1) inputs under the same title at the national economy level are very heterogenous, and many inputs--firm's R & D input, investments in upgrading equipment and human capital, and investment in management--considered important at a micro level never show up in the growth models; (2) regional variables external yet relevant to producers are irrelevant to an aggregate economy and not included in any growth model; (3) input substitutability at the producer level can be much lower than at the macro level, and the contribution each input makes to production and productivity growth of companies is less well known; and (4) a production function, which represents an input-output relationship for an aggregate economy, can cover a significant difference between different types of production. Thus, it seems necessary to develop a new analytical framework to examine the contributions of technology and regional factors to production and productivity growth.

Geographers have studied industrial growth and its spatial variations for more than a century. Unlike economists, geographers are more interested in the relationship between the regional environment and industrial location and the subsequent spatial diffusion than in the endogenous relationship between producer input and output. A century-old location theory(Thünen 1826, Weber 1909, and Lösch 1940[1]) and the later developed growth pole theory (Perroux 1950, 1955), as well as the product life cycle model (Vernon 1966), are the most important theoretical frames in geography to analyze and interpret the behavior of production location and growth in response to the regional business environment. According to location theory, transportation cost, labor cost, and agglomeration economy are the major factors affecting producers' locational decisions. The relative importance of each factor varies as the product market or the production technology changes. Development and application of growth pole theory and product life cycle theory reflect further appreciation of the interactive relationship between technological progress and the spatial location of production and regional growth. Both theories underscore spatially imbalanced economic growth resulting from growth in impulse or innovative industries. It is generally agreed that only those particular areas with sufficient entrepreneurial activities, technological externalities, and producer services may become growth centers. Furthermore, both growth pole theory and product life cycle theory agree that growth will diffuse to hinterland areas only when input-output links reach the sectors that are much less demanding for technological inputs or when production becomes standardized with no strong need for adjustment in production technology.

Empirical research has been conducted to classify locational patterns of technologically advanced industries and to identify the most important area-specific factors influencing innovative activities, technological adoptability, and regional growth. Although conclusions are far from consistency and unambiguity, earlier research findings often point out that high-tech industrial growth does not necessarily occur in the nation's largest metro areas. Earlier studies also indicate that no single locational variable can explain a significant part of the variations in high-tech industrial location and growth (Glasmeier et al. 1983, Rees 1986, Appold 1991). In some instances, researchers conclude that producers in earlier developed industrial areas tend to have a higher technological adoptability (e.g., Rees 1986) and that government programs are largely responsible for the current economic landscape of high-tech industrial location and growth (Markusen 1986, Scott et al. 1991).

Research techniques employed by geographers are often more intuitive than those used by economists. Besides case studies and descriptive analysis, a majority of empirical research in geography usually relates production location and growth to a set of regional contextual variables. Relying on the location theory, this type of linear model is flexible in examining area-specific variables. On the other hand, this type of model is unable to draw a complete picture of the interwined relationships between regional variables, factor productivity, factor inputs, and production and productivity growth because of the lack of a well specified structural form. Furthermore, without an explicit structural form, the functional form used to examine the relationships is usually inappropriate. As a result, estimates may be biased and real relationships between producer input/output variables and regional variables may not be revealed.

Regional science may be viewed as an interdisciplinary area[2] between economics, economic geography, and other disciplines with spatial interest. Regional scientists are concerned with endogenous relationship between economic variables within an economic functional unit and their spatial variations. Earlier research in this field usually follows the tradition of neoclassical economics, seeing capital and labor as the fundamental inputs of production and the primary contributors to production growth. In addition, regional variables are incorporated either as direct or as indirect inputs to production and growth. In Moomaw's work (1986, 1987), for instance, urbanization and localization enter production function as direct inputs of production, while in Sveikauskas' research (1975) population size of city is treated as a determinant of the neutral technical progress in a constant elasticity of substitution (CES) production function. A greater number of studies (e.g., Williams 1985, Uno 1986, Sasaki 1986, and Luger and Evans 1988) examine regional impact in an indirect manner. Frequently the same functional form is applied to different areas separately to show the differences in coefficients of production functions, total factor productivity, and neutral technological progress across different areas (or cities or states). These differences are interpreted as different joint impacts of regional factors on production across areas. Some earlier works (Beeson 1987, Moomaw and Williams 1991) also incorporate mainstream economists' measures of productivity with geographers' approach to estimate the effect of regional factors on production and productivity growth directly.

Empirical research findings support the proposition that regional factors contribute to production and productivity growth, and this contribution and its regional variations need to be distinguished from those caused by changes in producer inputs. On the other hand, there is mixed evidence about the contribution of each specific regional factor and the way each factor affects production growth. More importantly, a systematic theoretical framework of regional production growth has yet to be developed.

This study is built upon, and goes beyond earlier works by consolidating the relevant theories and methods in economics, geography, and regional science. The next chapter discusses the theoretical foundation and establishes an analytical framework to examine the production and productivity growth and the sources. Based on the analytical framework, the later chapters investigate direct and indirect contributions of technology and regional factors to production and productivity growth from several different angles. Each of the later chapters develops a mathematical model and estimates the operational equations in conjunction with critical review of the earlier research works in this field.

Notes

1. These theorists (also including Perroux, as well as Vernon who is less well-known) considered themselves economists and their work does indeed have an economic spirit. However, their works are by and large ignored by mainstream economists, especially English language economists. It is economic geographers who have inherited, employed, and spread these theories.

2. There has not been a clear definition of regional science. According to leading journals in this field such as *Journal of Regional Science* and *Regional Science and Urban Economics*, this discipline may be characterized as economic analysis of spatial phenomena using relatively advanced techniques. A majority of authors in this field have academic training in economics. In addition, some are from other fields of social science, e.g., geography, environmental science, agricultural economics, and anthropology.

2 Theoretical Framework
-- A Vision Beyond Capital and Labor

This chapter develops a theoretical framework to investigate the contributions of technological progress, technology-related inputs and regional contextual factors to production and productivity growth. Production theory and growth theory form the underlying basis of the framework and operational models. In the process of developing the micro growth model, the concepts that are the most important to the current research are clarified and emphasized. The first section synthesizes various types of technological progress in production and develops a general production function and growth equation with manageable expressions of technological progress embodied in capital and labor. The second section introduces regional contextual factors into the production function and the growth equation in line with production theory and the accumulated evidence in regional science research. The third section discusses implications of the micro growth model. The fourth section justifies a production function approach as an appropriate means to further investigate the impact of regional factors and company attributes on production and to examine the nature of technological progress. The final section summarizes the relationships between different groups of variables and presents an analytical framework of the research.

2.1. PRODUCTION GROWTH WITH TECHNOLOGICAL PROGRESS

Assuming only capital and labor are relevant inputs and retaining generality, a production function at time t can take on the form of equation (2.1),

(2.1)
$$Q_t = A_t \, F(K_t, L_t) \; ,$$

where Q_t is the output, K_t and L_t are the capital and the labor respectively, and A_t is an efficiency parameter. Differentiating (2.1) with respect to time and dividing both sides of the total differentiation equation by output level, the production growth can be easily expressed as

(2.3)
$$\frac{dQ_t}{Q_t dt} = \frac{dA_t}{A_t dt} + \left(\frac{\partial Q_t}{\partial K_t} \frac{K_t}{Q_t} \right) \frac{dK_t}{K_t dt} + \left(\frac{\partial Q_t}{\partial L_t} \frac{L_t}{Q_t} \right) \frac{dL_t}{L_t dt},$$

or in a neater form

(2.2')
$$\dot{Q}_t = a + \beta_k \dot{K}_t + \beta_L \dot{L}_t \; .$$

Dotted Q_t, K_t, and L_t designate the growth rates of output and inputs respectively. The growth equation says that for the given output elasticities of the inputs, β_k and β_L, the growth rate of output is a linear function of the growth rates of inputs. The intercept, $dA_t/(A_t dt)$, measures the effect of technological progress on output growth, and the other two terms measure the contributions of capital growth and labor growth to the output growth respectively. A non-zero intercept implies that the level of output will be higher over time for the fixed factor inputs.

2.1.1. Disembodied Technological Progress

Growth literature makes a distinction between embodied and disembodied technological progress to identify the sources of production growth and reveal the way technological progress affects output growth. A technological progress is said to be disembodied if the technological progress equally influences all capital and labor, new and old, in production. A technological progress is considered as embodied if the technological progress only applies to a particular set of inputs, usually new capital or newly trained workers. Disembodied technological progress can be further classified as neutral or non-neutral. A disembodied technological progress is neutral if it does not cause bias in the direction of either capital-saving or labor-saving; otherwise, the technological progress is non-neutral, capital-saving or labor-saving.

There are three cases of neutral technological progress in growth literature: Hicks neutral, Solow neutral, and Harrod neutral. Hicks neutral technological progress is the most obvious case, which may best fit in equations (2.1) and (2.2). Efficiency parameter A_t grows at an annual rate of $dA_t/(A_t dt)$ over time, resulting in a growth in output for given inputs. Total growth in output is the sum of contributions due to technological progress and input growth.

The second case is Solow neutral technological progress, where capital is more and more productive over time. In that case, an appropriate production function is

(2.1')
$$Q_t = F(A_t K_t, L_t) ,$$

where A_t indicates the efficiency parameter. Since A_t grows at $dA_t/(A_t dt)$ and capital becomes more efficient, output grows over time for a given level of inputs. It is obvious that equation (2.1') and (2.1) have similarity nature with respect to the technological progress-output growth relation if equation (2.1') is used to derive a growth equation,

(2.3)
$$\frac{dQ_t}{Q_t dt} = \left(\frac{\partial Q_t}{\partial A_t K_t}\frac{A_t K_t}{Q_t}\right)\frac{dA_t}{A_t dt} + \left(\frac{\partial Q_t}{\partial A_t K_t}\frac{A_t K_t}{Q_t}\right)\frac{dK_t}{K_t dt} + \left(\frac{\partial Q_t}{\partial L_t}\frac{L_t}{Q_t}\right)\frac{dL_t}{L_t dt}$$

or

(2.3')
$$\dot{Q}_t = \beta_{\alpha k} a + \beta_{\alpha k} \dot{K}_t + \beta_L \dot{L}_t .$$

It is usually assumed and generally verified in empirical study that production at the macro level is characterized by constant return to scale. It follows that coefficients of factor inputs add up to unity and $\beta_{\alpha k}$ is the same as β_k (Branson 1980). Therefore, equation (2.3') is different from (2.2') only by $(1 - \beta_k)*a$. The same rate of technological progress will contribute to a smaller amount of output growth in Solow neutral case than in Hicks case, but the way in which output growth is affected is the same. Some macroeconomists argue that Solow neutral form is not an appropriate representation of technological progress for macro growth models since macro growth models require a constant capital-output ratio in long run steady state growth to fit historical records (Allen 1967).

The third case is Harrod neutral progress, which assigns labor a coefficient of technological progress. Workers are all considered to become more and more knowledgeable and efficient. Output can increase over time for a given capital and a fixed number of natural units of labor. The production function and growth function with Harrod neutral technological progress are essentially the same as Solow neutral case except efficiency parameter A_t is now attached to variable L_t and the intercept in growth equation now is $\beta_L \alpha$. Since labor share is usually two or three times as much as capital share, the same rate of technological advance, $dA_t/A_t dt$ or α, will lead to higher growth in output.

Disembodied technological progress can be non-neutral, implying capital-saving, a very rare case, or, more likely, labor-saving in response to scarcity or cost of factors. Harrod (1956) and Hicks (1967) provide somewhat different schemes to classify non-neutral technological change. According to Harrod, if capital-output ratio rises over time while profit rate remains constant, the technological progress is labor-saving; if capital-output ratio falls, capital-saving technological progress is present. Using Hicks' scheme, a technological change is defined as labor-saving if the marginal rate of technical substitution of capital for labor is decreasing when the capital-labor ratio and relative price ratio remain constant; a technological change is said to be capital-saving if the marginal rate of substitution is increasing while the capital-labor ratio and relative price ratio are constant. For both classifications, the underlying cause for the biased technological change is the difference between capital and labor in the improvement of efficiency. Regardless of initial cause, if a technological change results in an increase in the marginal product of capital relative to labor, the marginal rate of substitution of capital for labor tends to decrease at original capital-labor ratio, a labor-saving technological change in Hicks' sense; given the improved efficiency of capital, the producers would use more capital intensive technology without sacrificing profit rate, resulting in higher capital-output ratio, a labor-saving technological change in Harrod's definition.

It may be expected that high wage industries and regions tend to develop labor-saving technologies. This non-neutral technological progress can generate different outcomes, which theory alone may not be able to predict.

First, neoclassical theory traditionally suggests that in the long term income distribution tends to be equalized among industries and among workers due to market equilibrium mechanism and institutional forces, and the income distribution tends to be dependent more on naturally equally distributed factors such as human physical and mental abilities than on unequally distributed factors like production capital and other inherited wealth. Therefore, capital share of income is suggested to fall or, at least, not to rise in the long term. This proposition has long been supported by historical records of relatively stable income shares going to capital and labor. However, labor-saving technologies can logically raise the capital share of total income. Consequently, the capital share of income in better paid industries and in better developed areas should be larger than average. This conceptually contradicts the well known inverse U curve relationship between equality of income distribution and economic development (Kuznets 1955).

Second, labor-saving technology can result in higher marginal product of labor. This may in turn lead workers to command a higher wage rate, thus giving producers an incentive to further develop labor-saving technology. The process, once put in motion, seems to be an endless circle. We could expect to see a secular progress in labor-saving technology and constant increases in capital-labor ratio and capital-output ratio if the argument is reasonable. Since these reasoning embodies a conflict within neoclassical theory, relevant hypothesis tests are more important than pure theoretical argument in revealing the nature of technological progress.

In general, modeling disembodied technological progress is straightforward. Most early studies take this approach in modeling production and productivity growth with technological progress. However, disembodied technological progress at best can only capture a part of the joint influence of a variety of technological progress on production in a vague fashion. Even if the notion of disembodied technology is useful, further break-down of disembodied technology and investigation are required to find precisely which factors are responsible for a higher level of output for given capital and labor. Most of these factors may reside outside production units and will be discussed later. If we take a close look at those cases of disembodied technological progress, some of them may not be very interesting. Particularly, both Solow neutral and Harrod neutral cases are not very relevant in developing micro growth models. Constant or near constant technological progress, $dA_i/A_i dt$ in the two cases, may be justified in a macro economic context but are very unlikely to be the case for any single producer. Once equipment is installed and workers are hired, the production technology represented by the set of factor inputs stays fairly constant. Any technological progress related to capital or labor must occur in spurt when some new investment or new hiring is undertaken. Technological progress should be represented only by these new capital goods and newly hired or trained employees. This situation is better expressed using the models of embodied technological change.

2.1.2. Embodied Technological Progress

As opposed to disembodied technological progress, the notion of embodied technological progress treats capital and labor as heterogeneous inputs and treats technological advance as a relevant concept only to new capital and labor. The 'embodiment' treatment can provide a better explanation of historical growth records (Solow 1960). The treatment can also conceptually organize early omitted factors in to an integrated theory.

An appropriate measure of embodied technology is crucial in developing a growth model. Growth literature repeatedly addresses the average age of capital as the most important proxy of embodied technology in capital. Newly designed machines are assumed to incorporate the latest technology available. This technology is theoretically available for the whole economy, but many economic agents do not really use it for various reasons. The most obvious reason is that they cannot easily discard machines already installed. Technology in practice is often not theoretically the best. Average age, thus, can be used as a measure of gap between the technology theoretically best available and the technology practically used.

Depending on different assumptions and the different ways to formulate the embodied technological progress, an average age of capital can enter a growth model with different theoretical significance. Earlier studies developed several models incorporating embodied technological progress (Jorgenson 1959, Solow 1960, and Nelson 1964) and tested the models empirically using national aggregate data. Heterogenous vintages of capital stocks and corresponding labor crews present a real challenge in both theoretical and empirical research. Earlier research suggests several measures of technological efficiency of different capital vintage (Solow 1962, Nelson 1964, Hulten and Wykoff 1984, Jorgenson 1989). All these measures essentially have the same flavor. It is assumed that technological progress is a steady process and only new capital goods incorporate up-to-date technology. Capital installed at different times have different technical specification with respect to complemental input such as labor. Therefore, each vintage or layer of capital stock may have a unique production function. Capital goods, once installed, is inelastic in supply. Thus, production is optimized according to labor input. Let $K_v(t)$ be the capital goods installed at time v and still in operation at time t, production function for capital vintage v is

(2.4)
$$Q_v(t) = A(t)F(L_v(t), K_v(t)) \ ,$$

where $K_v(t)$ is the capital vintage v, $Q_v(t)$ and $L_v(t)$ are, respectively, the output and the labor input corresponding to the capital vintage v, $A(t)$ is the parameter of neutral technology. Maximizing profit, which is the revenue of output minus cost, $Q_v - wL_v - pK_v$, with respect to labor input yields the first order condition of the optimization problem. From the first order condition, a labor demand function can be derived as (2.5),

(2.5)
$$L_v(t) = g_v(w, p, K_v(t)) \ .$$

Let I_v be the gross investment at time v, δ the depreciation rate, and λ_k the rate of technological progress. Suppose value of the capital remaining in place is determined by the depreciation rate, then

(2.6)
$$K_v(t) = I_v e^{-\delta(t-v) + \lambda_k v} \ .$$

Substitution of the labor demand function (2.5) and the capital vintage (2.6) into (2.1) gives rise to

(2.7)
$$Q_v(t) = A(t)F\left(g_v(w, p, I_v e^{-\delta(t-v) + \lambda_k v}), \ I_v e^{-\delta(t-v) + \lambda_k v} \right) \ .$$

Integration of the production over all the vintages yields a general form of aggregate production function with full description of technology built in each capital vintage,

$$(2.8) \qquad Q(t) = \int_{-\infty}^{t} A(t) F\left(g_v(w,p,I_v e^{-\delta(t-v)+\lambda_k v}), I_v e^{-\delta(t-v)+\lambda_k v}\right) dv \ .$$

This general form must be further manipulated in an empirical research.

Assuming a work force can always be reorganized to optimally work on all layers of the total capital stock (namely putty-putty case in growth literature, i.e., before and after installation of equipments it is always feasible to organize and reorganize workers according to technical specification of the equipments) and employing a constant return Cobb-Douglas production functional form allow Solow (1960) to develop an explicit aggregate production function (2.9)

$$(2.9) \qquad Q(t) = B e^{-\delta(1-\alpha)t} L(t)^\alpha J(t)^{1-\alpha} \ ,$$

where the capital J(t) is $\qquad J(t) = \int e^{(\delta + \frac{\lambda_k}{1-\alpha})v} I(v) dv,$

B is a constant, and δ is the rate of depreciation (see Solow 1960 for detail). Still, operating the model is formidable. Solow imposed outside estimates of α and δ to estimate the equation.

Focusing on the components of growth rate in capital jelly, Nelson (1964) developed a similar model of growth of capital jelly. A capital stock at time t is specified as

$$(2.10) \qquad J(t) = \sum_{0}^{t} K_v(t)(1+\lambda_k)^v \ .$$

$K_v(t)$ is the capital of vintage v remaining at time t after taking depreciation into account and λ_k is the rate of technological progress. An approximation[1] to the J_t is

(2.11) $J(t)=(1+\lambda_k)^{-A_0}(1+\lambda_k)^t K(t)\left(1+\lambda_k(A_0-A_t)\right)$,

where A_0 and A_t are average ages of capital at time 0 and $_t$. If λ_k is small and A_0 is not very different from A_t, differentiating (2.11) in logarithm form with respect to time, the growth rate of J(t) can be further approximated[2] by

(2.12) $$\frac{dJ(t)}{J(t)dt}=\frac{dK(t)}{K(t)dt}+\lambda_k-\frac{\lambda_k dA_t}{dt} \ ,$$

Where dA_t/dt is the change in the average age of capital. This equation says that the growth rate of capital stock is made up of three terms, a growth rate of gross capital stock, a constant growth rate of embodied technology (λ_k), and a product term of the growth rate of embodied technology and change in average age of capital stock ($-\lambda_k dA_t/dt$). Since λ_k is an unknown constant, it becomes a part of the intercept in the growth equation. The effect of λ_k on output growth is of Solow neutral, while $-\lambda_k dA_t/dt$ affects output growth in the same way physical capital does. Therefore, λ_k, the annual rate of technological progress, can be estimated given coefficient estimates for $dK(t)/K(t)dt$ and dA_t/dt.

Using age as a measure of embodied technology is only an approximation. Precise functional relationship between the age of capital and the level of embodied technology is hard to know. Using a general age-technology relationship, this study develops a measure of the embodied technology slightly different yet more manageable than Nelson's model. This age-technology relationship can be estimated simultaneously when the growth equation is estimated. If $I_v(t)$ is the gross investment made at time v and still working at time t, δ is the rate of depreciation, and λ_k is the rate of embodied technological progress, capital jelly at time t can be written as

(2.13) $$J(t)=\sum_{v=0}^{t} I_v(t)e^{-\delta(t-v)+\lambda_k v} \ .$$

Let value of vintage v at time t be $K_v(t)=I_v(t)e^{-\delta(t-v)}$, then (2.13) becomes

$$(2.14) \qquad J(t)=\sum_{v=0}^{t} K_v(t)e^{\lambda_k v}=K(t)\sum_{v=0}^{t}\left(\frac{K_v(t)}{K_t}\right)e^{\lambda_k v} .$$

In (2.14), $\Sigma_{v=0}(K_v(t)/K(t))e^{\lambda v}$ is nothing more than the weighted average of capital efficiency, i.e., technology embodied in capital stock, $T(t)$. Since capital stock and embodied technology both are variables, growth of output will depend on growth rates of both parts. Knowing that the younger the average age of capital, the more advanced technology is incorporated, the average age of capital stock should approximately have an inverse relation with the level of embodied technology. Mathematically, embodied technology is

$$T(t)=a(t)A(t)^{-\alpha_k} ,$$

where a(t) and α_k are unknown coefficients and A(t) is the average age of physical capital stock at time t. Since α_k is a unknown parameter determined by the proposed age-technology relationship, it may take any value greater than zero as long as the value produces a good fit in age-technology relationship for a particular economy or industry. Coefficient $a(t)$ is related to the level of embodied technology. If annual rate of technological progress embodied in new capital is λ_k, technology embodied in a capital stock at time t is $e^{\lambda_k t}$ times as advanced as that in a capital stock at time 0 if average age of the capital is constant. In general, the relationship between average age and technology embodied in capital can be specified as

$$T(t)=a_0 e^{\lambda_k t}K(t)A(t)^{-\alpha_k} .$$

Substitution of $T(t)$ and $K_v(t)$ in (2.4) yields

$$(2.14') \qquad J(t)=a_0 e^{\lambda_k t}K(t)A(t)^{-\alpha_k} .$$

The growth rate of capital jelly can be derived by differentiating logarithm of (2.14') and remembering the unknown constant a_0 and α_k,

$$(2.15) \quad \frac{dJ(t)}{J(t)dt} = \frac{da_0}{a_0 dt} + \lambda_k + \frac{dK(t)}{K(t)dt} - \alpha_k \frac{dA(t)}{A(t)dt} - LnA(t) \frac{d\alpha_k}{\alpha_k dt}$$

$$= \lambda_k + \frac{dK(t)}{K(t)dt} - \alpha_k \frac{dA(t)}{A(t)dt} \ .$$

The parameter specifying the age-technology functional relationship, α_k, can be computed from the parameter estimates of $dK(t)/K(t)dt$ and $dA(t)/A(t)dt$. From (2.14) one cannot develop a manageable growth model since (2.14) involves full description of distribution of all capital vintages and actual rate of depreciation that may vary from place to place (Luger 1986) and is not readily available. From (2.15), on the other hand, a growth equation similar to (2.2) can be derived without major difficulty and the contribution of embodied technology to growth, and the relationship between age and embodied technology can be estimated at the same time. Unfortunately, like form (2.12), λ_k cannot be identified and it will become a part of the intercept of a growth equation. As a result, $\alpha_k dA(t)/A(t)dt$ (multiplied by the parameter estimate) only reflects part of contribution of technological progress to growth as in the case of (2.12). Equation (2.12) and (2.15) are both employed for comparison in the research. In (2.12) absolute change in capital age may affect the growth rate of capital stock and output, while in (2.15) a relative change of the average age of capital stock may exert an influence on output growth.

Similarly, labor carries knowledge and skills. The levels of educational attainment and work experience are the most important characteristics of labor input. The more knowledgeable and the more experienced the workers, the more easily they can understand technical issues involved in production and adapt to technical change in production. Educational attainment and experience of technical, professional, and managerial personnel may have even more significant influence on production, because the technological capability of these personnel determines the level and the growth rate of technology adopted in their production. By decomposing a heterogeneous labor crew into many 'layers' according to educational attainment and work experience, a measurement similar to (2.15) can be developed.

Let $M(t)$ be the measure of efficiency units of labor input as opposed to natural units of labor $L(t)$. Let $L_{ts,te,t}$ be the 'layer' of labor with formal educational attainment of t_s years and work experience of t_e years. Let λ_s and λ_e be the rates of growth of efficiency due to increases in the numbers of years of standard education and work experience. Then labor input can be measured as (2.16)

(2.16)
$$M(t)=\sum_{t_s=0}^{Max(t_s)} \sum_{t_e=0}^{Max(t_e)} L_{t_s t_e}(t) e^{\lambda_s t_s} e^{\lambda_e t_e}$$

$$=L(t)\sum_{t_s=0}^{Max(t_s)} \sum_{t_e=0}^{Max(t_e)} \left(\frac{L_{t_s t_e}(t)}{L(t)}\right) e^{\lambda_s t_s} e^{\lambda_e t_e} \, ,$$

where $Max(t_s)$ and $Max(t_e)$ are the maximum numbers of years of education and work experience of employees. Assuming efficiency for workers to perform their job and ability for technical and managerial personnel to adopt a new technology are positively related to average levels of educational attainment and experience, a general functional form relating average educational attainment and work experience to knowledge and skill embodied in labor can be derived. Using $E_s(t)$ and $E_e(t)$ to represent average years of schooling and work experience respectively, the weighted average $\Sigma_{ts}\Sigma_{te}(L_{tste}/L(t))e^{\lambda_{sts}}e^{\lambda_{ete}}$ becomes $E_s(t)E_e(t)^3$. Under the assumption of a general positive relationship between educational attainment/work experience and embodied knowledge/technology, technology embodied in labor is $T_L(t)=\gamma(t)E_s^{\alpha_s}E_e^{\alpha_e}$, where α_s and α_e are unknown parameters empirically describing how and how much average years of schooling and average years of work experience affect efficiency of labor respectively.

It is also recognized that advance in knowledge, reflected by different contents or substances in education and work experience, can raise labor productivity even if average years of schooling and work experience remain constant over time. Let λ_L be the average annual rate of advance of knowledge and γ_0 an unknown constant; thus, technology in labor input at time t is $e^{\lambda_L t}$ times as advanced as that at time 0. The general expression of technology embodied in labor, therefore, can be rewritten as $T_L(t)=\gamma_0 e^{\lambda_L t}E_s^{\alpha_s}E_e^{\alpha_e}$. Substitution of $\Sigma\Sigma(L_{tste}(t)/L(t))e^{\lambda_{sts}}e^{\lambda_{ete}}=T_L(t)=\gamma_0 e^{\lambda_L t}E_s^{\alpha_s}E_e^{\alpha_e}$ into (2.16) yields the growth rate of labor input

$$(2.17) \quad \frac{dM(t)}{M(t)dt} = \frac{d\gamma_0}{\gamma_0 dt} + \lambda_L + \frac{dL(t)}{L(t)dt} + \alpha_s \frac{dE_s(t)}{E_s(t)dt} + LnE_s(t)\frac{d\alpha_s}{\alpha_s dt}$$

$$+ \alpha_e \frac{dE_e(t)}{E_e(t)dt} + LnE_e(t)\frac{d\alpha_e}{\alpha_e dt}.$$

Since γ_0, α_s, and α_e are unknown constants, (2.17) can be further reduced to

$$(2.18) \quad \frac{dM(t)}{M(t)dt} = \lambda_L + \frac{dL(t)}{L(t)dt} + \alpha_s \frac{dE_s(t)}{E_s(t)dt} + \alpha_e \frac{dE_e(t)}{E_e(t)dt} .$$

Because λ_L is underidentified in estimation, this term will become a part of the intercept.

It is important to tell empirically which type of labor inputs carries knowledge or skills that contribute to production and productivity growth significantly. It is desirable to have separate measures for production workers and technical/managerial personnel. Thus, two efficiency labor inputs similar to (2.18) should be used. Their efficiency parameters are expected to be different.

To simplify the notation, $Q(t)$, $J(t)$, $M(t)$, $K(t)$, $L(t)$, $E_s(t)$, and $E_e(t)$ are replaced with Q_t, J_t, M_t, K_t, L_t, E_{st}, and E_{et} respectively. Using by now the routine procedure of deriving a growth equation results in an equation similar to (2.2') and numbered as (2.19),

$$(2.19) \quad \dot{Q_t} = \alpha + \beta_k \dot{K_t} - \beta_k \alpha_k \dot{A_t} + \beta_L \dot{L_t} + \beta_L \alpha_s \dot{E_{st}} + \beta_L \alpha_e \dot{E_{et}} .$$

In (2.19), all dotted variables are measured in growth/change rate. The constant term α includes the contribution of the remaining neutral technological progress and a part of the effects of the technology and knowledge embodied in capital and labor, λ_k and λ_L, which cannot be independently estimated. From (2.19) a reduction in average age (i.e., a negative value on dotted A_t), implying an advance of embodied technology, is expected to raise the growth rate of output, while the magnitude of the effect is also dependent on β_k and α_k. An increase either in formal education or work experience is expected to contribute to growth in output. The strength of influences of education and experience also relies on the parameters α_s and α_e. From estimates of (2.19) we can easily derive the unknown parameters α_k, α_s and α_e describing empirical relationship between the direct measure (i.e., the average age of capital stock, the average years of formal education, and the average years of work experience) and embodied technology/ knowledge.

Besides the conventional inputs, labor and capital, endogenous growth theory emphasizes technological input as an intentional effort. This emphasis is more consistent with producers' profit maximizing behavior. Faced with the market incentive of a potentially higher rate of return, a producer may make a technological investment aiming at technological progress. Producer R & D input, patent purchase or license, input in computer and numerical control technology, investment in equipment upgrading, expenditure on worker training, and spending on management system should all be considered as the intentional efforts to advance or adopt technology and to promote output growth. Technological change resulting from these efforts can be embodied or disembodied depending on the influence of each of the inputs on other conventional inputs. Let Z_t be the vector of the technological inputs just mentioned, then the production function can be written as

$$(2.1\text{''}) \qquad Q_t = a_t F\left(a_0 e^{\lambda_k t} K_t A_t^{-\alpha_k},\ \gamma_0 e^{\lambda_t t} L_t E_s^{\alpha_s} E_e^{\alpha_e},\ Z_t\right),$$

where a_t denotes the remaining part of neutral efficiency term, Q_t, K_t, and L_t are the output, the capital stock, and the physical labor input respectively, $a_0 A_t^{-\alpha_k}$ and $\gamma E_s^{\alpha_s} E_e^{\alpha_e}$ are the efficiency factors of capital and the labor crew.

In growth models, the magnitude of the intercept measures the 'ignorance' about the sources of output growth. The intercept is also treated as neutral technological progress. Inclusion of these technological inputs should capture a part of unexplained growth. Consequently, neutral effect of technological progress in growth equation is expected to fall. Since one of objectives of growth theory is to reduce the unexplained residual (Griliches 1963), explicit allocation of growth among technological inputs is one step toward better understanding of the sources of production and productivity growth.

2.2. PRODUCTION GROWTH
WITHIN A REGIONAL CONTEXT

Regional business environment can significantly influence industrial production. This subsection establishes a production function with regional variables as additional dimensions.

Regional contextual factors may constitute a necessary condition for location and growth of production. According to product cycle theory, a technologically advanced industry may heavily rely on intensive input of technical personnel and prompt feedback of market information to adjust and improve its products in a timely fashion. Because a peripheral locality lacks the skilled labor force and adequate market services, it may be impossible for the locality to establish production of the industry no matter how low its prevailing wage rate and land rental might be. On the other hand, the peripheral area may attract an industry with standardized production and promote local production growth because of the low prices of labor and land inputs.

Many regional/social contextual factors are free or 'quasi-free' goods to producers, because they are essentially nonexcludable in nature. These regional factors include proximity to market, social infrastructure, economic structure, technological externalities, and physical environmental factors. In the meantime, other factors such as the price of land, the wage rate, congestion, and other external diseconomies may incur an additional cost of doing business in certain areas.

Depending on an industry's market orientation, input-output linkages with other industries, and production technology, the industry may more or less rely on contextual factors. One distinctive feature of a regional growth model should be to identify and quantify effects of regional factors on production growth. To accomplish this, earlier research on regional growth either uses a single variable such as population size or industry scale (Sveikauskas 1975, Moomaw 1986) or tests variations in efficiency parameters of inputs and total factor productivity (TFP) across regions without adding extra regional factors (Williams 1985, Sasaki 1986, Beeson 1987). At the company level, quality and combination of localized inputs, organization of production, and technology used in production can be more heterogeneous than at the regional aggregate level. Some industries grow selectively in particular areas and production technology varies among areas. This fact suggests that the influences of regional factors on company production growth are not neutral, and conventional inputs cannot easily replace regional variables. It remains to be known how and how much regional variables have facilitated or inhibited production growth and technological progress.

Regional factors can be better interpreted in terms of restricted inputs in production function. A forceful argument is that diminishing marginal product of capital or labor is due to the presence of some fixed input (Varian 1986). To many producers the fixed inputs are environmental rather than conventional inputs. Variable regional and environmental factors impose different restrictions on different areas. At an initial stage of production location, producers make investment and hiring decisions based on regional conditions. Later, if an area experiences new social overhead investment, the corresponding regional variables will change values. The new social-economic environment may result in a lower cost of production of individual producers while maintaining the level of production or in a higher output level at original producer cost. Accordingly regional factors contribute to production directly. Moreover, as marginal cost becomes lower, producers will naturally adjust their input levels until further expansion no longer brings in an additional profit. Producer inputs actually are partly determined by regional factors. In this case, regional factors make indirect contribution to production. Introducing a regional factor, R_t, production function can be rewritten as

$$(2.20) \quad Q_t = aF\left(a_0 e^{\lambda^k t} K_t(R_t) A_t^{-\alpha_k}, \; \gamma_0 e^{\lambda^l t} L_t(R_t) E_s^{\alpha_s} E_e^{\alpha_e}, \; Z_t(R_t), \; R_t\right),$$

where R_t indicates a relevant regional variable, which is externally determined and relatively stable to producers, assuming any individual producer under investigation is not large enough to significantly alter its regional context.

Producers determine internal inputs levels, $a_k e^{\lambda^k t} A_t^{-\alpha k} K_t(R_t)$, $\gamma_0 e^{\lambda^l t} E_s^{\alpha s} E_e^{\alpha e} L_t(R_t)$, $Z_t(R_t)$, following a profit maximizing or cost minimizing rule. Since R_t represents free goods to producers, the level of production is settled only by marginal productivity of paid factors. If the market is competitive, producer equilibrium can be characterized by first order condition of optimization with respect to output level,

$$(2.21) \qquad p - \frac{\partial C_i}{\partial Q_i} = 0 , \qquad i = 1, 2, 3, \ldots N ,$$

where $i = 1, 2, 3, 4 \ldots N$ indicate different producers, p is the price of output, and C_i and Q_i, respectively, are the cost and the output level of the ith producer. In the long run, marginal cost is also equal to average cost, i.e., $\partial C_i / \partial Q_i = C_i / Q_i$ for $i = 1, 2, 3, \ldots N$. Since price, p, is common to all producers, it follows that all producers operate with the same marginal and average products regardless of scale. Therefore, production in the whole industry appears to have a constant return to scale with respect to producer inputs. Under the condition of constant return, Euler's theorem holds:

$$(2.22) \qquad Q_t = a_0 e^{\lambda_k t} K_t A_t^{-\alpha_k} \left(\frac{\partial Q_t}{\partial (a_0 e^{\lambda_k t} K_t A_t^{-\alpha_k})} \right)$$
$$+ \gamma_0 e^{\lambda_{l} t} L_t E_s^{\alpha_s} E_e^{\alpha_e} \left(\frac{\partial Q_t}{\partial (\gamma_0 e^{\lambda_{l} t} L_t E_s^{\alpha_s} E_e^{\alpha_e})} \right) + Z_t \left(\frac{\partial Q_t}{\partial Z_t} \right) .$$

Regional factors can have positive or negative impact on production. For convenience and without losing any substance we temporarily assume that the regional variable, R_t, is productive factor, meaning $\partial Q_t / \partial R_t > 0$ (in the case of regional disamenities, we only need to change the direction of the inequality sign). If the regional factor increases from some base level by R_t, the inequality $R_t(\partial Q_t / \partial R_t) > 0$ holds. Inclusion of regional factor, R_t, in (2.22) yields an inequality

$$(2.23) \qquad Q_t < a_0 e^{\lambda_k t} K_t A_t^{-\alpha_k} \left(\frac{\partial Q_t}{\partial (a_0 e^{\lambda_k t} K_t A_t^{-\alpha_k})} \right)$$
$$+ \gamma_0 e^{\lambda_{l} t} L_t E_s^{\alpha_s} E_e^{\alpha_e} \left(\frac{\partial Q_t}{\partial (\gamma_0 e^{\lambda_{l} t} L_t E_s^{\alpha_s} E_e^{\alpha_e})} \right) + Z_t \left(\frac{\partial Q_t}{\partial Z_t} \right) + R_t \left(\frac{\partial Q_t}{\partial R_t} \right)$$

The relationships expressed by (2.22) and (2.23) have critical bearing on production location and production and productivity growth.

As long as R_t remains productive, a proportional increase in all factors including R_t will lead to a greater than proportional increase in Q_t, an increasing return to scale with all relevant factors. There can be two possibilities for the role R_t plays in production growth. First, an increase in R_t from a base level may directly contribute to production growth due to positive impact of $R_t(dQ_t/dR_t)$ on output. Second, the increase in R_t may result in an increase in marginal products of producer factor inputs. In either case producers would expand the scale of production until each marginal product falls back or close to the initial level. Therefore, R_t is a driving force for production location and regional growth. Despite the effect of regional factors on marginal products of producer inputs, the indirect influence of regional factors in (2.23) needs not be specified in the growth equation, since producers pay the cost of any internal input no matter if it is induced or not. Normally only (2.22) is observed in production, since R is free goods and does not enter producers' input-output accounting. An empirical estimation without regional factors may overstate the contribution of producer inputs to output. Inclusion of relevant regional variables reveals factor(s) which is a driving force to growth. One also may expect that as a producer becomes closer and closer to fullly utilizing the regional factor, the impact of the factor will be less and less significant. It may be expected that standardized production with stable technology is more likely to fulllly utilize regional factors than technologically dynamic production. A practical answer, however, must be derived from an empirical estimation.

Besides measuring contribution of regional factors to production growth, there are other important motives for inclusion of regional variables. First, to study the necessity of regional factors for production location and production and productivity growth, we must investigate substitutability between regional factors and producer inputs. For example, a better educated labor force in a region means less producer input in worker training; existence of a regional research center may have spillover effect in R & D activity, and the spillover may lead the relevant firms to invest more, if complementary, or less, if supplementary, in their own R & D (Spence 1984, Levin 1988). This suggests that regional inputs may be substitutable for conventional producer inputs. On the other hand, substitution of regional factors for producer internal inputs must be limited. Technically, if regional factors and producer inputs are perfectly substitutable for one another, production function could not be concave and there was no optimum point for producers to choose and, intuitively, monopolistic market was the only form that could exist, a result inconsistent with the fact. Obviously, it is desirable to better understand the relationship between regional variables and producer investment in technology and conventional inputs.

Second, the importance of including regional variables also resides in justifying the application of the same production function to many producers. Since each producer has a unique production function, the validity of using a single identical function with only two conventional inputs, capital and labor, in cross sectional analysis is doubtful. It is surprising that many early studies apply a single production function to cross sectional analysis without justification. It should be stressed that only when all relevant input and output variables are included, can a production function legitimately represent many different producers. More specifically, production function in its general form, transformation function, can include more types of inputs and outputs, and separation of movement along a conventional production function from shift of the function becomes meaningless, since the shift factors are included as additional dimensions of the transformation function. Frequently mentioned movement along a production frontier is equivalent to movement on the surface of the transformation function with constant shift variables, while shift of production frontier corresponds to variation in shift variables. The regional and some company-specific variables can serve both as inputs and as shift or control variables. Only in this case, can the same production function represent many companies' productions.

Third, regional inputs may incur no cost to producers, yet it may directly contribute to production. Omission of the regional inputs is inconsistent with macroeconomic accounting where all inputs and outputs are counted and aggregated. In empirical research where estimation is necessary, this omission in production functions may upward bias the effect of producer direct inputs on production and productivity growth. Inclusion of regional inputs, such as producer services, local infrastructure, and technological externalities can reduce the bias of estimates for producer inputs, explain locational advantage, test for inter-regional equilibrium, and reveal regional policy implication.

Several frequently addressed regional factors are educational attainment of labor force, accessibility, technological externalities, agglomeration (or separately measured by urbanization and localization), regional development level, metro size (or metro-non metro status) (see Sveikauskas 1972, Moomaw 1986, Harrington 1986, Rees 1986, Beeson 1987, Moomaw and Williams 1991). Some of these variables are closely related to each other and even conceptually similar. To demonstrate the derivation of a micro growth model, a vector of regional variables is used in the following equations.

After introducing regional variables, Hicks neutral efficiency term is expected to become much smaller. A general functional form has to be adopted if major internal and external factors, regardless of the natures of endogenous or exogenous, private goods or public goods, are included into production as input and shift variables. Maintaining generality, we can write production function as

$$(2.24) \qquad Q_t = a_t F\left(a_k K_t A_t^{-\alpha_k}, \; \gamma_0 e^{\lambda_L t} L_t E_s^{\alpha_s} E_e^{\alpha_e}, \; Z_t, \; R_t\right) ,$$

where all variables and coefficients are the same as in (2.1'') and R_t denotes a vector of regional contextual factors affecting production.

2.3. A PRODUCTION GROWTH MODEL AND IMPLICATIONS

2.3.1. Different Forms of Production Growth Equation

The growth equation can be routinely derived by differentiating function (2.24) with respect to time and dividing the total differentiation equation by output level,

(2.25)
$$\frac{dQ_t}{Q_t dt} = \frac{\partial Q_t}{\partial a_t} \frac{a_t}{Q_t} \frac{da_t}{a_t dt} + \frac{\partial Q_t}{\partial(a_0 e^{\lambda_k t} K_t A_t^{-\alpha_k})} \frac{a_0 e^{\lambda_k t} K_t A_t^{-\alpha_k}}{Q_t} \lambda_k$$

$$+ \frac{\partial Q_t}{\partial(a_0 e^{\lambda_k t} K_t A_t^{-\alpha_k})} \frac{a_0 e^{\lambda_k t} K_t A_t^{-\alpha_k}}{Q_t} \frac{dK_t}{K_t dt}$$

$$+ \frac{\partial Q_t}{\partial(a_0 e^{\lambda_k t} K_t A_t^{-\alpha_k})} \frac{a_0 e^{\lambda_k t} K_t A_t^{-\alpha_k}}{Q_t} (-\alpha_k) \frac{dA_t}{A_t dt}$$

$$+ \frac{\partial Q_t}{\partial(\gamma_0 e^{\lambda_L t} E_s^{\alpha_s} E_e^{\alpha_e} L_t)} \frac{\gamma_0 e^{\lambda_L t} E_s^{\alpha_s} E_e^{\alpha_e} L_t}{Q_t} \lambda_L$$

$$+ \frac{\partial Q_t}{\partial(\gamma_0 e^{\lambda_L t} E_s^{\alpha_s} E_e^{\alpha_e} L_t)} \frac{\gamma_0 e^{\lambda_L t} E_s^{\alpha_s} E_e^{\alpha_e} L_t}{Q_t} \frac{dL_t}{L_t dt}$$

$$+ \frac{\partial Q_t}{\partial(\gamma_0 e^{\lambda_L t} E_s^{\alpha_s} E_e^{\alpha_e} L_t)} \frac{\gamma_0 e^{\lambda_L t} E_s^{\alpha_s} E_e^{\alpha_e} L_t}{Q_t} (\alpha_s) \frac{dE_s}{E_s dt}$$

$$+ \frac{\partial Q_t}{\partial(\gamma_0 e^{\lambda_L t} E_s^{\alpha_s} E_e^{\alpha_e} L_t)} \frac{\gamma_0 e^{\lambda_L t} E_s^{\alpha_s} E_e^{\alpha_e} L_t}{Q_t} (\alpha_e) \frac{dE_e}{E_e dt}$$

$$+ \frac{\partial Q_t}{\partial Z_t} \frac{Z_t}{Q_t} \frac{dZ_t}{Z_t dt} + \frac{\partial Q_t}{\partial R_t} \frac{R_t}{Q_t} \frac{dR_t}{R_t dt} ,$$

or in a neater form

(2.25')
$$\dot{Q}_t = \beta_0 + \beta_1 \dot{K}_t - \beta_2 \dot{A}_t + \beta_3 \dot{L}_t + \beta_4 \dot{E}_s + \beta_5 \dot{E}_e + \beta_6 \dot{Z}_t + \beta_7 \dot{R}_t ,$$

where all dotted inputs and output are growth rates inputs and output and β_i are the elasticities of output with respect to the ith input, and $\beta_1=\beta_2/(-\alpha_k)$ and $\beta_3=\beta_4/\alpha_s=\beta_5/\alpha_e$. The influences of conventional input and the corresponding technologies embodied are different by a factor that describes the relationship between the original measure (i.e., average age of capital stock, average years of formal education, and average years of work experience) and embodied technology. Parameter β_i, $i>0$, suggests how much a given growth in an individual input, especially a technological input or a regional factor, may affect production growth. The constant β_0 is a combination of at least three terms:

$$(2.26) \qquad \beta_0 = \frac{\partial Q_t}{\partial a_t}\frac{a_t}{Q_t}\frac{da_t}{a_t dt} + \frac{\partial Q_t}{\partial(a_0 e^{\lambda_k t}KA_t^{-\alpha_k})}\frac{a_0 e^{\lambda_k t}KA_t^{-\alpha_k}}{Q_t}\lambda_k$$

$$+ \frac{\partial Q_t}{\partial(\gamma_0 e^{\lambda_t t}E_s^{\alpha_s}E_e^{\alpha_e}L_t)}\frac{\gamma_0 e^{\lambda_t t}E_s^{\alpha_s}E_e^{\alpha_e}L_t}{Q_t}\lambda_L \, ,$$

where the first term on the right hand side indicates the neutral effect of technology progress, the second and third terms are effects of embodied technological progress not captured by the terms on the right hand side. The parameters have rich meanings and can be individually or jointly used for theoretical and practical purposes.

It is sometimes argued (Adams 1990) that marginal product form of growth equation is more appropriate than output elasticity form, assuming a competitive market and a producer optimization behavior. Under these assumptions, marginal product of an input is a constant for all producers, i.e., the following first order optimization condition holds,

$$(2.27) \qquad \frac{\partial Q_a}{\partial X_j} = \frac{\partial Q_b}{\partial X_j} = \mu p_j \, , \quad a,b,=1,2,3..., \ a\neq b, \ j=1,2,3... \, ,$$

where Q_a and Q_b indicate output levels of two producers, X_j is the jth input, p_j is the price of input X_j, and μ is a constant (i.e., marginal product of producer's total inputs or Lagrangian multiplier in optimization problems). The relationship between output elasticity and marginal product is,

$$
(2.28) \qquad \frac{\partial Q_t}{\partial X_{jt}} \frac{X_{jt}}{Q_t} = Q_{jt} \frac{X_{jt}}{Q_t} ,
$$

where Q_{jt} is marginal product of input X_{jt}, and the subscript t indicates the period of interest. For capital jelly with embodied technology, since

$$
Q_{kt} = \frac{\partial Q_t}{\partial(a_0 e^{\lambda_k t} K_t A_t^{-\alpha_k})} \frac{d(a_0 e^{\lambda_k t} K_t A_t^{-\alpha_k})}{dK_t}
$$

$$
= \frac{\partial Q_t}{\partial(a_0 e^{\lambda_k t} K_t A_t^{-\alpha_k})} (a_0 e^{\lambda_k t} A_t^{-\alpha_k}) ,
$$

the following equation holds,

$$
(2.28') \qquad \frac{\partial Q_t}{\partial(a_0 e^{\lambda_k t} K_t A_t^{-\alpha_k})} \frac{a_0 e^{\lambda_k t} K_t A_t^{-\alpha_k}}{Q_t} = Q_{Kt} \frac{K_t}{Q_t} .
$$

A similar relationship can be expressed for the term of technology embodied in capital jelly by (2.28''),

$$
(2.28'') \qquad \frac{\partial Q_t}{\partial(a_0 e^{\lambda_k t} K_t A_t^{-\alpha_k})} \frac{a_0 e^{\lambda_k t} K_t A_t^{-\alpha_k}}{Q_t} (-\alpha_k) = Q_{At} \frac{A_t}{Q_t} .
$$

In general, a similar relationship exists for any other input with embodied technology. Thus equation (2.25) can be rewritten as

$$
(2.29) \qquad \frac{dQ_t}{dt} = Q_{at} \frac{da_t}{dt} + Q_{Kt} K_t \lambda_k + Q_{Kt} \frac{dK_t}{dt} + Q_{At} \frac{dA_t}{dt} + Q_{Lt} \frac{dL_t}{dt}
$$

$$
+ Q_{Ej} \frac{dE_{st}}{dt} + Q_{Ej} \frac{dE_{et}}{dt} + Q_{Zt} \frac{dZ_t}{dt} + Q_{Rt} \frac{dR_t}{dt} ,
$$

36   *Beyond Capital and Labor*

where Q_{i_t} is the marginal product of input i, but exponential parameters, α_k, α_s, and α_e, describing age-technology, schooling-knowledge, and experience-skill relationships can no longer be identified. The neater form of the equation (2.29) is

(2.29') $$\delta Q = b_0 + \sum_i b_i \delta X_i \, ,$$

where δ denotes the real growth over period dt, e.g., $\delta Q = dQ/dt$, $\delta X_i = dX_i/dt$, b_i is marginal product Q_{i_t}, and b_0 combines the first two terms in (2.29). Given data on real changes in input and output, b_i can be estimated, and the output elasticities for each producer can be computed according to (2.28).

2.3.2. Variable Output Elasticities and Determinants

The marginal product form of growth equation leads to the different output elasticities, β_j, across producers. The variation of the output elasticities may result from internal differences in technological progress and producer technological inputs. The output elasticity of an input is greater for a producer or an industry either because technological progress embodied in the input is faster than those in other inputs or because this producer or industry uses the input more efficiently relative to other inputs. Producer technological inputs can further affect the level of embodied technology and the efficiency of using internal inputs.

The variation of the output elasticities can also be caused by other factors. The differences in such regional substitutive and complemental factors as producer services, utility supplies, and technological spillovers can induce internal inputs and influence adoption of different technologies, thereby influencing the output elasticities. Producer characteristics such as internal organization, size, age, and mode of production may affect the output elasticities because these characteristics may determine the most appropriate technologies being adopted.

One way to examine the importance of technological inputs, regional factors, and producer characteristics to technological efficiency is to empirically test the relationship between these factors and the output elasticities. In practice, however, there can be many variable output elasticities, one for each input. It is more feasible to use summarized indicators, especially, total factor productivity, neutral technological progress, and economies of scale. This will be discussed in detail in section 2.3.5 and in chapter 6.

2.3.3. Income Distribution in Growth Context

Besides technological efficiency, the β_i and b_i have another important interpretation. If markets are competitive and producers are profit-maximizing, the coefficients b_i, $i>0$, are the rates of return to the factors and β_i should be close to share of income returning to the ith factor. Theoretically, relationships (2.25) and (2.29) dictate the distribution of income. There are two interesting questions about income distribution: (1) has income been distributed among factor inputs based on their contributions to output? (2) how is contribution of a regional factor to output reflected in income distribution?

The answer to the first question is straightforward. It is only subject to a comparison between marginal product b_i, $i>0$, and actual return to the same factor input (e.g., a comparison of marginal products of labor and capital with actual wage rate and capital rental). Marginal products and output elasticities can be estimated in the models and actual return to the factors are routinely documented. Therefore, we may properly answer the question by comparison.

The second question needs more effort to answer. Many regional factors are basically free inputs and, naturally, producers would make use of these factors as much as they can. In a perfect equilibrium, the marginal product of these regional factors may approach zero. Total income should be distributed among paid inputs and sum of income shares of all paid inputs should be equal to unity. However, growth in production implies a case of disequilibrium or a process toward equilibrium. Changes in regional contextual factors have been realized as one of disturbing (but not necessarily adverse) force to equilibrium. Growing production may have more or less benefitted from the improvement on these regional factors. It is interesting to find out where the contribution of regional factors goes in terms of income share. Obviously, the 'share' of free inputs may have been allocated to paid inputs. In the early stage of capital accumulation the 'share' largely went to capital. Due to institutional evolution over more than a hundred years, the current distribution of national income is very different from that in the early stage. In conjunction with actual records on wage rates and capital rental, study on β_i and b_i for different industries can reveal which factor inputs may have received income shares generated by regional external factors. The common experience of higher wage rates in well developed areas suggests that at least a significant part of the contribution of regional factors has translated to additional compensation for labor.

An in-depth comparative study would reveal sources of inter-industrial and interregional inequality of income distribution. The empirical estimates for the marginal product and the output elasticities of factor inputs may serve as some basis on which some policy consideration may be supported, especially faced with equality problem.

2.3.4. Non-Rivalry of Technology

Technological inputs have some features different from conventional factors. The most influential aspects are characterized by non-rival and partially non-excludable natures (Romer 1990). The non-rival nature allows a producer to apply a new technology over and over without incurring an additional cost, thereby resulting in non-concave production function. Existence of a spillover effect makes it difficult for an innovator to fully internalize the profit, causing technological investment lower than socially desired level.

Non-rivalry implies that, other things being equal, a firm with more advanced technology should have monopoly power in its product market. Although the existence and the nature of non-rivalry may not be directly measured, they may be indirectly detected to the extent that over proportional R & D input is a signal that technologically advanced producers may have taken advantage of the non-rival nature of technology to dominate part of their market. A more rigorous approach is to test an increasing marginal product of R & D input, since non-concavity is the most important sign of non-rivalry. Assuming that marginal output of R & D is increasing with the level of the input, a general relationship between R & D input and output is expressed as $Q_t = aF(..., Z', ...)$, $r > 1$, and the contribution of R & D input growth to output growth is

(2.30)
$$\frac{\partial Q_t}{\partial Z_t}\frac{Z_t}{Q_t}\frac{dZ_t}{Z_t dt} = r\frac{\partial Q_t}{\partial Z_t^r}\frac{Z_t^r}{Q_t}\frac{dZ_t}{Z_t dt}.$$

Unfortunately, unlike the cases for technology embodied in capital stock and knowledge in labor, the exponent, r, cannot be identified, because only one output elasticity term $\beta_T = r(\partial Q_i/\partial Z_i')(Z_i'/Q_i)$ can be estimated in growth equation. The only clue of non-rivalry nature of R & D input is a very high output elasticity of R & D input.

Underinvestment is more difficult to test, because social optimum level of input is usually unknown. Producer equilibrium only assures private return to R & D input equal to returns to other inputs. On the other hand, spillover itself may be detected if a producer's output is found to be related to other producers' technological input. Earlier research (Bernstein 1989) estimates that social return due to the spillovers effect is about twice the private return.

2.3.5. Growth of Productivity and Sources

Although production growth is important, in both economic theory and real life, it is productivity growth that is the most significant study subject. It is productivity that determines the amount of income possibly returning on each unit of human or non-human input, and it is the growth rate of productivity that determines the rate of improvement upon the welfare of a society.

There have been two general sets of productivity measures frequently used in early studies, average factor productivity and total factor productivity. Average factor productivity is also named partial productivity (Kendrick 1977), defined as output per unit of a specific input. It is apparent and understandable that in most cases researchers and practitioners are more interested in labor productivity than any other non-human factor productivity. Total factor productivity (TFP) refers to output per unit of combined measure of all conventional inputs. TFP has longer history in government publications than any partial productivity measures. Let us turn to TFP first due to the availability of the relevant measures derived in early sections.

The constant term, β_0, and output elasticities, β_j, $i > 0$, can be used to construct TFP, which is visualized in early studies as an important indicator of technological progress. If production is characterized by constant return to scale, growth rate of total factor productivity is simply equal to the intercept β_0, a case assumed in most growth models. One might expect that β_0 would drop substantially due to inclusion of technological input variables and embodied technology. Thus any concern over TFP might become insignificant. However, theory cannot tell us how much technological change can be embodied in producer inputs and how much should be in general social organization. Probably, there is always some observed 'residual' growth or 'neutral' technological progress due to improvement within the whole society. Moreover, production may or may not be a constant return to scale, and the economies of scale is a component of TFP. Investigation on TFP growth and its sources remains to be interesting.

The general measure of growth rate of TFP, taking any non-constant return to scale into account, is

(2.31)
$$TFP = \dot{Q} - \frac{\sum_j \beta_j \dot{X}_j}{\sum_j \beta_j} \; ,$$

where dotted X_j is the growth rate of the jth input, $\Sigma\beta_j$ is the sum of coefficients of inputs. There is ambiguity regarding the inputs involved in the computation. From producers' point of view, only paid inputs are relevant. Therefore, X_j designate paid inputs and $\Sigma\beta_j$ is the sum of coefficients of the paid inputs. In society's view, all internal and external inputs should be included to compute TFP growth. Since this study investigates production and productivity growth at company level, a measure consistent with producers' standpoint is adopted. This measure weights each input according to its impact on output growth. The growth rate of TFP is zero if growth rate of output and weighted average growth rate of inputs are the same. When favorable external factors exert their influence on production, the total factor productivity growth measured by (2.31) can continue to be positive. Cross sectional variations of the growth rate of TFP suggest differences between producers in efficiency of using the inputs. The variation also indicates different influences of external forces on TFP of different producers. Considering the possible causes of the variation in TFP growth, the variable growth rate of TFP can be explained by the variations in producer technological inputs, producer attributes, and regional complemental factors in an operational form[4].

Average factor productivity is another important measure. The most often used average factor productivity, or, partial productivity, is the average labor productivity. The average labor productivity, hereafter also simply called productivity, is defined as the output per unit of labor input, $q = Q/L$. Average productivity growth rate is the growth rate of output minus the growth rate of labor input, $dq/(qdt)=dQ/(Qdt)-dL/(Ldt)$. Dividing output and all paid inputs by amount of labor yields productivity and input intensity measures respectively. Factor intensive production function can be written as

(2.32)
$$q_t = a_t g_t (a_0 e^{\lambda_k t} k_t A_t^{-\alpha_k}, \gamma_0 e^{\lambda_L t} E_s^{\alpha_s} E_e^{\alpha_e}, z_t, R_t) ,$$

where q, k, and z_t are the output per unit of labor, the capital stock per unit of labor, and the technological inputs per unit of labor respectively, $a_k e^{\lambda_k t} A_k^{-\alpha_k}$ and $\gamma_0 e^{\lambda_L t} E_s^{\alpha_s} E_e^{\alpha_e}$ are efficiency factors of capital and labor respectively, and a_t, R_t are the same as in (2.24). Note that a_t and R_t are not divided by total labor input because they are treated as free goods. Using (2.32), an average productivity growth equation similar to (2.25) can be derived as,

(2.33)
$$\frac{dq_t}{q_t dt} = \frac{\partial q_t}{\partial a_t} \frac{a_t}{q_t} \frac{da_t}{a_t dt} + \frac{\partial q_t}{\partial(a_0 e^{\lambda_k t} k_t A_t^{-\alpha_k})} \frac{a_0 e^{\lambda_k t} k_t A_t^{-\alpha_k}}{q_t} \lambda_k$$

$$+ \frac{\partial q_t}{\partial(a_0 e^{\lambda_k t} k_t A_t^{-\alpha_k})} \frac{a_0 e^{\lambda_k t} k_t A_t^{-\alpha_k}}{q_t} \frac{dk_t}{k_t dt}$$

$$+ \frac{\partial q_t}{\partial(a_0 e^{\lambda_k t} k_t A_t^{-\alpha_k})} \frac{a_0 e^{\lambda_k t} k_t A_t^{-\alpha_k}}{q_t} (-\alpha_k) \frac{dA_t}{A_t dt}$$

$$+ \frac{\partial q_t}{\partial(\gamma_0 e^{\lambda_L t} E_s^{\alpha_s} E_e^{\alpha_e})} \frac{\gamma_0 e^{\lambda_L t} E_s^{\alpha_s} E_e^{\alpha_e}}{q_t} \lambda_L$$

$$+ \frac{\partial q_t}{\partial(\gamma_0 e^{\lambda_L t} E_s^{\alpha_s} E_e^{\alpha_e})} \frac{\gamma_0 e^{\lambda_L t} E_s^{\alpha_s} E_e^{\alpha_e}}{q_t} (\alpha_s) \frac{dE_s}{E_s dt}$$

$$+ \frac{\partial q_t}{\partial(\gamma_0 e^{\lambda_L t} E_s^{\alpha_s} E_e^{\alpha_e})} \frac{\gamma_0 e^{\lambda_L t} E_s^{\alpha_s} E_e^{\alpha_e}}{q_t} (\alpha_e) \frac{dE_e}{E_e dt}$$

$$+ \frac{\partial q_t}{\partial z_t} \frac{z_t}{q_t} \frac{dz_t}{z_t dt} + \frac{\partial q_t}{\partial R_t} \frac{R_t}{q_t} \frac{dR_t}{R_t dt} ,$$

or in a neater form

(2.33') $\dot{q}_t = \alpha_0 + \alpha_1 \dot{k}_t - \alpha_2 \dot{A}_k + \alpha_4 \dot{E}_{st} + \alpha_5 \dot{E}_{et} + \alpha_6 \dot{z}_t + \alpha_7 \dot{R}_t$.

Growth of labor productivity is a result of joint forces including the increase in capital intensity, the technological change embodied in capital, the increase in efficiency of labor, the technological change embodied or not embodied in labor, and all relevant regional variables. Given factor intensity measures and measures on technological progress and regional factors, the productivity growth equation can generate estimates for all the factors. However, it will be immediately clear that equation (2.33) is almost redundant, and its estimates are similar to the estimates of the equation of production growth, (2.25), with a restriction.

Given the fact,

(2.34)
$$\frac{dq_t}{q_t dt} = \frac{dQ_t}{Q_t dt} - \frac{dL_t}{L_t dt} \; ,$$

$$\frac{dk_t}{k_t dt} = \frac{dK_t}{K_t dt} - \frac{dL_t}{L_t dt} \; ,$$

$$\frac{dz_t}{z_t dt} = \frac{dZ_t}{Z_t dt} - \frac{dL_t}{L_t dt} \; .$$

Substituting (2.34) into (2.33') and rearranging terms for $(dL_t/dt)/L_t$ yields equation (2.35) equivalent to (2.33'),

(2.35) $\dot{Q}_t = \alpha_0 + \alpha_1 \dot{K}_t - \alpha_2 \dot{A}_k + (1 - \alpha_1 - \alpha_6)\dot{L}_t + \alpha_4 \dot{E}_{st} \alpha_5 \dot{E}_{et} + \alpha_6 \dot{Z}_t + \alpha_7 \dot{R}_t$,

or

(2.35') $\dot{Q}_t = \alpha_0 + \alpha_1 \dot{K}_t - \alpha_2 \dot{A}_k + \alpha_3 \dot{L}_t + \alpha_4 \dot{E}_{st} + \alpha_5 \dot{E}_{et} + \alpha_6 \dot{Z}_t + \alpha_7 \dot{R}_t$,

Subject to $\alpha_1 + \alpha_3 + \alpha_6 = 1$.

Comparing (2.35) with (2.25'), we can observe that the two equations have the identical specification and all the variables are measured in the same way. Therefore, the coefficients, α_i, in equation (2.35) or (2.34) are similar to the coefficients, β_i, in equation (2.25'), i.e., $\alpha_i \approx \beta_i$, $i = 0$, $1, 2, 3, 4, \ldots$. The difference between α_i and β_i results merely from the restriction, $\alpha_1 + \alpha_3 + \alpha_6 = 1$. Instead of calculating factor intensity measures and their growth rates for all producer inputs and estimating equation (2.33), one can use all original factor input growth measures and equation (2.35) or equivalently (2.25) with restriction $\beta_1 + \beta_3 + \beta_6 = 1$ to estimate all coefficients, α_i, for labor productivity growth. If production is characterized by constant return to producer physical input, the restriction, $\beta_1 + \beta_3 + \beta_6 = 1$, is redundant and empirical estimation will show an insignificant estimate for the Lagrangian multiplier of the restriction. In that case, the production growth equation and the productivity growth equation have identical parameters. Notably, interpretations of the parameters for equation (2.25) and (2.35) are different. In the labor productivity growth equation, parameter α_i, $i \neq 3$, is the elasticity of labor productivity with respect to input intensity, namely, partial contribution of one percent increase in intensity of factor input X_i, X_i/L, to the growth rate of labor productivity. It is also easy to see that, holding other things constant, a L_t percent increase in labor input will lower labor productivity by $\alpha_3 L_t$.

2.4. MORE ABOUT TECHNOLOGICAL CHANGE AND REGIONAL FACTORS: A PRODUCTION FUNCTION APPROACH

Using a production function to analyze the impacts of technology and regional variables on production and productivity can be an important part of a research of this type, supplemental to growth equation. There are at least two reasons that a production function approach may have advantages over growth equations.

First, many regional contextual variables do not change much over a short period. During such a period producers may have adjusted the combination of their inputs and chosen the most appropriate technology in accordance with their physical and technological environment. In this production growth context producer equilibrium implies that advantages of technology and regional factors may be realized and the marginal products of these external factors may have approached zero. Therefore, these variables can be insignificant in growth models. Unlike the case in growth context, the level of production at any time can be related to the levels of the technological inputs and regional factors directly and indirectly no matter whether these variables change over time or not. Theoretically, it is cross sectional differences in technology and physical environment that are responsible for different levels of production across areas. To fully understand the role technology and regional variables play, we need also to examine the proposed relationship within a production function framework. By the same token, a production function approach can estimate the impact on production of producer characteristics that do not change over time.

Second, a growth model using two periods' data can only generate one single parameter estimate for each input. An evaluation of dynamic change in the parameter has to rely on information over a longer period. This requires substantially more resources to conduct research. In contrast, a production function only uses one period's data to estimate the relationship between output and each input. Economics theory can provide crucial connection between these parameter estimates and many other economic variables of interest. Under a common assumption of a specific functional form, these estimates are transferable to the parameter estimates in the growth equation. In this sense, the application of a production function approach is an economical way to do empirical research provided an appropriate functional form can be specified. Moreover, given data measured for two periods, a production function approach can generate two sets of parameter estimates. The evaluation of technological change and variation of influence of regional factors over time becomes a easier task. Neutral and non-neutral technological changes can be distinguished without great difficulties.

Before discussing any specific production functional form, we need to clarify two points conceptually. First, a production function defines a technological possibility of producing maximum output for a given set of inputs, while empirically observed input-output relationship normally does not reflect the technological possibility. In other words, production in economics is an ex-ante expression reflecting the best technology available, but a realized input-output relationship in production is an ex-post picture more or less behind the best technology. Compared with theoretical production function, the realized input-output relationship can be named empirical production function. Both types of production functions are needed in economic research. A theoretical production function embodies a rigorous theoretical base, formulates an input-output technical relationship, and suggests well rooted hypotheses. An empirical production function provides a test for the hypotheses and discovers an average technology used.

Second, a production function with a set of specified parameters can only describe a single input-output relationship. This relationship changes cross-sectionally and inter-temporally. Empirically, no rigorous theoretical input-output relationship can possibly be examined. Since any empirical study must involve a technical issue of identifying parameters, many observations actually representing a range of production functions are required to establish a single empirical function. The resultant empirical function can only be an average of the range of input-output relationships across different producers (or over time if the study object stays the same).

In short, there are two implications in using a production function. First, revealed relationship is an empirical one that may not be the same as defined in economic theory. Second, the relationship represents an average technology used by the whole group of producers.

Unlike growth models, a general form of production function cannot be performed empirically. An important earlier research (Christensen, Jorgenson and Lau 1971, 1973) shows that transcendental logarithmic (Translog) function is the most general functional form that can provide a good local second-order approximation to any production frontier. It is proposed and demonstrated that a Translog functional form should be used when the knowledge about functional form is not available. Many empirical studies have followed this direction and empirically verified the value of the device. A Translog production function with two inputs and one output is

(2.36)
$$LnQ = \beta_0 + \beta_k LnK + \beta_L LnL + \frac{1}{2}\beta_{KK}(LnK)^2$$
$$+ \beta_{KL} LnK LnL + \frac{1}{2}\beta_{LL}(LnL)^2,$$

where Q, K, and L respectively are the levels of output, capital and labor input and β_i, $i=1,2...$, are the parameters to be estimated. Under assumptions of additivity (i.e., output is assumed to be linearly dependent on inputs) and homogeneity (i.e., $aQ=F(aK, aL)$), all quadratic terms are dropped and the general production function can be reduced to special cases, either CES function ($Q^\alpha=\beta K^\alpha + (1-\beta)L^\alpha$) or C-D function ($lnQ=\beta lnK + (1-\beta)lnL$). The Translog production function is the general form, which does not need the popular yet more restrictive assumptions. The only assumption remaining, when applying the Translog production function, is a producer equilibrium expressed as marginal product of input i equal to the price rate of input i. Specifically, taking derivative of (2.36) with respect to capital and labor respectively yields

(2.37)
$$\frac{dQ}{dK}\frac{K}{Q}=\beta_K+\beta_{KL}LnL+\beta_{KK}LnK \,,$$

$$\frac{dQ}{dL}\frac{L}{Q}=\beta_L+\beta_{KL}LnK+\beta_{LL}LnL \,.$$

Producer equilibrium implies marginal products dQ/dK and dQ/dL equal to the prices of capital and labor respectively and (2.37) can be rewritten as

(2.38)
$$\frac{rK}{Q}=\beta_K+\beta_{KL}LnL+\beta_{KK}LnK \,,$$

$$\frac{wL}{Q}=\beta_L+\beta_{KL}LnK+\beta_{LL}LnL \,,$$

where r and w are the interest rate and the wage rate respectively. Since income shares of capital and labor should add up to total value of output, namely, $rK+wL=Q$ or $rK/Q+wL/Q=1$, the following equations must hold

(2.40)
$$\beta_K+\beta_L=1, \ \beta_{KK}+\beta_{KL}=0, \ \beta_{KL}+\beta_{LL}=0 \,.$$

This defines a set of restrictions on the parameters of the Translog production function. In a more general case a Translog production function can include more inputs. All the terms in the function and a larger set of restrictions can be derived without technical difficulty.

Application of the Translog function, however, has a serious practical restriction if the number of inputs is relatively large. The number of parameters to be estimated is normally many times the number of inputs, resulting in multicollinear and insignificant parameter estimates. This may explain why earlier empirical research only includes few inputs. In an empirical research, evidence from estimates of growth equations and from pretests of functional form can be used to justify an appropriate production function.

2.5. ANALYTICAL FRAMEWORK OF GROWTH

The major causal relationships to be tested are impacts of technological progress, technological inputs, and regional factors on production and productivity growth. These relationships cannot be examined in any single equation. An analytical framework of this research consists of four relatively independent yet integrated groups of equations examining different aspects of the relationships between technological progress, technological inputs, regional factors, and production and productivity growth. First, a set of growth equations is used to evaluate the direct contribution of each technology related variable and regional factor to production and labor productivity growth. Second, the most important indicators of technological efficiency: TFP, scale economies, and neutral technological progress are computed for each producer, and the impacts of technological inputs, regional factors, and producer's attributes on technological efficiency measured by these indicators are examined. The impacts reflect a part of the indirect contribution of technology and regional factors to production and productivity growth. Third, additional indirect contribution of technology related variables and regional factors to growth are estimated using a set of producer input demand functions. Fourth, a production function is estimated for different periods, and a conventional comparison and a rigorous statistical test are performed. These estimates shed light on the contribution to growth of each important technological input and regional factor, the impact of these variables on technological progress, and the nature of technological change.

Because effects of many factors are confounded in the real world, the relationship between several groups of variables should be sorted out conceptually.

First, two types of major independent variables to measure embodied and disembodied technological progress need to be specified. The age distribution on production facilities is used as a proxy measure of technology embodied in capital stock. An empirical relationship between the age and embodied technology was specified in equation (2.14'). Educational attainment and professional experience of workers are used as measures of knowledge and skill of labor. Empirical forms similar to (2.16) are established. Production workers and technical/professional employees are measured separately. Technological inputs including producer R & D, patent purchase or license, investment in computer control system and in machine upgrading, spending on management system, and expenditure on training programs are introduced separately. From producer point of view, most of these inputs, except R & D, are similar to conventional inputs, because external economies of these investment are negligible. R & D stock is different from other inputs. R & D input may suffer from higher risk of failure and external economies. One may expect that only those companies that have strong technological position in their industry may afford this luxury, because they are more capable of appropriating benefit from R & D activities. According to Griliches (1986), the possibility is that 'rich' successful firms are both more productive and can afford to invest more in R & D.

Second, regional factors may be necessary inputs for production. The key regional variables to be studied are agglomeration including urbanization and localization, technological externalities from other producers in the same industry[5], producer services, regional affluence, consumer services, and amenities. In earlier research, all these variables were suggested to have influence on production growth, but precise relationships and quantitative impacts remain to be known. Some of the variables can be highly correlated. This will be tested empirically.

Third, conventional factor inputs, capital and labor, are almost always contributors of output growth. The value of capital stock and the physical units of labor have conventional meaning in production growth. The terms of capital and labor, assuming they are deprived of embodied technologies, are included to estimate their contribution to production growth at the company level. Also they serve as the most important control variables to investigate the contribution of technology related variables and regional factors.

Fourth, the producer's size, organization, age, type of ownership, and other attributes may affect the adoption of advanced technologies (Rees et al. 1986). It may be believed that these producer attributes may affect production growth directly or indirectly due to their influence on technological adoptability or adaptability.

Fifth, any policy related to R & D investment can affect technological inputs directly and output growth indirectly through changing the cost or profitability of the technological input. Therefore, whether or not a producer has enjoyed special public programs or policies such as R & D investment credit and technical support should be taken into account. In this study a dummy variable indicating whether or not a producer uses local R & D credit is included in production function and growth equation[6].

Finally, production and productivity growth can result either from an increase in all producer inputs and relevant regional inputs or from producer internal technological efficiency which is measured by total factor productivity, scale economies, and neutral technological progress. Internal technological efficiency cannot be directly observed but can be estimated. Technological efficiency may be also determined by producer technological input, producer attributes, and regional factors. The measures of technological efficiency are derived and used as a set of dependent variables in the research.

A conceptual framework is developed using the relationships between production/productivity and six groups of the variables. The framework is shown in Figure 2.1. An arrow points to the direction of influence. A line with two arrows at both ends indicates that the two groups of factors are mutually influenced.

The relationships between the variables in groups (i), (ii) and (iv) are the major interest of the study. With respect to these relationships, the variables in group (v), (vi), and (vii) serve as controls. The producer inputs in group (i) and (vi) are endogenous variables that are affected by each other and by variables in group (ii), (v), and (vii). These endogenous variables may cause simultaneous bias in estimating production functions. Simultaneous equations or instrument variables are desirable in mitigating the probable bias. On the other hand, internal validity for growth equations is less likely to

Figure 2.1. Conceptual Relationships of Various Variables

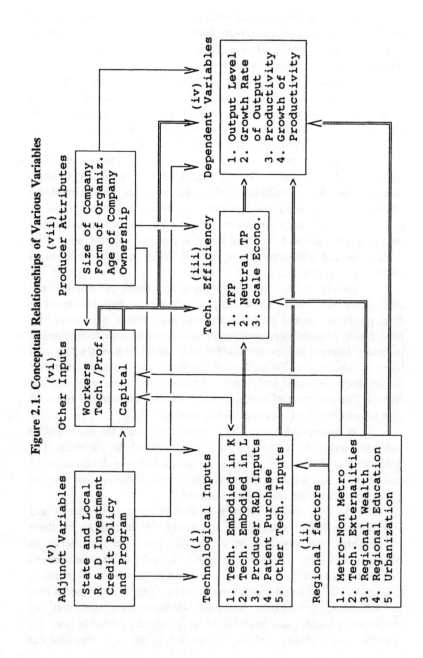

be threatened. The effects of regional factors on technological efficiency (TFP, scale economies, and neutral technological change) and technological inputs are also a basic concern, because this reflects the indirect contribution of regional factors to production growth.

The first group of operational equations is the growth model, which will be tested first. The variables in group (v) and (vii) are irrelevant, because the regional policy variables and the company attributes are constant in a short period, although some company attributes can be important to production function. The variables in group (iii) measuring internal technological progress of efficiency are not directly measurable.

To estimate the second group of the operational equations (determinants of internal technological efficiency), the variables in group (i), (ii), (vi), and (vii) are relevant. The measure of total factor productivity (TFP), economies of scale, and neutral technological progress are estimated. Technological efficiency is conceptually determined by producer technological inputs, conventional inputs, regional factors, and company characteristics.

The third group (determinants of producer technological inputs) is estimated using other internal inputs, regional factors, and company characteristics as independent variables. The specific form of the equations is determined by production function and producer optimization behavior. The equations will be derived in a later chapter. The relevant variables are in group (ii), (v), (vi), and (vii).

Finally, all measurable variables except those in group (iii) are used in establishing and estimating production function and examining the nature of the technological change.

Notes

1. The approximation may be shown as below

$$J(t) = \sum_0^t K_v(t)(1+\lambda_k)^v = (1+\lambda_k)^{-A_0}(1+\lambda_k)^t \sum_0^t K_v(t)(1+\lambda_k)^{v+A_0-t}$$

$$\approx (1+\lambda_k)^{-A_0}(1+\lambda_k)^t \ K(t)\sum_0^t \left(\frac{K_v(t)}{K(t)}\right)(1+\lambda_k v+\lambda_k A_0-\lambda_k t)$$

$$= (1+\lambda_k)^{-A_0}(1+\lambda_k)^t \ K(t)\left[1+\lambda_k A_0-\sum_0^t \left(\frac{K(t)}{K_t}\right)\lambda_k(t-v)\right]$$

$$= (1+\lambda_k)^{-A_0}(1+\lambda_k)^t \ K(t)[1+\lambda_k(A_0-A_t)] \ .$$

2. Taking logarithm of both sides yields

$$LnJ(t) = -A_0 Ln(1+\lambda_k)+tLn(1+\lambda_k)+LnK(t)+Ln(1+\lambda_k(A_0-A_t)).$$

Differentiating this logarithm function with respect to t results in the following form,

$$\frac{dJ(t)}{J(t)dt} = 0+Ln(1+\lambda_k)+\frac{dK(t)}{K(t)dt}+\frac{-\lambda_k d(A_t)}{(1+\lambda_k(A_0-A_t))dt}$$

$$\approx \lambda_k+\frac{dK(t)}{K(t)dt}-\lambda_k\frac{dA_t}{dt} \ .$$

3.

$$\sum_{t_s=0}^{Max(t_s)} \sum_{t_e=0}^{Max(t_e)} \left(\frac{L_{t_s t_e}(t)}{L(t)}\right)e^{\lambda_s t_s}e^{\lambda_e t_e} = \sum_{t_s=0}^{Max(t_s)} \sum_{t_e=0}^{Max(t_e)} \left(\frac{L_{t_s}(t)}{L(t)}\right)\left(\frac{L_{t_e}(t)}{L(t)}\right)e^{\lambda_s t_s}e^{\lambda_e t_e}$$

$$= \left[\sum_{t_s=0}^{Max(t_s)} \left(\frac{L_{t_s}(t)}{L(t)}\right)e^{\lambda_s t_s}\right]\times\left[\sum_{t_e=0}^{Max(t_e)} \left(\frac{L_{t_e}(t)}{L(t)}\right)e^{\lambda_e t_e}\right] = E_{t_s}(t)E_{t_e}(t)$$

4. In an early study (Beeson 1987) growth of TFP is divided into the economies of scale and neutral technological progress to

examine the relationship between these variables and urban agglomeration.

5. A full appreciation of technological externalities needs information on all aspects of the technological position of technological sender and recipient. If the technological positions of two producers are measured by two vectors consisting of the same variables, then dot product (i.e., cosine) of the two vectors can adequately measure technological proximity of the two agents. The proximity can measure impact of spillovers of technology (see Adam B. Jeffe, 1986, for detail). Due to the limited resource, this study uses size of the same industrial production and size of R&D service sector in the same area as measures of technological externalities, other regional service sectors such as communication and air transportation may also capture part of the influence of technological externalities on production and productivity growth though.

6. From a regional policy point of view, a more appropriate measure is a variable to indicate whether or not there exists a local R & D program or investment policy.

3 Variables, Data, and Sampling

Each industry has its unique bundle of products and distinct process of production. The technology used in production and the intensities of the technological inputs and conventional inputs can vary dramatically from industry to industry. The pace of technological change is also different among industries. More importantly, a distinction between technological leaders and technology recipients should be made--technological advance in the leading industries not only contributes to productivity growth of their own industries but also leads to growth of other related industries and the whole economy[1]. Technologically different industries also require different locational ingredients. As earlier research indicates, high-tech industries themselves are highly heterogeneous and display disparate spatial tendencies that can only be understood by analyzing disaggregated industries (Glasmeier et al., 1983).

To capture a wide range of technological attributes of producers and to examine the influence of regional factors on production and productivity growth of technologically different producers, this study chooses as study objects two technologically distinct industry groups, computer-electronics (SIC 357, 366, and 367) and textile-apparel (SIC 22 and 23). The computer-electronics group has experienced rapid accumulation in its technology. For instance, the annual rate of technological change measured by change in the price index of computer products is estimated as high as 20-30 percent[2] (Gordon 1989). Many final products in computer-electronics may have never reached a standardized mature stage before they are replaced by better products with more advanced technology. The technologies developed in this industry group are quickly transferred into most segments of the economy, particularly through its final products that are used as intermediate goods or capital goods in other industries. As a technological leader, this industry group has invested in R & D and

55

other technological inputs proportionally much more than the average for the whole economy. This group has also employed proportionally more technical and professional employees than most other industries. In 1985, for example, technical and professional employees in the machinery and electronics industry group, SIC 35 and SIC 36, accounted for 25 percent of total employees as opposed to 10 percent for all manufacturing and 4.6-6.2 percent for apparel and textile group (see Smith 1989). The ratio of technical and professional employees to production workers in the computer industry, SIC 357, can be even higher.

In contrast, the textile-apparel industries have mature products and have experienced more discrete technological progress. This industry group is essentially a recipient of new technologies developed by capital goods industries (Toyne, Arpan, Ricks, Shimp, and Barnett 1984). All notable technological changes in the industry, from innovation of newer machinery such as open end spinning, air jet and water jet shuttleless weaving to automation in textile mills and computer aided design in apparel plants, are initially made by capital goods industries. Final products of this industry do not make perceptible technological contribution to other segments of the economy. Besides the technology embodied in new or upgraded equipment, proportionally less investment has been devoted to technological progress. The textile manufacturing process is believed to bear many similarities to many nondurable consumer goods industries (Pack 1987).

According to the role in leading or following technological change in the whole economy, the speed at which technology proceeds, the intensity of the technological input including R & D input and technical and professional personnel input, and locational requirement, the two groups of industries can be visualized as two extremes of a broad range of production. Other industries can mostly fall in between. By studying these two industry groups the researcher will be in an appropriate position to understand inter-industrial variation in the contributions of technological progress, technological inputs, and regional factors to production and productivity growth. This chapter justifies variables included in the study, describes the process of data acquisition, examines the sample bias and reliability, and presents an overview of the sample data.

3.1. VARIABLES IN THE RESEARCH

Technological progress, producer technological inputs, and regional complemental or substitutive factors are three rather broad concepts with each having many relevant measures. An empirical study must select appropriate indicators to measure those concepts in order to maintain internal validity and test theoretical development. Early studies in the field have provided empirical evidence about the relevance of particular inputs to output. Those pieces of evidence serve as starting point for this research in choosing a specific set of variables. Because this research evaluates the contribution of relevant inputs to output growth, to large extent, success of the research depends on a construction of rigorous causal relationship. Only those factors that are direct inputs or complemental to or substitutive for direct inputs or affect productivity of direct inputs will be introduced into the model.

Producer direct inputs, capital and labor, are the most robust variables. Although many earlier studies treat all types of assets homogeneously, equipment is different from buildings in nature: the former is more liquid and easier to adjust in input level than the latter. A recent study (De Long and Summers 1991) using 61 countries' aggregate data revealed that the relationship between capital input and output growth becomes clear only after equipment and structure are separately measured, and that the reason many early studies found a weaker link between investment and growth is attributable to an inappropriate level of aggregation. In the current study, value of equipment and value of structure are measured separately to evaluate the contribution each type of capital made to growth. Labor input can be as heterogenous as capital. Manual labor normally cannot substitute for skilled labor, particularly in a place where sophisticated knowledge or high skill is a necessity to perform the job. Earlier research (Uno 1988) also found that both capital and well educated labor can easily substitute for less educated labor in developed areas and that aggregation of educated and less educated labor will generate estimate inconsistency with separate measures. It is an explicit effort of this study to examine the contribution to production growth of two different labor inputs; production workers and technical/ professional/ managerial employees.

Technology embodied in physical inputs is a major interest of the research. Theoretical and practical interest in the technology embodied in capital goods has stimulated a large volume of literature. Unfortunately, no direct measure of the embodied technology is available. As of today the best proxy is still the average age of capital stock. The empirical estimate of the contribution of embodied technology to production and productivity growth is inconclusive, particularly after Denison (1964, 1985) challenged the importance of embodied technology to growth. Later empirical research, however, did not stop investigating the relationship between embodied technology and growth, but the empirical tests generated mixed results (You 1976, McHugh and Lane 1983, 1987). As a proxy of technology embodied in capital, the weighted average age of the capital stock is used in this research. This study employs two different models of age-technology relationship. One was developed in the previous chapter and the other was proposed by Nelson (1964). Average age of equipment must be estimated before the two proxy measures of technology can be put in an equation. With the better measure of average age of capital, this study will generate a less biased estimate of the relationship between embodied technology and production and productivity growth or, more precisely, the relationship between capital age and growth.

It is less controversial to speak of the influence of educational attainment and professional experience of workers on production and productivity growth. A detailed and influential research (Denison 1985) indicates that based on national aggregate data, of labor productivity growth in the U.S. economy, about 16 percent is credited to the increased educational qualification of the average workers and 34 percent is attributed to growth of knowledge. These two closely related factors alone are responsible for one half of productivity growth. At the micro level, literature on wage differentials shows more evidence that industrial occupational differences and labor characteristics measured by educational attainment and experience are major sources of wage differentials. The same literature also reveals that market force tends to equalize the return to labor characteristics (i.e., Dickie and Gerking 1987, Farber and Newman 1989). Since growth of knowledge is a macro variable which is constant at any given time in a micro cross sectional analysis, no separate term will be used to measure general knowledge. The current study chooses four variables to measure educational attainment and work experience, two for production workers and two for technical/ professional/ managerial employees.

In addition to the conventional inputs and the technology embodied in the inputs, producers intentionally invest in technological activities. A part of the investment is devoted to R & D producing new technology and ultimately increasing productivity. The interest in the relationship between R & D and productivity growth has inspired many theoretical and empirical works. Research on R & D and its influence on productivity has become a distinct field of theoretical and applied economics. Most studies are concerned with the nature of R & D activities, the rate of return to R & D input, and effectiveness to promote growth through R & D investment. The R & D input is considered to differ from other producer inputs in nature because it generates considerable external economies. Unlike conventional inputs, the R & D investment normally cannot influence growth right away and the time lag or the period of gestation is less well known. These technological externalities and time lag of impact of R & D input put a heavy burden on researchers if social cost-benefit needs to be calculated and policy issues need to be addressed. Because of the limited resources, this research will only consider private return to R & D activities. The lag effect of R & D input on production and productivity growth can obscure the true relationship between R & D growth and productivity growth. Many empirical studies (i.e., Mansfield 1968, 1977, 1980, Pakes and Schankerman 1984) employed different research approaches to estimate the time lag between R & D investment and the market appearance of new technology and found that applied R & D has an average time lag of about 1.2 to 2.5 years, depending on the technology used in product or process and in different industries. In the current cross sectional study, the annualized growth rates of R & D capital and output computed over a 5-year period can partly mitigate the time lag problem. The 5-year annualized data will insure that the contribution of R & D input growth will be reflected in production and productivity growth measures, although the contribution may be underestimated.

The literature identifies another type of technological inputs that facilitates adoption of new technology. Inputs in patent purchase, computer or numerical control device/system, machine upgrading, improvement of management system, and employee training all fall in this category. These five inputs are different from R & D input, because there is basically no technological spillover from the inputs. The inputs are also different from conventional inputs, because these inputs may not be necessary for production, and the rates of return may vary widely. There exists little knowledge about their contribution to growth and the average return to these inputs, although there is a general appreciation about the importance of these technological inputs. Patent purchase can be considered as a substitution for a company's own R & D activities with less uncertainty. Patent purchase is also a crucial diffusion process which makes it possible for innovators to realize the return to uncertain R & D activities. At the producer level, the rate of return to the patent purchase is not well documented. We are in an early stage to understand the contribution of the intangible input to productivity growth. If the market functions well, the rate of return to the intangible input should be approximately the same as that to investment in other factors. An increase in patents used by a producer is expected to contribute positively to production and productivity growth. Similarly, all other technological inputs are expected to contribute to production and productivity growth. The five technological inputs listed earlier in this paragraph and measured by monetary units are selected to estimate their contribution to growth.

The contribution of regional factors to productivity growth is the second major part of the research. According to earlier research and conceptual justification, the current research introduces a set of regional factors into growth models. There are several conditions, under each of which a regional factor can be included. First, a regional factor is at least partly complemental to other internal inputs, because well established location theory suggests that some external factors are necessary conditions to production and that insufficient provision of the factor forms a bottleneck to production growth. Many variables measuring social infrastructure such as utilities, transportation, and communication are in this category. Second, a regional factor is substitutive for producer internal inputs. In this case, producers may utilize the external input and lower producer cost, resulting in production and productivity growth. A majority of producer services and technological externalities can play this role. Third, a regional factor may help to maintain or even upgrade producer internal inputs without incurring expense to producers. Regional amenities, health care services, education services, and social services may all function more or less in this way. Fourth, a regional factor may affect production and productivity growth adversely if presence of the factor or increase in the value of the factor incurs cost to producers. For instance, a higher wage rate tends to force producers to lower their labor input in order to raise their value of marginal product. The partial causal relationship in this case runs from higher wage to lower growth rate via cutting labor input.

Establishing a causal model in social research is always a difficult task, because many factors are mutually causally related. Interpretation of the estimates must be made cautiously. Taking the wage rate as an example, an estimated parameter may reflect a reversal of a proposed causal direction. If change in the wage rate shows a negative relationship with production and productivity growth, the causal direction is very likely to be from wage rate to production growth. Thus, the justified effect of the wage rate on growth is empirically verified. If the estimate shows a positive relationship between wage and growth, the actual causal direction may not run from wage to growth. It is possible that production growth leads to more employment in the relevant industry and at the same time productivity growth may raise the marginal product of labor input. These growths in combination provide a necessary and sufficient condition to raise wage rate in the industry. On the other hand, the efficiency wage theory (see, for example, Katz 1986) may explain that high wage rate results in high productivity--a causal direction from wage rate to productivity. In this circumstance, the direction of causal relation can be inconclusive.

The regional factors preselected in this research include: size of relevant industries (SIC 22, 23, 357, 366, 367 separately) to measure localization economies and external economies, air transportation services (SIC 45), other transportation services (SIC 47), communication services (SIC 48), utilities services (SIC 49), finance-insurance-securities-real estate-combinations services (SIC 60-66 combined), recreation and amusement services (SIC 79), health services (SIC 80), educational services (SIC 82), social services (SIC 83), engineering, accounting, R & D, management, and related services (SIC 87), and in particular, R & D and testing services (SIC 873) to measure regional services and the business environment. All the regional factors are measured by both the size and the growth rate of employment and the number of establishment. Only after extensive tests, a single measure for each regional factor will be retained in the growth models. The wage rates of relevant industries (SIC 22, 23, 357, 366, 367 separately) to measure factor cost are included. A population variable, a urban population percentage variable, and a metro area dummy are used to capture impact of agglomeration and influence of metro factors not specified. Percentage of people who are 25 years and older with a college degree is used to measure the quality of local labor force.

3.2. A NATIONWIDE MAIL SURVEY

The study population in this research is the U.S. textile-apparel and computer-electronics industries. The unit of analysis is individual manufacturer (establishment). Companies which have been in business for more than five years were sampled to obtain growth rate in the past five years. Data on regional factors are available in secondary form. A large amount of data, particularly the levels and the changes of capital stock and the age distribution, employees' educational attainment and work experience, producer R & D facilities, other technological inputs, and output in the past five years, had to be collected from the companies. *Ward's Business Directory of U.S. Private and Public Companies-1990* provided a list for textile-apparel and computer-electronics manufacturers in the nation (about 4,500 companies in textile-apparel industries and about 3,000 in computer-electronics). Given the reputation of the business directory, a study of a sample randomly generated from this sample frame should produce representative findings for the industries. However, the sample needs to be sufficiently large to cover enough variation in each important aspect to generate findings with internal and external validity.

Anticipating the difficulty of primary data collection, two questionnaires for the two industry groups were drafted and revised many times. A balance between accuracy of the measures and a higher response rate was made. Some questions were closed-ended, but supplemental open-ended questions were asked when accurate quantitative values were highly desirable. A pretest of a hundred-questionnaire survey was conducted in February 1991 to determine appropriateness of the questions and size of mailing sample. The result of the pretest showed that about ten percent of the respondents would complete the sophisticated questionnaire. From early June to mid-August 1991 a nationwide mail survey was conducted using a revised questionnaire. The questionnaire for computer-electronics manufacturers is shown in the appendix to this chapter. The questionnaire used for textile-apparel companies is similar to that for computer-electronics. This study basically employed Total Design Method (Dillman 1977) which has been proven in earlier studies to be one of the best survey techniques. From each of the two industry groups, 2,000 companies were randomly selected. Each company was sent a questionnaire with an individualized cover letter, and a week later an individualized follow-up reminder. After another two weeks a replacement of the questionnaire with yet another individualized letter was mailed to those who did not respond to early letters. Overall about 12,000 individualized correspondences were sent to 4,000 companies. That survey generated 489 completed questionnaires, with 210 in computer-electronics and 279 in textile-apparel industries. Due to limited research resources, bulk rate was used to send all the questionnaires. The biggest disadvantage is that the researcher cannot trace those companies who may have changed mailing address or gone out of business, and no feedback can be obtained from the post office. Results from an earlier survey (Rees 1991) suggests that up to 50 percent of companies may have changed addresses or gone out of business (his mailing addresses are from the Dun and Bradstreet files). An industry like computer-electronics whose technology may soon become obsolescent is expected to experience constant reorganization, because many companies may start up or close down at any given time. Therefore, of companies that are targeted in a survey, only about a half may remain accurate in the list. Given the nature as well as the number of the questions which demanded substantial effort from respondents, response rate of 489 out of the original 4,000 is a significant achievement.

3.3. EVALUATION OF SAMPLE DATA

3.3.1. Sample Bias

Non-response is one of the most formidable problems in primary data collection. Two types of non-response can be specified. One is a whole observation missing. The other is part of questions left unanswered. Both types of non-response can result in selection bias. A broad range of techniques is available to test and correct for these biases (Mitchell and Carson 1989). Weighted sample statistics are used to correct the first type of bias if the statistical method used is relatively simple. Sample bias can be detected when population distributions about their attributes are known. In this research *Ward's Business Directory of U.S. Private and Public Companies-1990* provides information on several key variables in the sampling frame. Notably, employment, total sale, location, ownership, and age of each company in the population can be used to check sample bias. If a bias is detected, interpretation of research findings should be made with caution. There exist more methods to handle the problem of missing values on single variables. Multivariate regression may be used to estimate the missing items, but a more objective way may be to do nothing on those missing values.

A series of efforts was made to check sample bias. Table 3.1 shows geographical distributions of population and sample data across states. A pairwise comparison was used to check the bias[3]. The sample distribution for computer-electronics industries closely resembles the distribution of the sampling frame across states. Sample percentage distributions for textile-apparel industries in most states are similar to the distributions of the sampling frame. In a few cases such as North Carolina and New York, the sample overrepresents one and underrepresents the other. In general, geographical distribution of the sample appears not to be seriously biased.

Table 3.2 evaluates sample bias with respect to different types of respondents. The sample for computer-electronics shows that public corporations in the sample are 11.1 percent as opposed to 23.6 percent in the sampling frame, while private companies in the sample are 55.8 percent compared with 36.8 percent in the sampling frame. The sample of textile-apparel industries have similar distribution as in the sampling frame.

Table 3.3 presents sampling frame and sample distributions across different sizes of employment. The sample of computer - electronics has higher percentage distributions than their counterparts in the population in three smaller categories, while the sample of textile-apparel industries does not show apparent bias.

Table 3.4 examines sample bias with respect to size of total sales. Small textile-apparel companies are slightly overrepresented, whereas large companies with sales more than $200 millions are underrepresented. Compared with the sample of textile-apparel industries, the sample of computer-electronics appears biased toward smaller companies with sales of $2 millions to $10 millions. All larger categories are underrepresented.

In combination, Table 3.2, Table 3.3, and Table 3.4 suggest that the sample of textile-apparel can reasonably represent the study population, while the sample of computer-electronics is biased against large public corporations. Research findings from this sample can be generalized to the whole textile-apparel industry in the nation, but findings for computer-electronics apply to smaller private producers better than to large public corporations.

**Table 3.1 Comparison of Sampling Frame and Sample Distribution
By Geographical Location**

	TEXTILE & APPAREL			COMPUTER & ELECTRONICS	
State Code	SAMPLING FRAME Percent	SAMPLE Percent	State Code	SAMPLING FRAME Percent	SAMPLE Percent
AL	3.4	3.4	AL	0.3	0.0
AR	0.7	1.1	AR	0.4	0.5
AZ	0.2	0.4	AZ	1.5	1.0
CA	6.0	6.1	CA	25.3	22.1
CO	0.2	0.0	CO	1.4	3.0
CT	1.3	1.5	CT	3.8	4.5
DE	0.2	0.0	DE	0.1	0.0
FL	1.3	1.5	FL	3.9	3.0
GA	8.2	5.7	GA	0.8	0.5
HI	0.1	0.0	IA	0.5	0.5
IA	0.4	0.4	ID	0.3	0.0
IL	2.1	1.5	IL	6.4	6.5
IN	0.8	0.4	IN	1.9	4.5
KS	0.2	0.4	KS	0.3	0.5
KY	1.3	1.9	KY	0.3	0.5
LA	0.6	0.4	LA	0.1	0.0
MA	3.1	2.3	MA	7.3	4.5
MD	0.6	0.4	MD	1.5	0.5
ME	0.6	0.4	ME	0.5	0.5
MI	0.9	1.5	MI	1.7	1.5
MN	1.1	0.8	MN	3.4	3.5
MO	1.8	1.1	MO	0.7	1.0
MS	2.7	1.1	MS	0.2	0.0
MT	0.0	0.4	MT	0.0	0.0
NC	14.0	20.8	MY	0.1	0.0
ND	0.0	0.4	NC	1.3	2.0
NE	0.1	0.0	NE	0.4	0.0
NH	0.4	0.0	NH	1.4	1.5
NJ	3.4	1.1	NJ	6.6	5.0
NM	0.1	0.0	NM	0.2	0.5
NV	0.0	0.0	NV	0.1	0.5
NY	14.5	9.1	NY	9.7	9.5
OH	1.3	2.7	OH	2.0	2.5
OK	0.5	1.1	OK	0.5	0.0
OR	0.2	0.4	OR	0.7	1.0
PA	8.7	8.0	PA	4.6	5.0
RI	0.8	1.5	RI	0.4	0.0
SC	6.5	5.7	SC	0.8	0.5
SD	0.1	0.0	SD	0.3	1.0
TN	3.9	5.3	TN	0.3	0.5
TX	3.4	4.2	TX	3.7	4.5
UT	0.4	0.4	UT	0.8	1.5
VA	1.9	2.3	VA	1.4	1.0
VT	0.1	0.4	VT	0.4	0.5
WA	0.7	0.4	WA	0.9	0.5
WI	0.9	1.1	WI	0.9	2.0
WV	0.2	0.8	WY	0.0	0.0

**Table 3.2 Comparison of Sampling Frame and Sample Distribution
By Type of Companies**

	TEXTILE & APPAREL			COMPUTER & ELECTRONICS	
TYPE	SAMPLING FRAME Percent	SAMPLE Percent	TYPE	SAMPLING FRAME Percent	SAMPLE Percent
A	0.2	0.4	A	0.3	0.0
D	28.3	25.8	D	20.2	15.1
J	0.0	0.0	J	0.1	0.0
P	2.4	1.5	P	23.6	11.1
R	58.2	64.8	R	36.8	55.8
S	10.9	7.6	S	19.0	16.6

Note: The definitions of the company types:
  A = Affiliate
  D = Division
  J = Joint Venture
  P = Public Corporation
  R = Private Corporation
  S = Subsidiary

**Table 3.3 Comparison of Sampling Frame and Sample Distribution
By Employment Size of Companies**

	TEXTILE & APPAREL		COMPUTER & ELECTRONICS	
EMPLOYMENT	SAMPLING FRAME Percent	SAMPLE Percent	SAMPLING FRAME Percent	SAMPLE Percent
<= 100	42.3	40.2	44.7	54.8
101- 200	19.9	25.8	13.8	19.1
201- 300	10.8	12.1	8.0	10.1
301- 400	6.7	6.1	5.0	4.0
401- 500	4.9	3.4	4.2	4.0
501- 600	2.5	2.7	2.7	0.5
601- 700	1.8	1.5	1.6	3.0
701- 800	1.6	1.5	2.0	0.5
801- 900	1.0	0.8	1.7	0.5
901-1000	1.3	1.1	1.5	1.5
1000+	7.3	4.9	14.8	2.0

Table 3.4 Comparison of Sampling Frame and Sample Distribution
By Total Sales of Companies

	TEXTILE & APPAREL		COMPUTER & ELECTRONICS	
SALE	SAMPLING FRAME Percent	SAMPLE Percent	SAMPLING FRAME Percent	SAMPLE Percent
<= 1000	5.2	5.3	4.6	3.5
1001- 2000	4.5	11.7	4.7	12.6
2001- 5000	16.2	18.2	16.8	25.1
5001- 10000	21.4	15.9	16.3	19.1
10001- 20000	23.9	19.3	16.1	14.1
20001- 50000	18.3	19.7	17.9	15.6
50001- 75000	3.4	3.4	4.7	2.5
75001-100000	1.7	2.7	3.4	1.0
100001-200000	2.6	2.7	6.7	4.5
200000+	2.6	1.1	8.7	2.0

Note:
Sales in thousand dollars.

3.3.2. Reliability of Sample Data

Assessment of the reliability of survey data is another crucial step in the research, since data from a questionnaire survey frequently suffer from the casual attitude of respondents. A test-retest method (Bohrnstedt 1983) was suggested to collect and assess data on a few key variables. Specifically, data on key variables could be surveyed twice for the same sample. Correlation between the values from the two surveys could be checked to assess the reliability of data. In practice, limited resources normally prohibit the effort of this kind. In this research data on several key variables furnished by the published business directory can serve the same purpose. Employment and total sales figures are analyzed to assess the reliability of the sample data.

The correlation coefficient between primary data and published information is greater than 0.8 for textile-apparel companies and greater than 0.7 for computer-electronics companies, both for employment and total sales variables. Further, simple regression analysis indicates that small textile-apparel companies with less than 200 employees as shown in the published list may have systematically reported their employment figures in the survey greater than those published. The same instance occurs in computer-electronics companies, with the breaking point at 175 employees. This may suggest that either the data from the survey or the data from business directory is inaccurate, or smaller companies who responded to the survey have experienced growth since the last survey conducted by the publisher of *Ward's Business Directory* (because the publisher must collect the data in 1989 or earlier for the 1990 directory). Smaller companies are generally less stable than big companies and are more likely to expand or contract the scale of production or even go out of business when the production technology or market changes. Naturally, declined small companies may be underrepresented, and disappearing companies cannot show up at all in the sample, resulting in an image of growth for small companies. Overall, results indicate that the survey data are fairly reliable. The internal validity of the research should not be seriously threatened by unreliable survey data.

3.4. PREPARATION OF SAMPLE DATA

To create the appropriate measures for variables in growth equations, the researcher must overcome several practical difficulties. First, original survey data show that a number of companies started technological investment after 1985. The growth rates on the inputs of these companies cannot be mathematically calculated, resulting in many missing values. Second, the rate of change in average age of capital stock is one of the key variables in the study. Since information contained in survey data only indicates age distribution over capital vintages in 1990, an age distribution for an earlier year must be determined in order to estimate the rate of change in average age. Third, given the sample of 489 cases for two industry groups consisting of four subgroups (textile, apparel, computer-telecommunication equipment[4], and electronics components) and some technological differences between two industries in each group, we must find a more efficient way to better use the sample data yet distinguish between the two industries in each group. Fourth, many technically not difficult yet conceptually important correction on original survey data must be performed. For instance, it is utilized capital, not gross stock, that should be used in production function and growth equation. Similarly, it is weighted average of schooling and experience of employees that should be used in empirical estimation. Finally, regional factors need to be measured at an appropriate aggregate level, and regional variables which are industry-specific need to be created.

3.4.1. Growth Rates of Technological Inputs

The sample data show that until 1985 many producers, especially textile-apparel manufacturers, did not invest in technological inputs. If these companies were omitted from the estimation of growth equations, the number of sample cases could shrink by about one half for textile-apparel companies and about one third for computer-electronics companies. To use the sample data efficiently, the following rule is adopted to save these observations. The growth rate of input is set to equal zero if the input is zero before and after 1985; the rate is set to equal the sample maximum if the investment is made only after 1985. The second part of the decision rule seems groundless, because the computed growth rate is actually infinity. The fact that a mathematically rigorous result is practically useless suggests that a compromise has to be made. Since mathematically any assignment to a missing value is equally arbitrary, the best approximation is to employ the information about the range of variation of the input growth rate. Therefore, the extreme value revealed in the sample is used to replace the missing values and the size of the sample is retained when moving from levels of inputs and output to growth rates of the inputs and output.

3.4.2. Average Age of Capital Stock

The sample data provide full description of age distribution over capital vintages only for 1990. Given the age distribution and capital vintages remaining in 1990, the average age of capital stock in 1990 can be computed according to the following relation,

(3.1)
$$A(t) = \sum_{v=0}^{t} \frac{K_v(t)}{K(t)} A_v(t) \; ,$$

where $A(t)$ is the average age of capital stock at time t, and $K_v(t)$, $K(t)$, and $A_v(t)$ are, respectively, the value of vintage v, the total value of capital stock, and the age of vintage v at time t. Because it is unrealistic in 1991 to request from respondents for detailed information about the age distribution for 1985, the relevant data have to be acquired indirectly. Data on percent change in the current value of total equipment over 1985-90 period are directly collected from all respondents. The information serves two purposes. One is to measure the growth of capital stock. The other is to control the estimate of the average age of capital stock in 1985. Assuming vintages retire according to their age (i.e., the oldest retires first, the second oldest second, etc.) and a new investment adds the newest vintage into capital stock at that time, a set of formulas is established to estimate average age of capital stock in 1985 using information on age distribution in 1990. Let $\Delta k(t)$ be the growth rate of capital stock in the 1985-90 period measured as proportion, $k_v(t)$ the percentage of capital stock accounted for by vintage v at time t, and $A_v(t)$ the age of vintage v at time t.

Case (1): If $\Delta k(t) > 0$ and $k_i(t) > \Delta k(t)/(1 + \Delta k(t))$, implying that part of investment in production capital in period t is replacement of retired production equipment, the average age of capital stock at time $t-1$ is

$$(3.2) \qquad A(t-1) = \sum_{v=\tau+1}^{t-1} \left(\frac{k_v(t)}{1 - \dfrac{\Delta k(t)}{1+\Delta k(t)}} A_v(t-1) \right)$$
$$+ \left(\frac{k_\tau(t)}{1 - \dfrac{\Delta k(t)}{1+\Delta k(t)}} + \frac{k_t(t)}{1 - \dfrac{\Delta k(t)}{1+\Delta k(t)}} - \Delta k(t) \right) A_\tau(t-1),$$

where τ is such that k_τ is the oldest vintage possible in period $t-1$. Note that $\Delta k(t)/(1 + \Delta k(t))$ is increased value of capital stock measured as proportion at time t. It follows that $k_v(t)/[1-\Delta k(t)/(1 + \Delta k(t))]$ converts the proportion of vintage v at time t to the proportion of vintage v at time $t-1$, i.e., $k_v(t)/[1-\Delta k(t)/(1+\Delta k(t))]=k_v(t-1)$. Notably, equation $k_\tau(t)/[1-\Delta k(t)/(1+\Delta k(t))]=\alpha k_\tau(t-1)$ holds, and the last term of the right hand side, i.e., $\{k_t(t)/[1-\Delta k(t)/(1+\Delta k(t))]-\Delta k(t)\}A_\tau(t-1)$, is equal to $(1-\alpha)k_\tau(t-1)$.

Case (2): If $\Delta k(t) > 0$ and $k_i(t) < \Delta k(t)/(1 + \Delta k(t))$, meaning that a part of investment in production capital in period t is to install production facilities which are not technologically most advanced. Under the assumption that the installed equipment is the next to the most advanced equipment in the company, the formula to estimate average age in the period $t-1$ is

(3.3)
$$A(t-1) = \sum_{v=\tau}^{t_0} \left(\frac{k_v(t)}{1 - \dfrac{\Delta k(t)}{1 + \Delta k(t)}} A_v(t) \right)$$
$$+ \left(\sum_{v=t_0}^{t} \frac{k_v(t)}{1 - \dfrac{\Delta k(t)}{1 + \Delta k(t)}} - \Delta k(t) \right) A_{t_0+1}(t-1),$$

where τ has the same meaning as in (3.2), t_0 is such that $\Sigma'_{v=t_0+1} k_v(t)/[1 - \Delta k(t)/(1 + \Delta k(t))] - \Delta k(t) < 0$ and $\Sigma'_{v=t_0+1} k_v(t)/[1 - \Delta k(t)/(1 + \Delta k(t))] - \Delta k(t) \geq 0$. Note that $\Sigma'_{v=t_0} k_v(t)/[1 - \Delta k(t)/(1 + \Delta k(t))] - \Delta k(t) = k_{t_0+1}(t-1)$.

Case (3): If $\Delta k(t) < 0$, indicating that new investment in period t is not enough to replace retired vintage, then the formula used is

(3.4)
$$A(t-1) = \sum_{v=\tau+1}^{t-1} \left(\frac{k_v(t)}{1 - \dfrac{\Delta k(t)}{1 + \Delta k(t)}} A_v(t-1) \right)$$
$$+ \left(\frac{k_t(t)}{1 - \dfrac{\Delta k(t)}{1 + \Delta k(t)}} - \Delta k(t) \right) A_\tau(t-1) .$$

The average age of capital stock in 1985 is calculated for all companies applying the formulas to sample data. Subsequently, it is a routine task to estimate absolute and relative changes in the average age of capital stock.

3.4.3. Industry-Adjustment Variables

Internal validity and statistical significance of cross sectional estimates of production function and growth equations are crucially dependent on the homogeneity of sample cases. Although the sample of 489 companies is divided into two groups, some technological characteristics may vary between two industries in each group. For instance, descriptive statistics show that textile mills are much more capital intensive than apparel manufacturers and computer-telecommunication equipment companies employ proportionally more technical and professional employees than electronic components producers. On the other hand, two industries in each group do share

many common features with each other. Further dividing each group
into two is neither conceptually necessary nor statistically desirable. A
strategy dealing with the dilemma is to use additional variables for
those inputs whose impacts on output vary between industries in the
same group while retaining the two industries together in each group.
Specifically, an industry dummy was created for apparel companies and
all relevant input variables were multiplied by this dummy, generating
a set of industry-adjustment variables. In model testing, an input that
contributes to output growth in two industries differently can show up
in a parameter estimate of its adjustment variable. For example, if
textile mills are more output elastic with respect to capital input than
apparel manufacturers and the difference is statistically significant, the
researcher should observe the larger positive parameter estimate for the
original measure of capital input and a smaller negative parameter
estimate for the apparel industry-adjustment variable. On the other
hand, if textile production is less output elastic than apparel, the
researcher should see a positive coefficient for the industry-adjustment
variable, which enlarges the output elasticity for apparel industry. To
maintain statistical efficiency, only after testing for the difference
across the industries, are the industry adjustment variables included in
the final growth equations.

3.4.4. Measures of Other Input Growths

A technically routine yet conceptually non-trivial task of
calculating utilized capital, weighted average years of schooling, and
weighted average years of work experiences of production workers and
technical/ professional/ management personnel as well as the growth
rates of these variables must be accomplished. Utilization of capital
input is one of the most important short run factors affecting production
and productivity. Difference in utilization across producers causes
distortion of input-output relationship estimated, resulting in less
significant or biased estimates. To mitigate the distortion, the value of
capital stock was adjusted according to utilization of each company's
equipment. Average years of schooling and average years of work
experience and the rates of change were computed separately for
production workers and professionals. All growth measures over the
1985-90 period were converted to annual growth rates adopting
exponential growth trend.

3.4.5. Data on Regional Factors

A regional contextual factor is exogenous to and independent from a company's production. This study treats regional factors as causal factors, and sees variation in companies' production and productivity growth as responses to the changes in regional factors and other independent variables. A causal examination requires that the change in the exogenous forces be prior to the change in respondents. Thus, in empirical studies the causal variables are usually measured for a period earlier than are dependent variables. A commonly used technique is changing time lag to find the best fit of the proposed relationship between a cause and its effect on the respondents. Since in this research the annual growth rate of production is measured as the geometric mean of the growth rate of the 1985-90 period and since the annual rates of changes in regional factors are means of change rate for the 1983-88 period, the individual producers had up to seven years to respond to exogenous changes. Data from *County Business Patterns* (CBP) and *County and City Data Book* (CCDB) for 1983 and 1988 are used to compute the levels and the growth rates of regional factors. The data were reorganized to reflect regional influence on production. The unit of region was metro area or rural county: in metro areas county level data were aggregated to generate metro level measures, while in rural areas county level data directly served the measure of regional factors.

Many regional factors such as factor input cost and technological externalities are industry-specific. For instance, the variation of the wage rate in the apparel industry may not have direct influence on textile production. To better capture the regional impact yet efficiently use sample data, industry dummies are used to multiply industry-specific regional factors. Specifically, factor cost measured by the wage rate in each industry and technological externalities and localization measured by the size of employment and the number of establishment in the industry in the same area are computed and then multiplies by an industry dummy such that these industry-specific variables can only affect the observations which belong to the industry group in the following econometric estimates. By the same token, industry-specific regional variables for another industry in the same group are also created and included in the single consolidated production function and growth equation. This approach allows for a more accurate measure of the impact of regional factors on production.

3.5. OVERVIEW OF SAMPLE DATA

A label system is used for all the variables. K- indicates that a variable is capital related; W- production worker related; and P- technical/ professional employees related. Capital input, technological inputs, and value added are measured in $1,000. Employment variables are measured in number of persons. All growth variables are measured in annualized percentage growth over the five-year period. These data can be summarized with a few notes. Table 3.5 lists variables and definitions. Table 3.6 presents means and standard deviations of selected variables in the sample.

Table 3.5   Selected Variables and Definitions

Variable	Definition
VALUE90	Value added in 1990, measured in $1,000
VALUEGROW	Annualized percentage growth rate of value added in 1985-90 period
PRDCTVTY	Labor productivity in 1990, measured in value added per employee
PRTY-GRW	Annualized percentage growth rate of labor productivity in 1985-90 period
W-EMP90	Number of production workers in 1990
W-EMPGROW	Annualized percentage growth rate of production workers in 1985-90 period
P-EMP90	Number of technical and professional employees in 1990
P-EMPGROW	Annualized percentage growth rate of technical and professional employees in 1985-90 period
W-EDUC90	Weighted average years of formal education of production workers in 1990
W-EDGROW	Annualized percentage growth rate of years of formal education of workers in 1985-90 period
W-EXP90	Weighted average years of work experience of production workers in 1990
W-EXPGROW	Annualized percentage growth rate of years of work experience of workers in 1985-90 period
P-EDUC90	Weighted average years of formal education of technical and professional employees in 1990

Table 3.5 Selected Variables and Definitions (Con.)

Variable	Definition
P-EDGROW	Annualized percentage growth rate of weighted average years of formal education of technical and professional employees in 1985-90 period
P-EXP90	Weighted average years of professional experience of technical and professional employees in 1990
P-EXPGROW	Annualized percentage growth rate of years of professional experience of technical and professional employees in 1985-90 period
K-EQ90	Value of production equipment in 1990, in $1,000
K-EQGROW	Annualized percentage growth rate of value of production equipment in 1985-90 period
UTI-RATE	Utilization of equipment in 1990, in percentage
K-UTLZ90	Value of utilized production capital in 1990, in $1,000
K-UTLGROW	Annualized percentage change in utilized production capital in 1985-90 period
K-AGE90	Weighted average age of utilized production capital in 1990
K-AGEGROW	Annualized percentage change in average age of utilized production capital in 1985-90 period
K-BD90	Value of structure in 1990, in $1,000
K-BDGROW	Annualized percentage change in value of structure in 1985-90 period
K-R&D90	Value of R & D capital in 1990, in $1,000
K-R&DGROW	Annualized percentage change in value of R & D capital in 1985-90 period
K-CC8590	Accumulated value of input in computer control technology in 1985-90 period, in $1,000
K-MCN8590	Accumulated value of input in machine upgrading in 1985-90 period, in $1,000
K-MNG8590	Accumulated value of input in management improvement in 1985-90 period, in $1,000
K-TRN8590	Accumulated value of spending in employee training in 1985-90 period, in $1,000
PATNT90	Accumulated value of patent purchase and license in 1985-90 period, in $1,000

3.5.1. Input and Output Levels

First, companies in the two industry groups, textile-apparel and computer-electronics, are similar in average size with means of value added in 1990 of $14 million and $16 million and means of employees of 350 and 200 for the two industry groups respectively. Breaking down into four subgroups, textile, apparel, computer, and electronics components, reveals a considerable difference in size between computer and electronics producers. An average computer maker is twice as big as a typical electronics producer. There is a substantial deviation of company size for the four subgroups.

Second, the average labor productivity (PRDCTVTY) varies across the industries. Computer companies have a productivity that is more than twice as high as apparel's. Cross sectional variation of productivity within each industry is very different. Within textile industry some companies are extraordinarily high and some others very low in labor productivity, implying heterogeneity of technology or capital intensity in the industry. On the other hand, the apparel industry shows the smallest variation in productivity, suggesting the similarity of technology and factor input intensities across apparel companies. The cross sectional variations of labor productivity for computer and electronics companies are in-between.

Third, the ratio of technical and professional employees to production workers differs across the industries. Technical and professional personnel account for more than 40 percent of employees in computer companies. This figure is much higher than for the whole machinery industry (25 percent in machinery in 1985, see Smith 1989). The same type of occupations only accounts for about 11 percent of total employees in textile and apparel companies.

Fourth, educational attainment of employees is approximately the same for all companies, although computer and electronics production workers received one more year of formal education. Work experience on the average is also similar for workers in all the industries, but across companies there is more variation in experience than in educational attainment.

Fifth, the capital input level of the textile companies, on the average, is $8.4 million as opposed to $5.6 million for computer companies, $3.7 million for electronics companies, and $2.5 million for apparel companies. The input levels, however, vary widely across producers. After adjustment for employment size, the capital intensity

Table 3.6 Sample Means and Standard Deviations

Variable	TEX.& APP. N=279 Mean	TEX. N=133 Mean	APP. N=146 Mean	COMP.& ELE. N=210 Mean	COMP. N=72 Mean	ELE. N=138 Mean
VALUE90	14276	14376	14185	16184	26751	10671
	(33252)	(32856)	(33722)	(31275)	(45772)	(17806)
VALUEGROW	2.788	3.035	2.564	4.173	5.150	3.659
	(8.156)	(7.240)	(8.929)	(9.999)	(10.565)	(9.689)
PRDCTVTY	53.089	64.863	42.363	73.340	90.356	64.462
	(147.62)	(211.78)	(26.625)	(74.406)	(67.502)	(76.504)
PRTY-GRW	3.859	3.253	4.412	4.459	5.462	3.932
	(7.557)	(6.385)	(8.469)	(8.659)	(7.295)	(9.278)
W-EMP90	295.513	283.547	306.686	122.976	144.374	111.629
	(660.99)	(649.50)	(673.75)	(178.83)	(234.71)	(140.28)
W-EMPGROW	-0.967	-0.099	-1.776	-1.057	-2.888	-0.120
	(7.128)	(6.696)	(7.442)	(14.909)	(18.668)	(12.543)
P-EMP90	40.537	39.835	41.197	60.547	100.160	39.541
	(107.96)	(92.548)	(121.02)	(99.019)	(142.52)	(55.341)
P-EMPGROW	-0.065	-0.040	-0.088	0.759	0.046	1.144
	(10.252)	(9.121)	(11.247)	(11.412)	(11.730)	(11.265)
W-EDUC90	10.942	11.067	10.823	11.721	11.495	11.835
	(1.204)	(1.350)	(1.036)	(1.743)	(2.683)	(0.970)
W-EDGROW	0.890	1.099	0.701	0.796	0.750	0.820
	(2.138)	(2.298)	(1.971)	(1.805)	(1.764)	(1.833)
W-EXP90	8.492	8.950	8.063	8.382	8.609	8.274
	(5.533)	(5.646)	(5.412)	(4.938)	(5.540)	(4.645)
W-EXPGROW	1.315	1.611	1.048	3.443	3.742	3.289
	(6.567)	(5.623)	(7.326)	(5.726)	(5.787)	(5.709)
P-EDUC90	15.315	15.271	15.356	15.247	15.411	15.164
	(1.399)	(0.971)	(1.704)	(1.270)	(1.274)	(1.265)
P-EDGROW	0.792	0.991	0.617	1.142	1.059	1.186
	(1.890)	(2.177)	(1.582)	(2.958)	(1.635)	(3.457)
P-EXP90	14.040	13.678	14.383	12.772	12.385	12.969
	(7.721)	(6.746)	(8.554)	(6.359)	(5.899)	(6.594)
P-EXPGROW	2.235	2.535	1.961	2.573	3.312	2.190
	(5.168)	(5.345)	(5.004)	(5.261)	(6.326)	(4.592)
K-EQ90	5335	8427	2462	4379	5626	3728
	(20300)	(28003)	(7216)	(9883)	(13772)	(7034)
K-EQGROW	1.436	1.748	1.151	3.179	2.583	3.498
	(6.613)	(6.401)	(6.810)	(9.232)	(10.727)	(8.353)
UTI-RATE	80.286	81.070	79.564	66.568	64.297	67.703
	(15.588)	(14.388)	(16.636)	(19.690)	(22.752)	(17.955)
K-UTLZ90	4283	6832	1959	2915	3617	2524
	(16298)	(22702)	(5741)	(6579)	(8855)	(3224)
K-UTLGROW	1.351	2.046	0.718	2.064	-0.270	3.241
	(8.292)	(7.944)	(8.577)	(12.335)	(14.959)	(10.650)
K-AGE90	10.824	11.693	9.981	8.220	7.336	8.684
	(4.840)	(4.894)	(4.652)	(4.117)	(3.687)	(4.266)
K-AGEGROW	1.033	0.646	1.405	-3.423	-4.919	-2.613
	(10.612)	(7.808)	(12.761)	(13.292)	(14.254)	(12.729)
K-BD90	4360	6308	2550	4470	6206	3577
	(19290)	(27197)	(5163)	(7702)	(9538)	(6420)

Table 3.6   Sample Means and Standard Deviations (Con.)

Variable	TEX.& APP. Mean	TEX. Mean	APP. Mean	COMP.& ELE. Mean	COMP. Mean	ELE. Mean
K-BDGROW	2.4802	2.258	2.680	2.541	3.203	2.195
	(5.793)	(5.575)	(5.996)	(6.425)	(7.248)	(5.949)
K-R&D90	155	216	95	864	1521	517
	(611)	(747)	(433)	(3939)	(6342)	(1529)
K-R&DGROW	1.051	0.890	1.209	2.700	2.978	2.555
	(5.298)	(6.605)	(3.608)	(8.355)	(9.150)	(7.946)
K-CC8590	326	391.870	265	363	543	269
	(1047)	(1106)	(989)	(1017)	(1414)	(721)
K-MCN8590	2544	4542	648	1019	1480	784
	(18858)	(26873)	(1817)	(2869)	(4363)	(1639)
K-MNG8590	194	201	188	242	382	171
	(690)	(722)	(661)	(961)	(1489)	(509)
K-TRN8590	102	119	86	114	182	78
	(256)	(304)	(202)	(463)	(731)	(214)
PATNT90	0.536	0.690	0.394	0.508	0.879	0.321
	(2.442)	(3.079)	(1.641)	(1.441)	(2.019)	(0.994)

is similar for textile mills and computer-electronics manufacturers, with $25,000 per employee, but much lower for apparel factories, with $7,000 per employee. Capital stock in the computer industry is much younger than in textile (7.3 years vs. 11.7 years) and apparel manufacturers (10 years). Taking into account the lower rate of capital utilization in the computer industry (64%) and the higher rate in textile (81%), the researcher infers that the average age of the capital stock actually used in production has even wider variation across industries.

Sixth, the R & D investment level of computer-electronics companies is 5.5 times as high as that of textile-apparel companies and the difference is even more substantial if an adjustment for employment level is considered. In particular, the computer subgroup can be easily characterized by a intensive R & D input with $1.5 millions devoted to R & D for an average company. By comparison, apparel producers made very little effort in R & D, as a typical producer spent only $95,000 per year in research and development.

Seventh, all the four industries, textile, apparel, computer, and electronics components, made inputs in computer or numerical control system, machine upgrading, management improvement, and worker training. A notable difference is that the textile mills on the average invested more in upgrading their production facilities, while computer producers spent relatively more on improving management system.

3.5.2. The Growth Measures

First, the annual growth rate of value added is 2.8 percent for the textile-apparel group and 4.2 for the computer-electronics group. Producers in the computer industry enjoyed the highest growth rate (5.2 percent per year), and the apparel factories experienced relatively lower growth rate (2.6 percent per year). Also notably, high standard deviations indicate a considerable variation in the growth rate across producers in all the industry groups.

Second, there appears not much inter-industrial variation in the average growth rate of productivity with an average annual growth rate of 3.9% for textile-apparel manufacturers and 4.5% for computer-electronics manufacturers. However, variation across individual producers is considerably larger in each industry. Once again a comparison among the four industries shows that productivity in the computer industry grew faster than in the other three industries.

Third, textile-apparel companies declined in the number of employees, including both production workers and professionals; computer-electronics companies also declined in the number of production workers; however, their technical/professional crew expanded. The average educational attainment of employees did not change much for all the four subgroups. Work experience increased more in computer-electronics companies than in textile-apparel companies.

Fourth, the annual growth rate of capital stock is 3.2 percent for computer-electronics and 1.4 percent for textile-apparel. After adjusting for the rate of utilization, the annual growth rate of capital stock utilized in production is 3.2 for electronics components manufacturers, 2.0 for textile, 0.7 for apparel, and about zero for computer producers. Considering the highest rate of reduction in the average age of capital stock in computer companies, the researcher infers that computer firms made significant investment, and that a large part of the investment was to replace less advanced equipment in order to maintain technological competitiveness.

Finally, there is an apparent inter-industrial variation in the growth rate of capital stock in R & D. The R & D capital stock in computer-electronics industries grew more than 2.5 times as fast as in textile-apparel industries. The heavy investment in R & D and fast growth in R & D capital means that the producers in this group are faced with intensive technological competition and that their activities are closely related to development of new technology. On the other hand, intensive input might lower marginal productivity of the input if R & D input shares the common feature with conventional inputs. Unfortunately, we do not know to what extent R & D input is unique and to what extent it is common in input-output relationship. The nature of R & D input will be empirically examined using growth equations and production functions.

In short, computer-electronics companies, especially computer producers, have intensive inputs in technical/ professional employees, new equipment, and R & D investment, whereas textile-apparel manufacturers have much smaller technical/professional crews, older equipment, and little R & D capital input. Among the four subgroups, apparel companies are especially low in capital intensity and R & D investment. The inter-industrial gaps in technical personnel, new equipment, and R & D input have been widening, given the different growth rates across the industries. As a result, the growth rate of productivity in computer-electronics is expected to be continuously higher than in textile-apparel manufacturing.

Standard deviations for each group or subgroup show that growth rates of all inputs and output vary substantially across individual producers and that distribution of growth rates across producers is very skewed. This may well suggest that individual manufacturers are using different technologies to produce similar products. There are two possible reasons that producers with diverse technologies and different productivity can coexist: (1) there exist many small market segments in each industry, and competition between producers in the different segments is not strong enough to force less advanced producers to make more technological progress or to go out of business; (2) many regional social economic factors may play important roles in raising productivity of individual producers to help effectively compete with producers in other areas.

Appendix 3 Survey Questionnaire

Please answer the following questions as completely as you can. If exact data are not readily available for some answers, provide your best, educated guess.

Q-1 Which type is your establishment? *(Please circle number)*
    1 SOLE PROPRIETORSHIP OR PARTNERSHIP
    2 PRIVATE CORPORATION
    3 PUBLIC CORPORATION

Q-2 Where are your headquarters located? *(Please circle number)*
    1 SAME COUNTY AS ESTABLISHMENT
    2 SAME STATE, DIFFERENT COUNTY
    3 U.S.A., NOT THE SAME STATE
    4 FOREIGN COUNTRY

Q-3 Which of the following decisions are made at establishment level? *(Circle number, please circle all that apply)*
    1 TYPE AND LEVEL OF MAINTENANCE SPENDING ON EXISTING
        PLANT AND EQUIPMENT
    2 EXPANSION OF PRODUCTION
    3 CHOICE OF PRODUCTION TECHNOLOGY
    4 CHOICE OF PRODUCT MIX
    5 LEVEL OF R&D TO IMPROVE PRODUCTION PROCESS
    6 LEVEL OF R&D LEADING TO NEW/BETTER PRODUCTS
    7 PURCHASE OF PRODUCTION TECHNOLOGY/PATENTS
    8 PROVISION OF ON-SITE LABOR SKILL TRAINING
    9 MARKETING
    10 OTHER *(Please specify)*

Q-4 Have any decisions in Q-3 allowed you to meet the certification requirements imposed by industrial buyers of your output? *(Circle number)*
    1 YES   2 NO

    If YES, which decisions have allowed you to meet the requirement? *(Circle number, please circle all that apply)*
    1 TYPE AND LEVEL OF MAINTENANCE SPENDING ON EXISTING
        PLANT AND EQUIPMENT
    2 EXPANSION OF PRODUCTION
    3 CHOICE OF PRODUCTION TECHNOLOGY
    4 CHOICE OF PRODUCT MIX
    5 LEVEL OF R&D TO IMPROVE PRODUCTION PROCESS
    6 LEVEL OF R&D LEADING TO NEW/BETTER PRODUCTS
    7 PURCHASE OF PRODUCTION TECHNOLOGY/PATENTS
    8 PROVISION OF ON-SITE LABOR SKILL TRAINING
    9 MARKETING
    10 OTHER

Q-5 What products are produced in your establishment? (*Please circle all that apply*)
   1 MAINFRAME COMPUTING EQUIPMENT
   2 MICRO COMPUTING EQUIPMENT
   3 COMPUTING PERIPHERAL DEVICES
   4 COMPLETE SETS OF TELECOMMUNICATION EQUIPMENT
   5 TELECOMMUNICATION EQUIPMENT COMPONENTS
        (EXCEPT SEMICONDUCTOR)
   6 SEMICONDUCTORS
   7 OTHER PRODUCTION(*Please specify*)

Q-6 Which modes of production are carried out in your establishment? (*Please circle all that apply*)
   1 CUSTOMIZED
   2 INTERMITTENT(BATCH)
   3 CONTINUOUS MASS PRODUCTION
   4 OTHER(*Please specify*)

Q-7 In what year did this establishment open here or in some previous location?
   19___

Q-8 On average, how many employees were in your establishment in 1990?
   AVERAGE TOTAL EMPLOYEES IN 1990 WAS ___

Q-9 Relative to total employment in your establishment in 1985, was your workforce in 1990:   (*Circle number and fill out relevant space*)
   1 HIGHER; by approximately what percent? ___ %
   2 ABOUT THE SAME
   3 LOWER; by approximately what percent? ___ %

Q-10 Indicate percentage of each category of workers to total employment in your establishment. (*Note: each column should add to 100%*)

	1985	1990
Production workers	___	___
Professional/managerial	___	___
Others	___	___

Q-11 Approximately what percentage of all <u>production</u> workers in 1990 completed
   1 ONLY 8 GRADE OR LESS _____ %
   2 SOME HIGH SCHOOL _____ %
   3 HIGH SCHOOL GRADUATE _____ %
   4 SOME COLLEGE _____ %
   5 COLLEGE GRADUATE _____ %
   6 GRADUATE OR PROFESSIONAL SCHOOL _____ %
   (*Note: the sum of the above should be* = <u>100%</u>)

Q-12 Between 1985 and 1990, did the average education level of <u>production</u> workers in your establishment (*Please circle number and fill out relevant space*):
   1 INCREASE; by approximately how many grades? ___

2 STAY ABOUT THE SAME
3 DECREASE; by approximately how many grades? ___

Q-13   Approximately what percentage of all <u>professional/managerial</u> personnel in 1990 completed
1 SOME COLLEGE OR LESS _____ %
2 COLLEGE GRADUATE _____ %
3 GRADUATE OR PROFESSIONAL SCHOOL _____ %
(*Note: the sum of the above should be* = <u>100%</u>)

Q-14   Between 1985 and 1990, did the average education level of <u>professional /
managerial</u> workers in your establishment (*Please circle number and fill out
relevant space*):
1 INCREASE; by approximately how many grades? ___
2 STAY ABOUT THE SAME
3 DECREASE; by approximately how many grades? ___

Q-15   On average, how much work experience did all <u>production</u> workers have in 1990?
___ YEARS AND ___ MONTHS

Q-16   Relative to 1985, did the average work experience of production workers (*Circle
number and fill out relevant space*)
1 INCREASE; by approximately how much? __ YEARS AND __ MONTHS
2 STAY ABOUT THE SAME
3 DECREASE; by approximately how much? __ YEARS AND __ MONTHS

Q-17   On average, how much work experience did all <u>professional/managerial</u> personnel
have in 1990?
___ YEARS AND ___ MONTHS

Q-18   Relative to 1985, did the average work experience of <u>professional / managerial</u>
personnel (*Circle number and fill out relevant space*)
1 INCREASE; by approximately how much? __ YEARS AND __ MONTHS
2 STAY ABOUT THE SAME
3 DECREASE; by approximately how much? __ YEARS AND __ MONTHS

Q-19   We need to know the age and 'market value' of all the equipment you used in
1990 in production. This 'market value' can be estimated in two ways, either
as (1) the original value less depreciation, or (2) your best guess of how much
you can sell all the equipment for in an auction. You can choose either
method.
THE MARKET VALUE OF THE EQUIPMENT WAS ABOUT: $___
You may circle an approximate location on this scale instead of answering
#19:

```
  $100K  $500K  $1M  $2.5M  $5M  $10M  $25M   $50M+
  ----|-----|-----|-----|-----|-----|-----|-----
```

Q-20 Please indicate as closely as possible the age distribution of your equipment in 1990 (excluding research and development equipment):
0-2 YEARS _____ %
3-5 YEARS _____ %
6-10 YEARS _____ %
11-15 YEARS _____ %
16-20 YEARS _____ %
20+ YEARS _____ %
(Note: the sum should be = 100 %)

Q-21 Between 1985 and 1990, did the average value of your equipment *(Circle number and fill out relevant space)*:
1 INCREASE; by approximately what percent? ___ %
2 STAY ABOUT THE SAME
3 DECREASE; by approximately what percent? ___ %

Q-22 What was the utilization of all your equipment in 1990 compared with the designed capacity?
THE UTILIZATION OF EQUIPMENT WAS ABOUT ___ %

Q-23 What was the utilization of all your equipment in 1985 compared with the designed capacity?
THE UTILIZATION OF EQUIPMENT WAS ABOUT ___ %

Q-24 We need to know the age and 'market value' of all the buildings you used in 1990 in production regardless of ownership of the buildings. This 'market value' can be either (1) the original value less depreciation, or (2) your best guess of how much all the buildings can be sold for. You can use either method.
THE MARKET VALUE OF ALL THE BUILDINGS WAS ABOUT: $___

You may check an appropriate location on this scale instead of answering #24:

```
$100K $500K  $1M  $2.5M  $5M  $10M  $25M  $50M+
----|-----|-----|-----|-----|-----|-----|-----
```

Q-25 Between 1985 and 1990, did the value of your buildings *(Circle number and fill out relevant space)*:
1 INCREASE; by approximately what percent? ___ %
2 STAY ABOUT THE SAME
3 DECREASE; by approximately what percent? ___ %

Q-26 Approximately how many patents/copyrights/blueprints did your company purchase or license for production each year in the 1985-90 period? *(Please fill out relevant space)*
____ # PATENTS/LICENSES, APPROXIMATE VALUE: $____

Q-27 Did your company ever purchase or license patents/copyrights/blueprints for production before <u>1985</u> ? (*Please circle number and fill out relevant space*)
    1 YES __# PATENTS/LICENSES, APPROXIMATE VALUE: $__
    2 NO

Q-28 Some companies conduct their own research and development (R&D) either to improve production process or to develop new products. If your company conducts product or production process R&D, what is the market value of the R&D facilities in <u>1990</u> in your establishment (market value is defined the same way as before)?
    THE MARKET VALUE WAS ABOUT $_____

    You may circle an appropriate location on this scale instead of answering #28:

```
    $50K   $250K $500K $750K  $1M   $2.5M  $5M    $10M+
 ---|-----|-----|-----|-----|-----|-----|-----|----
```

Q-29 Approximately, what was the percentage age distributions of all R&D equipment in <u>1990</u> ?
    < 2   YEARS ____%
    2-5   YEARS ____%
    6-10 YEARS ____%
    11-15 YEARS ____%
    15+   YEARS ____%
    (*Note: Sum = <u>100%</u>*)

Q-30 Between 1985 and 1990, did the value of your R&D equipment (*Circle number and fill out relevant space*):
    1 INCREASE; by approximately what percent? ____%
    2 STAY ABOUT THE SAME
    3 DECREASE; by approximately what percent? ____%

Q-31 Approximately, how much did your establishment invest in on-line computer control production technology in the 1985-90 period? $_____
    You may circle an appropriate location on this scale instead of answering #31:

```
    $50K  $250K $500K $750K   $1M   $2.5M  $5M    $10M+
 ----|-----|-----|-----|-----|-----|-----|-----|----
```

Q-32 Did your establishment ever invest in on-line computer control production technology <u>before 1985</u>? (*Circle number and fill out relevant space*)
    1 YES. Approximately how much in total? $_____
    2 NO

Q-33 Did your establishment ever invest in upgrading production machinery (other than automation) <u>before 1985</u>? (*Circle number and fill out relevant space*)
1 YES. Approximately how much in total? $_____
2 NO

Q-34 Approximately, how much did your establishment invest in upgrading (other than automation) production machinery in the 1985-90 period?
$_____

You may circle an appropriate location on this scale instead of answering #34:

```
$50K $250K $500K $750K  $1M   $2.5M  $5M     $10M+
---|-----|-----|-----|-----|-----|-----|-----|----
```

Q-35 Approximately, how much did your establishment invest in improving management (e.g., factory data statistical analysis, market analysis/ inventory/ distribution information system, introduction to and/or implementation of computer management system or expert system, etc.) in the 1985-90 period?
$_____

You may circle an appropriate location on this scale instead of answering #35:

```
$5K    $25K   $50K $75K  $100K $250K $500K  $1M+
----|-----|-----|-----|-----|-----|-----|-----|----
```

Q-36 Did your establishment ever invest in improving management (e.g., factory data statistical analysis, market analysis/ inventory/ distribution information system, introduction to and/or implementation of computer management system or expert system, etc.) <u>before 1985</u>? (*Circle number and fill out relevant space*)
1 YES. Approximately how much in total? $_____
2 NO

Q-37 Approximately, how much did your establishment invest directly in training programs for production and support workers in 1985-90 period?
$_____

You may circle an appropriate location on this scale instead of answering #37:

```
$5K    $25K   $50K  $75K $100K $250K $500K  $1M+
---|-----|-----|-----|-----|-----|-----|-----|----
```

Q-38 Did your establishment ever invest in training program for production and support workers <u>before 1985</u>? (*Circle number and fill out relevant space*)
1 YES. Approximately how much in total? $_____
2 NO

Q-39 Approximately, how much did your establishment spend in raw material and intermediate inputs (including utilities) in 1990?
$_____

You may circle an appropriate location on this scale instead of answering #39:

$500K	$1M	$2.5M	$5M	$10M	$25M	$50M	$100M+

Q-40 Of all good and products purchased in 1990 as direct production inputs, approximately what percentage was acquired from: (*Circle all that apply and fill out relevant space*)
1 FIRMS THAT YOU OR OTHERS CERTIFIED AS SUPPLIERS____%
       (NUMBER OF SUPPLYING FIRMS CERTIFIED BY YOU __)
2 ALL OTHER FIRMS THAT SELL DIRECTLY TO YOU ......____%
3 WHOLESALERS, DISTRIBUTORS, ETC.___%
(*Note: the sum of the above should be* = <u>100%</u>)

Q-41 Approximately, the amount of total sales in 1990 was:
$_____

You may circle an appropriate location on this scale instead of answering #41:

$500K	$1M	$2.5M	$5M	$10M	$25M	$50M	$100M+

Q-42 Did total sales between 1985 and 1990 (*Circle number and fill out relevant space*):
1 INCREASE by what percent? ____%
2 STAY ABOUT THE SAME
3 DECREASE by what percent? ____%

Q-43 Of your firm's total value of 1990 production, approximately what percentage of output was sold: (*Circle number and fill out relevant space*)
1 TO FIRMS FOR WHICH YOU ARE A CERTIFIED SUPPLIER....___%
(NUMBER OF FIRMS THAT CERTIFY YOUR PRODUCTION __)
2 TO ALL OTHER FIRMS THAT YOU SUPPLY DIRECT INPUTS..___%
3 TO FINAL MARKET USERS (DIRECT SALES, WHOLESALE, DISTRIBUTORS, ETC.) ___%
(*Note: the sum of the above should be* = <u>100%</u>)

Q-44 Has your establishment ever used the:
       (a) Federal R&D tax credit? (*Check one*)   YES ____   NO ____
       (b) Any state or local R&D incentive program (e.g., tax credit, loans, subsidies, etc.)?
       (*Check one*)   YES ____   NO ____

       If YES, please name and describe the single most important incentive:

Thank you for your help! Please fold the completed questionnaire in half so our address on the back shows. You only need to tape or staple the questionnaire together and mail it. We will pay the postage.

Notes

1. Capital goods sectors are historically an engine for technological progress and productivity growth in other sectors, while consumer goods sectors are essentially followers and beneficiaries of technological progress (Rosenberg 1974).

2. R.J. Gordon (1989) conducted a survey on price and performance of various computers. Mainframes' price declined at the rate of 22.1% in 1954-65, 12.7% in 1965-77, and 26.5% in 1977-84, and PC's price declined at an average annual rate of 26.3% over 1981-87, or 32.7% when a shift to PC 'clones' was included.

3. Since the Chi Square statistic increases with the number of total counts and the number of categories, it is not a reliable test for biasedness when many thousands of cases are involved in the calculation of the statistic. Although not very reliable, the Chi Square statistics are calculated based on the population data of about 4,500 companies and sample data of 279 for textile-apparel industries and population of about 3,000 companies and a sample of 210 cases for computer-electronics. Resultant Chi Square statistics are as follows
   Textile-apparel
   (1). Geographic distribution: 99.34, df=41
   (2). Company type distribution: 6.557, df=4
   (3). Employment size distribution: 9.339, df=10
   (4). Sale size distribution: 37.886, df=9
   Computer-electronics
   (5). Geographic distribution: 42.24, df=41
   (6). Company type distribution: 36.716, df=4
   (7). Employment size distribution: 43.029, df=10
   (8). Sale size distribution: 50.978, df=9
Among these statistics, (1) and (3) are very unreliable, while (4), (6), (7), and (8) suggest some bias of the sample if the Chi Square statistic can be used as a valid test.

4. Companies in this subgroup include 25 telecommunication equipment makers. Since these companies are more similar to computer makers than to electronics components companies in product technology and production process, they are combined with computer companies.

4 A Descriptive Analysis
of U.S. Textile-Apparel and
Computer-Electronics Companies

This chapter takes a first look at the variation of production and productivity growth across different producers and different areas. Descriptive statistics are employed to scan the producer characteristics and regional variables that may be responsible for the variation in the growth. Bivariate relationships between these producer attributes/ regional factors and producer technological inputs (i.e., R & D and inputs in adoption of advanced technologies) are examined. Results of the analysis can be compared with earlier research of this type (e.g., Rees et. al. 1986).

4.1. WHO GREW?
VARIATIONS OF GROWTHS OF OUTPUT AND
TECHNOLOGICAL INPUTS ACROSS PRODUCERS

Producers' behavior in investment and response to external change can be affected by their inherent attributes including organization, ownership, age, size, and marketing practice. These attributes can be used to classify companies so that variation of growth across individual producers can be evaluated according to the attributes. Correlation analysis and Chi Square statistics are used respectively to evaluate linear and nonlinear relationships between input and output growth and producer attributes. The correlation coefficient analysis may also identify the categories of companies who experienced higher growth or, conversely, lower or negative growth.

Included in the correlation coefficient analysis are annualized growth rates of value added and labor productivity, growth rate of R & D capital, and other technological inputs. All the producer input and output variables are defined in Table 3.5, except that SALE90 is total sales value in 1990, measured in $1,000. A set of producer attribute variables and their definition is listed in Table 4.1.

Table 4.2 presents the correlation coefficients of these input, output, and company attribute variables. Several points can be highlighted in Table 4.2.

Table 4.1 Company Attribute Variables and Definitions

Variable	Definition
PARTNER	Dummy variable, it equals 1 if a company is a sole proprietorship, 0 otherwise
PRIVATE	Dummy variable, it equals 1 if a company is a privately owned company, 0 otherwise
PUBLIC	Dummy variable, it equals 1 if a company is a public corporation, 0 otherwise
HQ-CNTY	Dummy variable, it equals 1 if a company's headquarters are in the same county as the company, 0 otherwise
HQ-STATE	Dummy variable, it equals 1 if a company's headquarters are in the same state (but a different county) as is the company, 0 otherwise
HQ-US	Dummy variable, it equals 1 if a company's headquarters are in U.S.A. but not in the same state as the company, 0 otherwise
HQ-FRGN	Dummy variable, it equals 1 if a company's headquarters are in a foreign country, 0 otherwise
CUSTOMIZE	Dummy variable, it equals 1 if a company conducts customized production, 0 otherwise
BATCH	Dummy variable, it equals 1 if a company conducts intermittent production, 0 otherwise
STANDARD	Dummy variable, it equals 1 if a company conducts standardized mass production, 0 otherwise
BUYCRTF	Dummy variable, it equals 1 if a company buys intermediate inputs from a certified suppliers, 0 otherwise
SALECRTF	Dummy variable, it equals 1 if a company is a certified supplier, 0 otherwise.

Table 4.2 Correlation Coefficient Analysis
COMPUTER & ELECTRONICS

	VALUE GROW	PRTY -GRW	K-R&D GROW	K-CC 8590	K-MCN 8590	K-MNG 8590	K-TRN 8590	PATNT90
VALUEGROW	1.000	0.274	0.315	-0.040	-0.084	-0.061	-0.066	0.053
	0.000	0.000	0.000	0.570	0.232	0.387	0.343	0.459
PRTY-GRW	0.274	1.000	0.015	0.047	-0.030	-0.015	0.055	-0.007
	0.000	0.000	0.834	0.503	0.671	0.830	0.430	0.917
K-R&DGROW	0.315	0.015	1.000	0.092	0.076	0.157	0.157	0.092
	0.000	0.834	0.000	0.211	0.304	0.034	0.033	0.213
K-CC8590	-0.040	0.047	0.092	1.000	0.655	0.246	0.732	-0.014
	0.570	0.503	0.211	0.000	0.000	0.000	0.000	0.838
K-MCN 8590	-0.084	-0.030	0.076	0.655	1.000	0.316	0.724	0.025
	0.232	0.671	0.304	0.000	0.000	0.000	0.000	0.728
K-MNG 8590	-0.061	-0.015	0.157	0.246	0.316	1.000	0.258	0.044
	0.387	0.830	0.034	0.000	0.000	0.000	0.000	0.543
K-TRN 8590	-0.066	0.055	0.157	0.732	0.724	0.258	1.000	0.027
	0.343	0.430	0.033	0.000	0.000	0.000	0.000	0.702
PATNT90	0.053	-0.007	0.092	-0.014	0.025	0.044	0.027	1.000
	0.459	0.917	0.213	0.838	0.728	0.543	0.702	0.000
PARTNER	-0.021	-0.021	-0.017	-0.046	-0.049	-0.047	-0.048	-0.056
	0.759	0.756	0.814	0.518	0.483	0.501	0.494	0.430
PRIVATE	-0.094	0.010	0.044	-0.175	-0.169	0.041	-0.142	-0.006
	0.173	0.884	0.550	0.013	0.015	0.559	0.041	0.928
PUBLIC	0.109	0.000	-0.036	0.208	0.203	-0.017	0.174	0.037
	0.114	0.989	0.619	0.003	0.003	0.805	0.012	0.600
HQ-CNTY	-0.022	0.074	-0.102	-0.223	-0.165	-0.012	-0.221	-0.024
	0.748	0.285	0.166	0.001	0.018	0.860	0.001	0.731
HQ-STATE	-0.030	0.010	0.132	0.037	0.074	-0.002	0.066	0.006
	0.660	0.879	0.074	0.596	0.292	0.968	0.344	0.928
HQ-US	-0.013	-0.085	0.025	0.232	0.173	0.022	0.204	0.044
	0.849	0.218	0.735	0.001	0.013	0.750	0.003	0.536
HQ-FRGN	0.155	0.037	-0.026	0.002	-0.022	-0.015	-0.000	-0.034
	0.024	0.591	0.726	0.969	0.750	0.829	0.992	0.630
AGE- CMPNY	-0.018	-0.001	0.042	-0.027	0.003	-0.016	0.008	-0.005
	0.792	0.986	0.575	0.707	0.965	0.813	0.908	0.938
COSTOMIZE	0.109	-0.018	0.102	-0.047	0.029	0.086	0.034	0.108
	0.118	0.796	0.169	0.512	0.684	0.224	0.624	0.132
BATCH	0.023	-0.031	-0.039	-0.000	0.016	0.029	0.046	0.082
	0.735	0.655	0.597	0.997	0.820	0.677	0.514	0.256
STANDARD	-0.126	-0.093	0.033	0.191	0.169	0.076	0.155	-0.087
	0.071	0.182	0.654	0.007	0.016	0.281	0.027	0.227
SALE90	0.010	0.032	0.081	0.433	0.512	0.314	0.366	0.055
	0.884	0.645	0.273	0.000	0.000	0.000	0.000	0.440
BUYCRTF	-0.100	-0.004	0.064	0.017	0.079	0.089	0.060	-0.003
	0.146	0.952	0.384	0.805	0.259	0.202	0.386	0.960
SALECRTF	0.070	-0.028	0.046	-0.029	-0.053	-0.107	-0.105	-0.078
	0.307	0.683	0.526	0.682	0.451	0.127	0.132	0.272

Table 4.2 Correlation Coefficient Analysis (Con.)
TEXTILE & APPAREL

	VALUE GROW	PRTY -GRW	K-R&D GROW	K-CC 8590	K-MCN 8590	K-MNG 8590	K-TRN 8590	PATNT90
VALUEGROW	1.000	0.559	0.135	0.056	0.032	0.033	0.016	0.110
	0.000	0.000	0.026	0.359	0.598	0.591	0.783	0.067
PRTY-GRW	0.558	1.000	0.108	0.048	0.019	0.051	0.040	0.036
	0.000	0.000	0.077	0.432	0.753	0.397	0.509	0.550
K-R&DGROW	0.135	0.108	1.000	0.035	0.049	0.063	0.042	0.000
	0.026	0.077	0.000	0.565	0.427	0.306	0.499	0.999
K-CC8590	0.056	0.048	0.035	1.000	0.419	0.632	0.405	0.106
	0.359	0.432	0.565	0.000	0.000	0.000	0.000	0.079
K-MCN8590	0.032	0.019	0.049	0.419	1.000	0.364	0.232	-0.001
	0.598	0.753	0.427	0.000	0.000	0.000	0.000	0.974
K-MNG8590	0.032	0.051	0.063	0.632	0.364	1.000	0.233	0.241
	0.591	0.397	0.306	0.000	0.000	0.000	0.000	0.000
K-TRN8590	0.016	0.040	0.042	0.405	0.232	0.233	1.000	0.123
	0.783	0.509	0.499	0.000	0.000	0.000	0.000	0.045
PATNT90	0.110	0.036	0.000	0.106	-0.001	0.241	0.123	1.000
	0.067	0.550	0.999	0.079	0.974	0.000	0.045	0.000
PARTNER	-0.096	-0.021	0.052	-0.052	-0.026	-0.019	-0.073	-0.051
	0.108	0.716	0.390	0.389	0.670	0.746	0.227	0.399
PRIVATE	0.077	0.038	-0.060	-0.193	-0.164	-0.225	-0.127	-0.006
	0.197	0.527	0.322	0.001	0.007	0.000	0.037	0.914
PUBLIC	-0.041	-0.051	0.039	0.263	0.205	0.262	0.196	0.035
	0.495	0.396	0.514	0.000	0.000	0.000	0.001	0.561
HQ-CNTY	-0.012	-0.029	-0.024	-0.232	-0.125	-0.121	-0.149	-0.051
	0.831	0.623	0.686	0.000	0.041	0.045	0.014	0.393
HQ-STATE	-0.057	0.015	-0.054	0.217	0.191	0.065	0.131	-0.026
	0.336	0.803	0.377	0.000	0.001	0.285	0.031	0.660
HQ-US	0.026	0.052	0.067	0.087	-0.006	0.068	0.063	0.070
	0.658	0.386	0.268	0.151	0.911	0.263	0.298	0.245
HQ-FRGN	0.128	-0.073	0.013	0.085	0.013	0.052	0.042	0.020
	0.032	0.225	0.829	0.162	0.821	0.392	0.491	0.741
AGE- CMPNY	-0.081	0.010	0.043	0.053	0.133	0.115	0.057	0.081
	0.184	0.859	0.489	0.384	0.033	0.063	0.357	0.186
SALE90	0.050	0.008	0.060	0.322	0.142	0.194	0.507	0.034
	0.402	0.889	0.320	0.000	0.020	0.001	0.000	0.571
BUYCRTF	0.088	0.087	-0.001	0.081	0.074	0.084	0.054	0.040
	0.139	0.145	0.985	0.181	0.229	0.165	0.374	0.505
SALECRTF	0.075	0.049	0.025	0.133	0.089	0.079	0.017	0.011
	0.208	0.410	0.680	0.028	0.145	0.192	0.772	0.847

First, company attributes have little to do with growth in value added and productivity, implying that considerable variations of company production and productivity growth are attributable to other variables not included in the table. There are two exemptions in production growth: (1) companies with headquarters located in foreign countries (HQ-FRGN) tend to grow faster than domestically headquartered companies in both textile-apparel and computer-electronics industries; and (2) computer-electronics companies conducting mass production (STANDARD) seem to have experienced slower growth.

Second, most technological inputs are positively related to each other, suggesting that a company that was aware of the importance of technological progress to production may make an extensive technological effort through investment in several types of inputs. If most companies who made the investment were technologically more advanced producers, the technological gap should be widening. On the other hand, if most companies who made the inputs were less advanced producers, the result should be just opposite. The insignificant correlation coefficients between growth rates of production and productivity and these technological inputs convey the message that these technological inputs are not systematically related to producers' technological positions.

Third, privately owned companies made less technological investment than other types of producers, while public corporations tend to have made more technological input. The behavioral difference of technological inputs between private and public corporations may result from different expectations on return to technological input-- privately owned companies may have narrower considerations regarding return to the investment. Considering that public corporations tend to be larger than private ones, the difference also can reflect the impact of different scales of production on technological inputs, since large companies are more likely to benefit from technological inputs due to the larger scale of production and larger market share.

Fourth, local owned companies (HQ-CNTY) appear to have invested less in technological inputs in both industry groups. In textile-apparel industries multi-establishment firms headquartered in the same state but in a different county (HQ-STATE) seem to have made more technological inputs in their branch companies located in the same state, while in computer-electronics multi-establishment firms with headquarters in the U.S.A. but in a different state (HQ-US) are likely to have contributed to more technological input. This means that ties between headquarters and branch companies in textile-apparel industries are tight only within the same state, but in the computer-electronics group there seems to be nationwide close ties between headquarters and their plants. Probably, this is because computer-electronics industries have better integrated production and market nationwide.

Fifth, older companies in textile-apparel industries tend to have made more effort in upgrading machinery (K-MCN8590) and improving management (K-MNG8590). This indicates that, instead of replacing all of the older facilities with brand new equipment, those older companies may have chosen to incorporate new devices into older machines to make them productive. This is a cost-effect investment strategy for an industry whose technology proceeds discretely, and a major part of the technology in production remains effective and only part of its facilities needs to be technologically updated.

Sixth, in the computer-electronics group the mode of standardized mass production (STANDARD) shows a positive relationship with inputs in computer and numerical control (K-CC8590), machine upgrading (K-MCN8590), and employee training programs (K-TRN8590). In connection with the insignificant relationship between technological inputs and the mode of customized or batch production, these positive relationships suggest that expected return from the technological inputs is higher in standardized mass production than in other more flexible modes of production. An interesting question is why the companies conducting mass production made more technological inputs, given the high rate of technological obsolescence in the industries. A possible answer is that mass production is still a major means to grasp a lion share of profit in this technologically very dynamic industry, and profit rate is so high that technological investment can be reimbursed in a very short period.

Seventh, unlike most other technological inputs, R & D measured in growth rate of research and development capital (K-R&DGROW) has no apparent relationship with producer attributes. Only in the computer-electronics group did producers with headquarters in the same state and different counties seem to invest more in R & D, but the relationship is significant only at 90% level.

Finally, the evidence that larger companies invested more in technological inputs is much stronger than all other relationships discussed, given the higher correlation coefficients. In particular, big companies in textile-apparel industries show a strong tendency to make more investment in employee training (K-TRN8590). Probably, this is because employees in large textile-apparel companies are more stable, so the companies are willing to spend more in training their workers.

However, all the positive relationships may simply indicate a positive input-output relationship if technological inputs are treated as conventional inputs, and the relationships also may reflect an increasing return to scale with respect to technological inputs as suggested in chapter 2.

The correlation analysis projects the first impression that producer attributes merely have moderate influence on technological inputs and almost no effect on production growth. To explore possible nonlinear relationships between the producer attributes and production and productivity growth and technological inputs, frequency distributions of growth rates and technological inputs across different categories of companies are examined and the Chi Square test is performed.

To conduct the Chi Square test, all variables must be categorical. Company attributes are mostly categorical variables. Type of ownership (OWNER) is coded in three categories: sole proprietorship, privately owned corporation, and public corporation. Headquarters location (HEADQUARTER) has four codes: headquarters in the same county as the establishment, headquarters in a different county but in the same state as the establishment, headquarters in a different state in the USA, and headquarters in a foreign country. Two certification dummy variables, BUYCRTF and SALECRTF, are measured the same way as in Table 4.1. Other variables including output growth and company age and size have to be converted from interval to ordinal measures. The conversion will inevitably lose some information, but this is the only feasible way to observe distribution of a variable across categories. A univariate analysis is performed to determine the breaking points so the companies can spread in a reasonable number of categories. Since textile-apparel and computer-electronics companies have different distributions by size and input level, different breaking points are used in conversion.

For textile-apparel companies, the growth rate of value added is divided into five ranges: negative growth (Growth < 0), zero growth (Growth = 0%), moderate growth (0% < Growth ≤ 2%), relatively high growth (2% < Growth ≤ 6%), and very high growth (Growth > 6%). Labor productivity growth rate is also divided into negative growth (Growth < 0), zero growth (Growth = 0%), moderate growth (0% < Growth ≤ 3%), relatively high growth (3% < Growth ≤ 6%), and very high growth (Growth > 6%). Age of companies are divided into four categories: youngest companies (AGE < 10 years old), young companies (10 years ≤ AGE < 20 years), old companies (20 years ≤ AGE < 30 years), and oldest companies (AGE ≥ 30 years). Company size is broken down to four categories: very small (employees < 70 and sales < $4 millions), small (70 ≤ employees < 160, $4 millions ≤ sales < $10 millions), large (160 ≤ employees < 320, $10 millions ≤ sales < $25 millions), and very large (employees ≥ 320 and sales ≥ $25 millions).

For computer-electronics companies, the growth rate of value added is also divided into five ranges with breaking points 3.5% and 8.5% to divide moderate growth, relatively high growth, and very high growth. Labor productivity growth rate is divided into the same five categories as the growth rate of value added. Company age has the same four categories as for textile-apparel companies. Company size has four categories: very small (employees <40, sales <$3 millions), small(40 ≤ employees < 90, $3 millions ≤ sales < $7.5 millions), large (90 ≤ employees < 250, $7.5 millions ≤ sales < $25 millions), and very large (employees ≥ 250, sales ≥ $25 millions).

Actual and expected frequency distributions of growth rates and technological inputs are presented in Appendix 4A to this chapter and only Chi Square statistics of the frequency distribution tables are shown in Table 4.3 and Table 4.4. An examination of the contingency table (Appendix 4A) reveals the directions and magnitudes of the distributional bias of growth and technological inputs across different categories of producers. Corresponding Chi Square statistics show statistical significance levels of the possible biases.

**Table 4.3   Chi Square Statistics of Growth Rates
by Company Attributes**

GROWTH RATE OF VALUE ADDED

Company Attribute	TEXTILE & APPAREL			COMPUTER & ELECTRONICS		
	DF	Chi Sq.	Prob	DF	Chi Sq.	Prob
OWNER	8	8.547	0.382	8	8.153	0.419
HEADQUARTER	12	15.800	0.201	12	12.492	0.407
AGE-CMPNY	12	10.093	0.608	12	15.520	0.214
EMP90	12	26.845	0.008**	12	9.817	0.632
SALES	12	29.491	0.003**	12	11.840	0.459
BUYCRTF	4	1.901	0.754	4	7.704	0.103
SALECRTF	4	1.687	0.793	4	4.338	0.362

Table 4.3   Chi Square Statistics of Growth Rates
by Company Attributes (Con.)

GROWTH RATE OF LABOR PRODUCTIVITY

Company Attribute	TEXTILE & APPAREL			COMPUTER & ELECTRONICS		
	DF	Chi Sq.	Prob	DF	Chi Sq.	Prob
OWNER	8	6.393	0.603	8	4.523	0.807
HEADQUARTER	12	4.239	0.979	12	9.047	0.699
AGE-CMPNY	12	17.394	0.135	12	11.771	0.464
EMP90	12	24.075	0.020**	12	9.899	0.625
SALES	12	19.980	0.067*	12	13.360	0.343
BUTCRTF	4	1.757	0.780	4	7.687	0.104
SALECRTF	4	1.128	0.890	4	0.249	0.993

Note: * and ** indicate statistically significant at 90% and 95% levels respectively.

The statistics in Table 4.3 indicate that in textile-apparel industries, size of companies, measured by number of employees and total sales, seems to be related to production and productivity growth. The distribution table (Appendix 4A) shows that large companies tend to have grown more. In the computer-electronics industries, all attribute variables appear to be irrelevant to production and productivity growth. This suggests that observed production and productivity growth result exclusively from changes in factor input variables and external forces.

To examine whether company attributes make a difference in technological inputs, frequency distribution of the technological inputs across different categories and Chi Square statistics for all distribution tables are computed. The distribution tables are documented in Appendix 4A. The corresponding Chi Square statistics are presented in Table 4.4. Unlike technological input variables in correlation coefficient analysis where interval measures are used, technological input variables are recoded as dummies to observe qualitative difference in producers' behavior. If a producer made investment in a technological input, the input variable is coded 1, otherwise 0. All producer attributes are coded using the same categories as in Table 4.3.

Table 4.4 provides three pieces of information. First, company size measured in employment and total sales makes a significant difference in technological inputs. In textile-apparel industries, the six inputs are all related to producer size. Proportionally many more large companies made efforts to improve their technology. Since technology

**Table 4.4 Chi Square Statistics of Technological Input
by Company Attributes**

	TEXTILE & APPAREL			COMPUTER & ELECTRONICS		
	DF	Chi Sq.	Prob	DF	Chi Sq.	Prob
by OWNER						
K-R&DGROW	2	8.340	0.015**	2	0.304	0.859
PATNT90	2	6.486	0.039**	2	0.263	0.877
K-CC8590	2	11.314	0.003**	2	2.656	0.265
K-MCN8590	2	0.564	0.754	2	3.259	0.196
K-MNG8590	2	4.179	0.124	2	0.153	0.926
K-TRN8590	2	1.772	0.412	2	5.049	0.080*
by HEADQUARTER						
K-R&DGROW	3	1.317	0.725	3	1.040	0.791
PATNT90	3	6.124	0.106	3	0.620	0.892
K-CC8590	3	6.788	0.079*	3	6.098	0.107
K-MCN8590	3	0.456	0.928	3	7.359	0.061*
K-MNG8590	3	3.177	0.365	3	3.472	0.324
K-TRN8590	3	9.444	0.024*	3	4.007	0.261
by Company AGE						
K-R&DGROW	3	2.607	0.456	3	10.217	0.017**
PATNT90	3	1.380	0.710	3	1.623	0.654
K-CC8590	3	2.603	0.457	3	0.996	0.802
K-MCN8590	3	2.571	0.463	3	4.005	0.261
K-MNG8590	3	3.018	0.389	3	1.333	0.721
K-TRN8590	3	1.133	0.769	3	4.599	0.204
by EMP90						
K-R&DGROW	3	19.206	0.000**	3	6.048	0.109
PATNT90	3	16.613	0.001**	3	6.117	0.106
K-CC8590	3	34.199	0.000**	3	14.332	0.002**
K-MCN8590	3	13.326	0.004**	3	20.062	0.000**
K-MNG8590	3	21.787	0.000**	3	6.799	0.079*
K-TRN8590	3	31.892	0.000**	3	33.603	0.000**
by SALE90						
K-R&DGROW	3	21.220	0.000**	3	12.998	0.005**
PATNT90	3	17.306	0.001**	3	1.718	0.633
K-CC8590	3	21.879	0.000**	3	21.577	0.000**
K-MCN8590	3	12.484	0.006**	3	17.818	0.000**
K-MNG8590	3	25.943	0.000**	3	15.105	0.002**
K-TRN8590	3	29.806	0.000**	3	21.158	0.000**
by BUYCRTF						
K-R&DGROW	1	4.487	0.034**	1	4.226	0.040**
K-PATNT90	1	0.158	0.691	1	0.678	0.410
K-CC8590	1	7.805	0.005**	1	7.493	0.006**
K-MCN8590	1	4.035	0.045**	1	10.331	0.001**
K-MNG8590	1	3.515	0.061*	1	9.581	0.002**
K-TRN8590	1	10.465	0.001**	1	6.414	0.011**
by SALECRTF						
K-R&DGROW	1	6.503	0.011**	1	1.316	0.251
PATNT90	1	0.418	0.518	1	0.015	0.902
K-CC8590	1	2.966	0.085*	1	0.578	0.447
K-MCN8590	1	3.091	0.079*	1	1.944	0.163
K-MNG8590	1	2.707	0.100	1	0.066	0.798
K-TRN8590	1	12.885	0.000**	1	0.366	0.545

Note: * and ** indicate statistically significant at 90% and 95% level respectively.

related inputs are coded as dummies, the statistics reveal a qualitative relationship between company size and the company's behavior in technological inputs. Company size plays a stronger role in the textile-apparel group than in the computer-electronics group. By comparison, in the computer-electronics group patent purchase is not related to company size, implying that either patent purchase is less important in the industries or that small companies could be as knowledgeable and aggressive as large manufacturers in purchasing and applying advanced technology. Overall, large companies in both groups are more willing to invest in technological input than small ones.

Second, product certification[1], labeled by BUYCRTF and SALECRTF, is the second important attribute affecting technological inputs. In both industry groups, producers who are buyers (BUYCRTF) of intermediate inputs produced by certified suppliers are more likely to make investment in a wide range of technological inputs: R & D, computer and numerical control system, machine upgrading, management system improvement, and employee training. This reflects a complemental effort made by the companies, because intermediate goods from certified suppliers are more reliable in quality and in timing of shipment and probably more expensive. Only internally well organized production can fully realize the benefit of buying intermediate goods from certified suppliers. On the other hand, textile-apparel companies who are certified suppliers (SALECRTF) are likely to make investment in employee training and R & D. This suggests that R & D input and employee training are the most important producer technological inputs in order to meet the certification requirement. This also implies that the potential of improving product and maintaining quality and timing is embodied in R & D activities and in work crews. Unexpectedly, certified computer-electronics suppliers (SALECRTF) did not make an extra effort in technological inputs. This may be attributable to the greater speed of technological obsolescence in the industry. To follow the general pace of technological progress of the industry, a computer-electronics producer has to constantly upgrade its facilities and work force regardless of certification. Compared with certified suppliers, buyers of certified products (BUYCRTF) are technologically more active for both industry groups. An interpretation of the difference may be that the suppliers and the buyers of the certified products are facing different incentives in making technological investment. The suppliers are faced with a ceiling in raising revenue or profit, because the price and shipment of their products are presettled. They make efforts only to meet the predetermined requirement. On the other hand, the buyers of the certified products have greater incentives to make best use of the inputs at the given cost.

Third, other attributes either have very limited influence or no influence at all on the technological inputs. As shown in correlation analysis, the public corporations in textile-apparel industries are more likely to purchase patent/ technology and invest in computer and numerical control devices. The contingency table analysis and Chi Square test also show that public corporations and to less extent partnership are more likely to make investment in R & D than privately owned corporations. Proportionally more textile-apparel companies headquartered in the same counties as the establishments (most are the single establishment firms) do not invest in computer and numerical control systems and in employee training. The age of companies in the textile-apparel group has no impact on the inputs. Compared with textile-apparel companies, computer-electronics manufacturers are even less affected by ownership and location of headquarters in making technological inputs. Age of companies in computer-electronics industries shows a significant influence on R & D input but no impact on all other technological inputs. The computer-electronics companies of 30 years and older are more likely to make an investment in R & D. Because R & D investment usually results in new technology, the older companies have a stronger technological position and contribute more to technological progress in the industry. On the other hand, because the other five technological inputs are all indicators of adoption of new technology, age of companies appears to have no influence on technological adoptability.

A tentative conclusion is drawn from the analysis. Company size is the most important attribute affecting technological inputs and production and productivity growth. Large companies are more likely to invest in a broad array of technological inputs aiming at development *and* adoption of new technology. As a result, the large companies tend to grow faster in production and productivity. Product certification is the second most important factor. Producers using intermediate input provided by certified suppliers tend to make investment to adopt *and* develop new technology. All other producer attributes either have limited influence or no influence at all on technological inputs and production and productivity growth.

4.2. WHERE DID GROWTH OCCUR? GEOGRAPHICAL VARIATIONS OF GROWTHS OF OUTPUT AND TECHNOLOGICAL INPUTS

This section examines the regional patterns of technological inputs and growth of existing companies. Metro size and census regions are used to test the geographical difference in production and productivity growth and difference in propensity to technological investment[2]. The variable metro size takes four values in the test. The metro size is set to 0 if a company is in non metro area; the metro size is equal to 1 if a company is in a metro area with population under 500 thousands; the metro size is 2 if a company is in a metro area with population equal to or greater than 500 thousand and less than 1.5 millions; and the metro size is 3 if a company is in a metro area with population equal to or greater than 1.5 million. The production and productivity growth measures and technological input measures are the same as in the preceding section: production growth is measured by annualized percentage growth rate and labeled as VALUE; productivity growth is annualized percentage growth rate of labor productivity and labeled as PRDCTVTY; and so on. This section compares observed distributions with expected distributions and computes Chi Square statistics to examine the direction, the magnitude, and the significance of the interregional difference. Because of the large number of possible combinations, this book only documents in Appendix 4B those distribution tables that show statistically significant Chi Squares. Table 4.5 presents Chi Square statistics for all regional distribution tables.

Metro size has made some difference in producers' propensity to investment in technological inputs, but not in production and productivity growth. Textile-apparel companies in the large metro areas with population more than 1.5 million are more likely to buy patent and technology (PATNT90) than their counterparts in any other area. There are many factors which can make economic agents technologically more active in large metro areas: demonstration effect resulting from large numbers and high density of relevant economic agents, information about profitability of new technology, and better communication and other regional services. However, no parallel evidence is discovered for computer-electronics companies. Metro area size also appears to have made difference in investment in equipment upgrading (K-MCN8590). Surprisingly, both textile-apparel and computer-electronics companies

Beyond Capital and Labor

Table 4.5 Chi Square Statistics of Production and Productivity Growth and Technological Input by Region

	TEXTILE-APPAREL			COMPUTER-ELECTRONICS		
	DF	Chi Sq.	Prob	DF	Chi Sq.	Prob
by METRO						
VALUEGROW	12	11.808	0.461	12	18.549	0.100
PRTY-GRW	12	8.532	0.742	12	14.588	0.265
K-R&DGROW	3	3.825	0.281	3	2.693	0.441
PATNT90	3	7.588	0.055*	3	1.298	0.730
K-CC8590	3	2.388	0.496	3	3.276	0.351
K-TRN8590	3	7.987	0.046**	3	9.108	0.028**
K-TRN8590	3	2.421	0.490	3	9.503	0.023**
by NE region						
VALUEGROW	4	8.288	0.082*	4	15.030	0.005**
PRTY-GRW	4	0.832	0.934	4	5.453	0.244
K-R&DGROW	1	0.682	0.409	1	0.000	0.988
PATNT90	1	8.081	0.004**	1	3.120	0.077*
K-CC8590	1	3.514	0.061*	1	0.333	0.564
K-MCN8590	1	2.716	0.099*	1	1.248	0.264
K-MNG8590	1	0.000	0.988	1	0.368	0.544
K-TRN8590	1	8.330	0.004**	1	1.499	0.221
by MW region						
VALUEGROW	4	3.163	0.531	4	3.330	0.504
PRTY-GRW	4	5.184	0.269	4	1.955	0.744
K-R&DGROW	1	0.361	0.548	1	1.474	0.225
PATNT90	1	0.172	0.678	1	5.445	0.020**
K-CC8590	1	0.130	0.719	1	1.624	0.202
K-MCN8590	1	0.349	0.555	1	3.785	0.052*
K-MNG8590	1	1.050	0.306	1	3.696	0.055*
K-TRN8590	1	2.423	0.120	1	2.431	0.119
by SOUTH region						
VALUEGROW	4	7.114	0.130	4	4.466	0.347
PRTYGRW	4	2.058	0.725	4	2.561	0.634
K-R&DGROW	1	0.286	0.592	1	3.204	0.073*
PATNT90	1	5.386	0.020**	1	0.014	0.905
K-CC8590	1	3.158	0.076*	1	0.723	0.395
K-MCN8590	1	0.767	0.381	1	0.098	0.754
K-MNG8590	1	0.015	0.903	1	0.103	0.748
K-TRN8590	1	2.517	0.113	1	1.356	0.244
by WEST region						
VALUEGROW	4	0.362	0.986	4	5.450	0.244
PRTY-GRW	4	13.260	0.010**	4	2.195	0.700
K-R&DGROW	1	0.324	0.569	1	0.006	0.936
PATNT90	1	0.085	0.771	1	0.536	0.464
K-CC8590	1	0.093	0.761	1	2.703	0.100
K-MCN8590	1	0.081	0.776	1	0.555	0.456
K-MNG8590	1	0.751	0.386	1	2.878	0.090*
K-TRN8590	1	0.383	0.536	1	4.307	0.038**

Note: * and ** indicate statistically significant at 90% and 95% levels respectively.

in large metro areas are more likely to have made no investment in upgrading their machines during the 1985-90 period. There may be two interpretations for the statistical results: (1) because companies in the large metro areas are likely to own better facilities, they need no substantial inputs in the recent years; (2) because part of the companies in large metro areas perform functions other than routine production. Metro size is also negatively related to computer-electronics producers' spending in their employee training. The findings can be interpreted very differently--one interpretation is of a substitution of vocational schools, universities' evening schools, and other educational opportunities in the large metro areas for private training programs which could incur a great cost for individual companies, and the other is of less stable staff that could make employers reluctant to train their employees.

Table 4.5 shows that production and productivity growth and technological inputs have no strong regional patterns, although several Chi statistics are statistically significant. Following is a detailed variable-by-variable review of the findings.

Production and productivity growth shows an inter-regional difference between the northeast region and other regions. Chi Square statistics and distribution tables (compiled in Appendix 4B) show that companies in the NE region are more likely to contract or expand. Because risk ventures and innovative activities can be major reasons of drastic rise and fall, northeastern companies may have been involved in the risk and innovative activities more than the companies in other regions. In the short term, Northeastern computer-electronics industries may experience more fluctuation, but in the long run they may gain a technological edge. In addition, Table 4.5 suggests that proportionally more Western textile-apparel companies experienced faster productivity growth. However, the Chi Square test is not very appropriate, since there are five categories of growth rate and only 21 companies in the west region and many cells have very small expected counts. The researcher concludes that the productivity growth has no strong regional pattern and that production growth is more likely to fluctuate among northeastern companies.

Patent purchase or license (PATNT90) is a technological input relatively more sensitive to regional location: proportionally more textile-apparel companies in the NE region purchased patent and technology, but proportionally fewer computer-electronics companies in the same region made the similar effort. As opposed to NE region companies, proportionally more midwest (MW) region computer-electronics companies purchased patents and technology. South region textile-apparel companies created another regional pattern--proportionally, these companies are less likely to buy patents and new technology. This is an unhappy finding for the south region, because the region has hosted many textile-apparel companies, and the local economy in many places is heavily dependent on this industry group.

The next technological input sensitive to location is input in employee training (K-TRN8590). In the NE region, proportionally fewer textile-apparel companies spent money in training. Also considering larger fluctuation of production of these companies, the researcher tends to interpret the bias toward not spending on training as a result of an unstable work force. The lower tendency of spending on training can be also a reflection of urbanization dominating the region. Since the NE region is the most populous one with many large metro areas, the companies may have tried to use some substitutes provided by the metro areas. A similar case is found in the West region where proportionally fewer computer-electronics companies made investment to train their employees. A further break-down of the region reveals that companies in California are the cause of the regional pattern.

At a lower significance level (90%), proportionally more southern textile-apparel companies established or improved computer numerical control production systems (K-CC8590), while proportionally more southern computer-electronics companies chose not to invest in R & D (K-R&DGROW). Although the first case is welcome to the south region, the second case is a disappointing sign. If this regional pattern of R & D investment remains unchanged over time, southern computer-electronics industries will be farther behind their counterparts in other regions.

In general, most technological inputs are not very sensitive to current regional location. This conclusion pertains to areas where the production is actually located. However, this does not mean that locational ingredients are irrelevant to production and productivity growth and producer technological inputs. An appropriate hypothesis is that location and investment decisions of these companies are sensitive to regional conditions, which should be measured by individual regional factors rather than census regions.

4.3. DID R & D INVESTMENT CREDIT POLICY AFFECT TECHNOLOGICAL INPUT AND GROWTH?

External economies or loose appropriability of some R & D activities and its products (i.e., technology) leads private companies to invest less in R & D than a socially optimum level. R & D investment credit policies or programs encourage more R & D activities. Since state and local R & D investment credit lowers the cost of R & D and pushes the marginal cost curve of R & D products downward, policy intervention should be positively related to companies' R & D input. In this study, information on state or local R & D investment credit policies is collected. A dummy variable, R&DCRDT, is used to classify companies, R&DCRDT=1 if a company used state or local R & D credit, R&DCRDT=0 otherwise. Frequency and expected frequency tables and Chi Square tests are used to examine the relationship. The contingency tables are compiled in Appendix 4C and Chi Square statistics are presented in Table 4.6. Growth and technological input measures are the same as in Table 4.5.

Table 4.6 Chi Square Statistics of Production and Productivity Growth and Technological Input by R & D Credit Policy

	TEXTILE-APPAREL			COMPUTER-ELECTRONICS		
	DF	Chi Sq.	Prob	DF	Chi Sq.	Prob
by R&DCRDT						
VALUEGROW	4	3.675	0.452	4	1.848	0.764
PRTY-GRW	4	0.677	0.954	4	1.212	0.876
K-R&DGROW	1	6.027	0.014**	1	2.888	0.089*
PATNT90	1	0.123	0.725	1	0.829	0.362
K-CC8590	1	2.241	0.134	1	1.610	0.205
K-MCN8590	1	9.283	0.002**	1	0.944	0.331
K-MNG8590	1	10.054	0.002**	1	3.934	0.047**
K-TRN8590	1	6.656	0.010**	1	2.581	0.108

Note: * and ** indicate statistically significant at 90% and 95% levels respectively.

The Chi Square statistics clearly indicate that investment in R & D (K-R&DGROW) is related to state and local R & D credit policies. Moreover, state and/or local R & D credit policies are closely related to many other technological inputs, especially in textile-apparel industries. Textile-apparel companies that used state and local R & D credit are also likely to invest in machine upgrading, management improvement, and worker training. Since R & D credit cannot reduce the cost of other technological inputs, the findings reflect an induced effect of credit policies on the three technological inputs that are complementary to R & D and other producer inputs. The companies that made R & D investment tend to be technologically more conscious. When they explore the opportunity of R & D credit, they also make complemental investment to fully materialize the investment credit. Because of the induced complemental inputs, the R & D investment credit policies can be effective for textile-apparel companies.

Computer-electronics producers are less strongly affected by R & D credit. First, the direct relationship between R & D input and R & D credit is weaker than in textile-apparel. At the 90 % significance level, R & D input is positively related to state and local R & D credit. Second, R & D credit induced other technological inputs are mostly not significant at commonly acceptable level. Only machine upgrading is positively associated with the R & D credit. Because of the high rate of technological obsolescence and high return to more advanced technology in the industries, computer-electronics companies are constantly pushed and pulled to make a wider scope of technological inputs and, as a result, additional policy intervention can only add small marginal incentive to induce additional inputs. Thus, government intervention to R & D investment is less effective for computer-electronics companies than for textile-apparel companies.

These interpretations are only tentative. In the nationwide survey, information about the use of local R & D credit was collected as a proxy of state and local R & D credit policies or programs. There is an unknown gap between the existence and the use of a local R & D credit policy. Some companies that made R & D investment may not use R & D credit due to the certain cost of applying for and using the credit. If a local R & D credit policy is expected to be effective, the cost of applying for and using the credit should be low. Assuming the gap is small, the researcher infers that state and local R & D credit is an effective tool to induce private investment in R & D with variation of the effectiveness across industries. In textile-apparel industries, the R & D credit policies and programs have direct and indirect impacts on technological progress--in addition to more investment in R & D, the policy also induces other technological inputs. In computer-electronics industries, the policy is likely to have direct influence to induce more R & D investment but no effect on other technological inputs.

Appendix 4A: Frequency Distribution of Production and Productivity Growths and Technological Inputs by Company Attributes

(Statistically very insignificant tables are not shown to save space)

(1) Distributrion of Growth by Company Attributes

Textile-Apparel

Growth of Value Added	Emp<70	EMP90 70<=Emp <160	160<=Emp <320	Emp >320	Total
Growth < 0%	18	18	9	11	56
	13.448	14.452	14.05	14.05	
Growth = 0%	27	14	21	12	74
	17.771	19.097	18.566	18.566	
0%<Growth<=2%	3	7	5	4	19
	4.5627	4.9032	4.767	4.767	
2%<Growth<=6%	7	14	20	17	58
	13.928	14.968	14.552	14.552	
Growth > 6%	12	19	15	26	72
	17.29	18.581	18.065	18.065	
Total	67	72	70	70	279

Chi-Square (df=12): 26.845, Prob.: 0.008

Growth, Labor Productivity	Emp<70	EMP90 70<=Emp <160	160<=Emp <320	Emp >320	Total
Growth < 0%	9	17	18	9	53
	12.728	13.677	13.297	13.297	
Growth = 0%	21	8	10	8	47
	11.287	12.129	11.792	11.792	
0%<Growth<=3%	8	10	15	13	46
	11.047	11.871	11.541	11.541	
3%<Growth<=6%	15	17	9	21	62
	14.889	16	15.556	15.556	
Growth > 6%	14	20	18	19	71
	17.05	18.323	17.814	17.814	
Total	67	72	70	70	279

Chi-Square (df=12): 24.075, Prob.: 0.020

Growth of Value Added	SALE90				Total
	Sale<$4M	$4M<= Sale<$10M	$10M<=Sale<$25M	Sale> $25M	
Growth < 0%	19	9	19	9	56
	12.645	11.642	17.462	14.251	
Growth = 0%	24	20	15	15	74
	16.71	15.384	23.075	18.832	
0%<Growth<=2%	4	3	9	3	19
	4.2903	3.9498	5.9247	4.8351	
2%<Growth<=6%	8	11	23	16	58
	13.097	12.057	18.086	14.76	
Growth > 6%	8	15	21	28	72
	16.258	14.968	22.452	18.323	
Total	63	58	87	71	279

Chi-Square (df=12): 29.491,   Prob.: 0.003

Growth, Labor Productivity	SALE90				Total
	Sale<$4M	$4M<= Sale<$10M	$10M<=Sale<$25M	Sale> $25M	
Growth < 0%	12	12	16	13	53
	11.968	11.018	16.527	13.487	
Growth = 0%	17	11	13	6	47
	10.613	9.7706	14.656	11.961	
0%<Growth<=3%	8	10	19	9	46
	10.387	9.5627	14.344	11.706	
3%<Growth<=6%	17	7	17	21	62
	14	12.889	19.333	15.778	
Growth > 6%	9	18	22	22	71
	16.032	14.76	22.14	18.068	
Total	63	58	87	71	279

Chi-Square (df=12): 19.980,   Prob.: 0.067

Computer-Electronics

Growth of Value Added	EMP90				Total
	Emp<40	40<=Emp < 90	90 <=Emp <250	Emp >250	
Growth < 0%	12	12	13	12	49
	11.2	13.3	10.733	13.767	
Growth = 0%	12	12	8	10	42
	9.6	11.4	9.2	11.8	
0%<Grow<=3.5%	3	3	2	6	14
	3.2	3.8	3.0667	3.9333	
3.5%<Gr<=8.5%	16	20	13	14	63
	14.4	17.1	13.8	17.7	
Growth >8.5%	5	10	10	17	42
	9.6	11.4	9.2	11.8	
Total	48	57	46	59	210

Chi-Square (df=12): 9.817,   Prob.: 0.632

Growth, Labor Productivity	EMP90				
	Emp<40	40<=Emp < 90	90 <=Emp <250	Emp >250	Total
Growth < 0%	9	12	13	10	44
	10.057	11.943	9.6381	12.362	
Growth = 0%	3	10	6	8	27
	6.1714	7.3286	5.9143	7.5857	
0%<Grow<=3.5%	7	10	10	14	41
	9.3714	11.129	8.981	11.519	
3.5%<Gr<=8.5%	15	13	7	16	51
	11.657	13.843	11.171	14.329	
Growth >8.5%	14	12	10	11	47
	10.743	12.757	10.295	13.205	
Total	48	57	46	59	210

Chi-Square (df=12): 9.899, Prob.: 0.625

Growth of Value Added	SALE90				
	Sale<$3M	$3M<= Sale<$7.5M	$7.5M<=Sale<$25M	Sale> $25M	Total
Growth < 0%	16	11	12	10	49
	12.133	12.367	12.133	12.367	
Growth = 0%	11	11	12	8	42
	10.4	10.6	10.4	10.6	
0%<Grow<=3.5%	2	4	3	5	14
	3.4667	3.5333	3.4667	3.5333	
3.5%<Gr<=8.5%	18	17	15	13	63
	15.6	15.9	15.6	15.9	
Growth >8.5%	5	10	10	17	42
	10.4	10.6	10.4	10.6	
Total	52	53	52	53	210

Chi-Square (df=12): 11.840, Prob.: 0.459

Growth, Labor Productivity	SALE90				
	Sale<$3M	$3M<= Sale<$7.5M	$7.5M<=Sale<$25M	Sale> $25M	Total
Growth < 0%	10	17	8	9	44
	10.895	11.105	10.895	11.105	
Growth = 0%	6	9	5	7	27
	6.6857	6.8143	6.6857	6.8143	
0%<Grow<=3.5%	7	8	14	12	41
	10.152	10.348	10.152	10.348	
3.5%<Gr<=8.5%	16	10	10	15	51
	12.629	12.871	12.629	12.871	
Growth >8.5%	13	9	15	10	47
	11.638	11.862	11.638	11.862	
Total	52	53	52	53	210

Chi-Square (df=12): 13.360, Prob.: 0.343

(2) Distribution of Technological Inputs
By Company Attributes
Textile-Apparel   Computer-Electronics

PATA NT90	OWNERSHIP			OWNERSHIP		
	Propriet orship	Private corporat	Public corporat	Propriet orship	Private corporat	Pu lic co porat
No	14	198	33	12	101	56
Yes	0	22	9	2	25	14
Chi-Sq. (df=2):			6.486			0.263
Prob.:			0.039			0.877

K-CC 8590	OWNERSHIP			OWNERSHIP		
	Propriet orship	Private corporat	Public corporat	Propriet orship	Private corporat	Public corporat
No	9	71	7	2	40	17
Yes	5	149	35	12	86	53
Chi-Sq. (df=2):			11.314			2.656
Prob.:			0.003			0.265

K-CC 8590	HEADQTR				HEADQTR			
	HQ-CNTY	HQ-STATE	HQ-US	HQ-FRGN	HQ-CNTY	HQ-STATE	HQ-US	HQ-FRGN
No	67	6	13	1	49	2	5	2
Yes	116	25	46	2	102	10	32	5
Chi-Sq. (df=3):			6.788				6.098	
Prob.:			0.079				0.107	

K-MCN 8590	HEADQTR				HEADQTR			
	HQ-CNTY	HQ-STATE	HQ-US	HQ-FRGN	HQ-CNTY	HQ-STATE	HQ-US	HQ-FRGN
No	41	6	12	1	42	1	5	0
Yes	142	25	47	2	109	11	32	7
Chi-Sq. (df=3):			0.456				7.359	
Prob.:			0.928				0.061	

K-MNG 8590	HEADQTR				HEADQTR			
	HQ-CNTY 1	HQ-STATE 2	HQ-US 3	HQ-FRGN 4	HQ-CNTY 1	HQ-STATE 2	HQ-US 3	HQ-FRGN 4
No	44	4	11	0	31	1	5	0
Yes	139	27	48	3	120	11	32	7
Chi-Sq. (df=3):			3.177				3.472	
Prob.:			0.365				0.324	

Textile-Apparel   Computer-Electronics

K-TRN 8590	HEADQTR				HEADQTR			
	HQ-CNTY	HQ-STATE	HQ-US	HQ-FRGN	HQ-CNTY	HQ-STATE	HQ-US	HQ-FRGN
No	65	5	12	0	36	2	5	0
Yes	118	26	47	3	115	10	32	7
Chi-Sq. (df=3):				9.444				4.007
Prob.:				0.024				0.261

PATNT 90	EMP90				EMP90			
	Emp<70	70<=Emp<160	160<=Emp<320	Emp>320	Emp<40	40<=EmP<90	90<=EmP<250	Emp>250
No	67	66	58	56	38	52	35	44
Yes	0	6	12	14	10	5	11	15
Chi-Sq. (df=3):				16.613				6.117
Prob.:				0.001				0.106

K-CC 8590	EMP90				EMP90			
	Emp<70	70<=Emp<160	160<=Emp<320	Emp>320	Emp<40	40<=EmP<90	90<=EmP<250	Emp>250
No	35	30	16	7	23	15	12	9
Yes	32	42	54	63	25	42	34	50
Chi-Sq. (df=3):				34.199				14.332
Prob.:				0.000				0.002

K-MCN 8590	EMP90				EMP90			
	Emp<70	70<=Emp<160	160<=Emp<320	Emp>320	Emp<40	40<=EmP<90	90<=EmP<250	Emp>250
No	23	18	12	7	22	9	10	7
Yes	44	54	58	63	26	48	36	52
Chi-Sq. (df=3):				13.326				20.062
Prob.:				0.004				0.000

K-MNG 8590	EMP90				EMP90			
	Emp<70	70<=Emp<160	160<=Emp<320	Emp>320	Emp<40	40<=EmP<90	90<=EmP<250	Emp>250
No	24	20	11	4	14	9	8	6
Yes	43	52	59	66	34	48	38	53
Chi-Sq. (df=3):				21.787				6.799
Prob.:				0.000				0.079

K-TRN 8590	EMP90				EMP90			
	Emp<70	70<=Emp<160	160<=Emp<320	Emp>320	Emp<40	40<=EmP<90	90<=EmP<250	Emp>250
No	34	28	12	9	24	8	5	6
Yes	33	44	58	61	24	49	41	53
Chi-Sq. (df=3):				31.892				33.603
Prob.:				0.000				0.000

Textile-Apparel   Computer-Electronics

PATNT 90	Sale <$4M	SALE90 4M<=Sale<10M	SALE90 10M<=S.<25M	Sale>25M	Sale <$3M	SALE90 3M<=Sa<7.5M	SALE90 7.5M<=S.<25M	Sale>25M
No	63	53	76	55	44	44	41	40
Yes	0	5	11	16	8	9	11	13
Chi-Sq. (df=3):				17.306				1.718
Prob.:				0.001				0.633

K-CC 8590	Sale <$4M	SALE90 4M<=Sale<10M	SALE90 10M<=S.<25M	Sale>25M	Sale <$3M	SALE90 3M<=Sa<7.5M	SALE90 7.5M<=S.<25M	Sale>25M
No	33	21	22	12	26	17	9	7
Yes	30	37	65	59	26	36	43	46
Chi-Sq. (df=3):				21.879				21.577
Prob.:				0.000				0.000

K-MCN 8590	Sale <$4M	SALE90 4M<=Sale<10M	SALE90 10M<=S.<25M	Sale>25M	Sale <$3M	SALE90 3M<=Sa<7.5M	SALE90 7.5M<=S.<25M	Sale>25M
No	22	13	18	7	22	13	6	7
Yes	41	45	69	64	30	40	46	46
Chi-Sq. (df=3):				12.484				17.818
Prob.:				0.006				0.000

K-MNG 8590	Sale <$4M	SALE90 4M<=Sale<10M	SALE90 10M<=S.<25M	Sale>25M	Sale <$3M	SALE90 3M<=Sa<7.5M	SALE90 7.5M<=S.<25M	Sale>25M
No	24	15	18	2	18	9	5	5
Yes	39	43	69	69	34	44	47	48
Chi-Sq. (df=3):				25.943				15.105
Prob.:				0.000				0.002

K-TRN 8590	Sale <$4M	SALE90 4M<=Sale<10M	SALE90 10M<=S.<25M	Sale>25M	Sale <$3M	SALE90 3M<=Sa<7.5M	SALE90 7.5M<=S.<25M	Sale>25M
No	33	22	19	9	22	9	7	5
Yes	30	36	68	62	30	44	45	48
Chi-Sq. (df=3):				29.806				21.158
Prob.:				0.000				0.000

K-CC8590	BUYCRTF No	BUYCRTF Yes	BUYCRTF No	BUYCRTF Yes
No	55	33	No 29	30
Yes	85	106	Yes 44	107
Chi-Sq. (df=1):		7.805		7.493
Prob.:		0.005		0.006

Textile-Apparel   Computer-Electronics

K-MCN590	BUYCRTF No	Yes		No	BUYCRTF Yes
No	37	23	No	26	22
Yes	103	116	Yes	47	115
Chi-Sq. (df=1):		4.035			10.331
Prob.:		0.045			0.001

K-MNG590	BUYCRTF No	Yes		No	BUYCRTF Yes
No	36	23	No	21	16
Yes	104	116	Yes	52	121
Chi-Sq. (df=1):		3.515			9.581
Prob.:		0.061			0.002

K-TRN590	BUYCRTF No	Yes		No	BUYCRTF Yes
No	54	29	No	22	21
Yes	86	110	Yes	51	116
Chi-Sq. (df=1):		10.465			6.414
Prob.:		0.001			0.011

K-CC8590	SALECRTF No	Yes		No	SALECRTF Yes
No	58	30	No	22	37
Yes	105	86	Yes	48	103
Chi-Sq. (df=1):		2.966			0.578
Prob.:		0.085			0.447

K-MCN8590	SALECRTF No	Yes		No	SALECRTF Yes
No	41	19	No	20	28
Yes	122	97	Yes	50	112
Chi-Sq. (df=1):		3.091			1.944
Prob.:		0.079			0.163

K-TRN8590	SALECRTF No	Yes		No	SALECRTF Yes
No	62	21	No	16	27
Yes	101	95	Yes	54	113
Chi-Sq. (df=1):		12.885			0.336
Prob.:		0.000			0.545

Beyond Capital and Labor

Textile-Apparel   Computer-Electronics

K-R&D GROW	OWNERSHIP			OWNERSHIP		
	PROPRIET	PRIVATE	PUBLIC	PROPRIET	PRIVATE	POUBLIC
No	10	197	32	9	84	49
Yes	4	23	10	5	42	21
Chi-Sq. (df=2):			8.340			0.304
Prob.:			0.015			0.859

K-R&D GROW	COMPANY AGE				COMPANY AGE			
	Age<10	10<=Age<20	20<=Age<30	Age>=30	Age<10	10<=Age<20	20<=Age<30	Age>=30
No	20	31	41	149	13	42	53	34
Yes	3	4	3	28	6	20	13	29
Chi-Sq. (df=3):				2.607				10.217
Prob.:				0.456				0.017

K-R&D GROW	EMP90				EMP90			
	Emp<70	70<=Emp<160	160<=Emp<320	Emp>320	Emp<40	40<=EmP<90	90<=EmP<250	Emp>250
No	63	63	65	50	39	38	27	38
Yes	4	9	5	20	9	19	19	21
Chi-Sq. (df=3):				19.206				6.048
Prob.:				0.000				0.109

K-R&D GROW	SALE90				SALE90			
	Sale<$4M	4M<=Sale<10M	10M<=S.<25M	Sale>25M	Sale<$3M	3M<=Sa<7.5M	7.5M<=S.<25M	Sale>25M
No	59	54	78	50	40	43	28	31
Yes	4	4	9	21	12	10	24	22
Chi-Sq. (df=3):				21.220				12.998
Prob.:				0.000				0.005

K-R&DGROW	BUYCRTF		BUYCRTF	
	No	Yes	No	Yes
No	127	114	56	86
Yes	13	25	17	51
Chi-Sq. (df=1):		4.487		4.226
Prob.:		0.034		0.040

K-R&DGROW	SALECRTF		SALECRTF	
	No	Yes	No	Yes
No	148	93	51	91
Yes	15	23	19	49
Chi-Sq. (df=1):		6.503		1.316
Prob.:		0.011		0.251

Appendix 4B: Frequency Distribution of Production and Productivity Growths and Technological Inputs by Metro Size and Region

(Statistically very insignificant tables are not shown to save space)

Textile-Apparel   Computer-Electronics

PATNT 90	METRO SIZE 0	1	2	3	0	METRO SIZE 1	2	3
No	87	44	59	57	21	38	32	78
Yes	11	3	4	14	6	6	9	20
Chi-Sq. (df=3):				7.588				1.298
Prob.:				0.055				0.730

K-MCN 8590	METRO SIZE 0	1	2	3	0	METRO SIZE 1	2	3
No	19	4	18	19	6	9	3	30
Yes	79	43	45	52	21	35	38	68
Chi-Sq. (df=3):				7.987				9.108
Prob.:				0.046				0.028

K-TRN 8590	METRO SIZE 0	1	2	3	0	METRO SIZE 1	2	3
No	24	15	19	25	4	5	5	29
Yes	74	32	44	46	23	39	36	69
Chi-Sq. (df=3):				2.421				9.503
Prob.:				0.490				0.023

PRTY-GROW	NE Region No	Yes	NE Region No	Yes
G < 0	40	16	29	20
G = 0	65	9	38	4
0<G<=2	15	4	4	5
2<G<=6	43	15	30	11
G > 6	50	22	44	25
Chi-Sq. (df=4):		8.288		15.030
Prob.:		0.082		0.005

PATNT 90	NE Region No	Yes	NE Region No	Yes
No	195	52	112	57
Yes	18	14	33	8
Chi-Sq. (df=1):		8.081		3.120
Prob.:		0.004		0.077

Textile-Apparel   Computer-Electronics

K-CC 8590	NE Region No	NE Region Yes	NE Region No	NE Region Yes
No	61	27	39	20
Yes	152	39	106	45
Chi-Sq. (df=1):		3.514		0.333
Prob.:		0.061		0.564

K-MCN 8590	NE Region No	NE Region Yes	NE Region No	NE Region Yes
No	41	19	30	18
Yes	172	47	115	47
Chi-Sq. (df=1):		2.716		1.248
Prob.:		0.099		0.264

K-TRN 8590	NE Region No	NE Region Yes	NE Region No	NE Region Yes
No	54	29	33	10
Yes	159	37	112	55
Chi-Sq. (df=1):		8.330		1.499
Prob.:		0.004		0.221

PATNT 90	MW Region No	MW Region Yes	MW Region No	MW Region Yes
No	222	25	136	33
Yes	28	4	26	15
Chi-Sq. (df=1):		0.172		5.445
Prob.:		0.678		0.020

K-MCN 8590	MW Region No	MW Region Yes	MW Region No	MW Region Yes
No	55	5	42	6
Yes	195	24	120	42
Chi-Sq. (df=1):		0.349		3.785
Prob.:		0.555		0.052

K-MNG 8590	MW Region No	MW Region Yes	MW Region No	MW Region Yes
No	55	4	33	4
Yes	195	25	129	44
Chi-Sq. (df=1):		1.050		3.696
Prob.:		0.306		0.055

	Textile-Apparel		**Computer-Electronics**	

K-R&D GROW	SOUTH Region		SOUTH Region	
	No	Yes	No	Yes
No	103	138	116	26
Yes	18	20	62	6
Chi-Sq. (df=1):		0.286		3.204
Prob.:		0.592		0.073

PATNT 90	SOUTH Region		SOUTH Region	
	No	Yes	No	Yes
No	101	146	143	26
Yes	20	12	35	6
Chi-Sq. (df=1):		5.386		0.014
Prob.:		0.020		0.905

K-CC 8590	SOUTH Region		SOUTH Region	
	No	Yes	No	Yes
No	45	43	52	7
Yes	76	115	126	25
Chi-Sq. (df=1):		3.158		0.723
Prob.:		0.076		0.395

PRTY-GROW	WEST Region		WEST Region	
	No	Yes	No	Yes
G < 0	53	0	29	15
G = 0	40	7	19	8
0<G<=2	41	5	24	9
2<G<=6	61	1	34	9
G > 6	63	8	43	20
Chi-Sq. (df=4):		13.260		2.195
Prob.:		0.010		0.700

K-MNG 8590	WEST Region		WEST Region	
	No	Yes	No	Yes
No	53	6	22	15
Yes	205	15	127	46
Chi-Sq. (df=1):		0.751		2.878
Prob.:		0.386		0.090

K-TRN 8590	WEST Region		WEST Region	
	No	Yes	No	Yes
No	78	5	25	18
Yes	180	16	124	43
Chi-Sq. (df=1):		0.383		4.307
Prob.:		0.536		0.038

Appendix 4C: Frequency Distribution
of Technological Inputs by R & D Credit Policy
(Statistically very insignificant tables are not shown to save space)

Textile-Apparel

K-R&D GROW	R&DCRDT No	R&DCRDT Yes	K-MCN 8590	R&DCRDT No	R&DCRDT Yes
No	213	28	No	59	1
Yes	28	10	Yes	182	37
Chi-Sq. (df=1):		6.027	Chi-Sq. (df=1):		9.283
Prob.:		0.014	Prob.:		0.002

K-MNG 8590	R&DCRDT No	R&DCRDT Yes	K-TRN 8590	R&DCRDT No	R&DCRDT Yes
No	57	2	No	80	3
Yes	184	36	Yes	161	35
Chi-Sq. (df=1):		6.656	Chi-Sq. (df=1):		10.054
Prob.:		0.010	Prob.:		0.002

Computer-Electronics

K-R&D GROW	R&DCRDT No	R&DCRDT Yes	K-TRN 8590	R&DCRDT No	R&DCRDT Yes
No	122	20	No	40	3
Yes	52	16	Yes	134	33
Chi-Sq. (df=1):		2.888	Chi-Sq. (df=1):		3.934
Prob.:		0.089	Prob.:		0.047

Notes

1. Strictly speaking, certification practice may not be a producer characteristics. Certification variables are included in the group of producer characteristics for convenience.

2. Regional patterns of production and productivity growth and technological inputs across census divisions are also examined. Many categories in both the textile-apparel and the computer-electronics groups have very small counts in several divisions. Contingency table and Chi square tests become inappropriate methods. Therefore, the statistics based on census divisions are not presented.

5 Modeling Production and Productivity Growth With Spatial Differentiation

This chapter employs the model developed in chapter 2 to systematically estimate the contribution of technology and regional factors to production and productivity growth. Figure 5.1. shows the conceptual relationship and the major groups of variables included in the empirical study. The relationship is obviously a part of the whole conceptual structure shown in Figure 2.1. The first section of this chapter presents the estimates of the growth equations and qualitative and quantitative interpretations. The second section estimates the labor productivity growth equations. The third section discusses the implications of the findings.

5.1. PRODUCTION GROWTH

5.1.1. Estimation of Production Growth

Equation (2.25) is the basic form used to estimate coefficients of production growth, but many justifiable variables are included in estimation and testing. The neater form of equation (2.25), namely, (2.25') is rewritten as (5.1) for convenience,

$$(5.1) \qquad \dot{Q}_t = \beta_0 + \beta_1 \dot{K}_t - \beta_2 \dot{A}_t + \beta_3 \dot{L}_t + \beta_4 \dot{E}_{st} + \beta_5 \dot{E}_{et} + \beta_6 \dot{Z}_t + \beta_7 \dot{R}_t \, ,$$

where dotted variables are annualized growth rates of output, producer inputs, and regional factors.

Practically, there are many possible candidates to measure each regional factor (e.g., a regional service sector, technological externality, and agglomeration). Statistically, inclusion of irrelevant

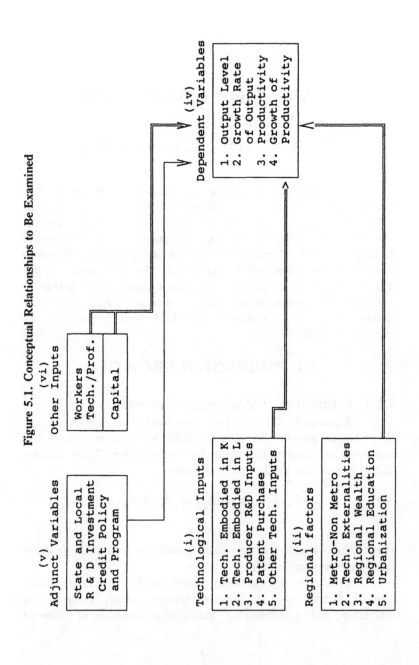

Figure 5.1. Conceptual Relationships to Be Examined

(vi)
Other Inputs

Workers
Tech./Prof.
Capital

(v)
Adjunct Variables

State and Local
R & D Investment
Credit Policy
and Program

(i)
Technological Inputs

1. Tech. Embodied in K
2. Tech. Embodied in L
3. Producer R&D Inputs
4. Patent Purchase
5. Other Tech. Inputs

(ii)
Regional factors

1. Metro-Non Metro
2. Tech. Externalities
3. Regional Wealth
4. Regional Education
5. Urbanization

(iv)
Dependent Variables

1. Output Level
2. Growth Rate
   of Output
3. Productivity
4. Growth of
   Productivity

variables leads to inefficient parameter estimates--greater standard errors of parameter estimates, making rejection of null hypotheses unnecessarily difficult. To avoid including irrelevant variables, the growth equations are estimated and tested in two steps. First, producer input growth variables including industry-adjustment variables are tested. Insignificant industry-adjustment variables are removed from the models. All producer input and remaining industry-adjustment variables are carried to the second step. Second, conceptually justifiable competing regional variables are examined. Only those regional variables that are conceptually distinctive and statistically more significant than the competing variables are allowed to enter the model. Each regional service sector is measured using two variables--growth rate of employment and growth rate of establishment. After extensive testing, only one variable, mostly employment growth rate, is retained for each regional service sector in the final model. Producer input variables and their definitions can be found in Table 3.5 of chapter 3. Regional variables and their definitions are listed in Table 5.1. Only growth measures of these variables are used in the production and productivity growth equations.

Table 5.1 Regional Variables and Definitions

Variables	Definition
TXTLEW88	Average annual wage rate in the area textile industry in 1988
TEXWAGGROW	Annualized percentage change in the area textile industry wage rate in 1983-88 period
APPLW88	Average annual wage rate in the area apparel industry in 1988
APPWAGGROW	Annualized percentage change in the area apparel industry wage rate in 1983-88 period
CMPTRW88	Average annual wage rate in the area computer industry in 1988
CMPWAGGROW	Annualized percentage change in the area computer industry wage rate in 1983-88 period
ELECW88	Average annual wage rate in the area electronics components industry in 1988
ELEWAGGROW	Annualized percentage change in the area electronics components industry wage rate in 1983-88 period

Table 5.1 Regional Variables and Definitions (Con.)

Variables	Definition
R&DCRDT	Dummy variable, it equals 1 if a company is in an area with state or local R & D credit, 0 otherwise
PCMINC85	Area average personal annual money income in 1985
COLLEGE	College degree holders as percentage of area population in 1986
METRO	Dummy variable, it equals 1 if a company is located in a metropolitan area, 0 otherwise
POP86	Area population in 1986
URBANPOP	Urban population as percentage of area population in 1986
TOTEMP88	Total area employment in 1988
TOTEST88	Total number of establishments in 1988
TXTLEE88	Employment in the area textile industry as percentage of area employment in 1988
TEXEMPGROW	Annualized percentage change in the area textile industry employment in 1983-88 period
TEXESTGROW	Annualized percentage change in the number of the area textile establishments in 1983-88 period
APPLE88	Employment in the area apparel industry as percentage of area employment in 1988
APPEMPGROW	Annualized percentage change in the area apparel industry employment in 1983-88 period
APPESTGROW	Annualized percentage change in the number of the area apparel establishments in 1983-88 period
CMPTRE88	Employment in the area computer industry as percentage of area employment in 1988
CMPEMPGROW	Annualized percentage change in the area computer industry employment in 1983-88 period
CMPESTGROW	Annualized percentage change in the number of the area computer establishments in 1983-88 period
ELECE88	Employment in the area electronics components industry as percentage of area employment in 1988
ELEEMPGROW	Annualized percentage change in the area electronics components industry employment in 1983-88 period

Table 5.1 Regional Variables and Definitions (Con.)

Variables	Definition
ELEESTGROW	Annualized percentage change in the number of the area electronics components establishments in 1983-88 period
AIR88	Employment in the area air transportation sector as percentage of area employment in 1988
AIREMPGROW	Annualized percentage change in the employment of the area air transportation sector in 1983-88 period
TRNSVC88	Employment in area transportation services other than air transportation as percentage of area employment in 1988
TSVEMPGROW	Annualized percentage change in the employment of the area transportation services other than air transportation in 1983-88 period
CMMNCT88	Employment in the area communication sector as percentage of area employment in 1988
CMUEMPGROW	Annualized percentage change in employment of the area communication sector in 1983-88 period
UTILIT88	The number of establishments in the area utilities sector in 1988
UTIESTGROW	Annualized percentage change in the number of the area utilities establishments in 1983-88 period
ENGNRG88	Employment in the area engineering services other than R & D and testing as percentage of area employment in 1988
ENGEMPGROW	Annualized percentage change in employment of the area engineering services in 1983-88 period
R&DTSVC88	Employment in the area R & D and testing services as percentage of area employment in 1988
R&DEMPGROW	Annualized percentage change in employment of the area R & D and testing services in 1983-88 period
BUSSVC88	Employment in the area business services sector as percentage of area employment in 1988
BUSEMPGROW	Annualized percentage change in the employment of the area business services in 1983-88 period
FIRE88	The number of establishments in the area finance, insurance, real estate, and security services in 1988
FIRESTGROW	Annualized percentage change in the number of the area utilities establishments in 1983-88 period

Table 5.1 Regional Variables and Definitions (Con.)

Variables	Definition
AMUSE88	Employment in the area recreation and amusement sector as percentage of area employment in 1988
AMSEMPGROW	Annualized percentage change in the employment of the area amusement and recreation services in 1983-88 period
HEALTH88	Employment in the area health care services sector as percentage of area employment in 1988
HLTEMPGROW	Annualized percentage change in the employment of the area health care services in 1983-88 period
EDUCAT88	Employment in the area education services sector as percentage of area employment in 1988
EDUEMPGROW	Annualized percentage change in the employment of the area education sector in 1983-88 period
SCLSVC88	Employment in the area social services sector as percentage of area employment in 1988
SOCEMPGROW	Annualized percentage change in the employment of the area social services in 1983-88 period
PHYSIC85	Number of physicians in the area in 1985
HOSPIT85	Number of hospital in the area in 1985

The growth equation is estimated for the two industry groups. Table 5.2 and Table 5.3 represent the empirical models for textile-apparel and computer-electronics industries respectively. Functional form (2.15) developed in this study is used in Equation 1, Equation 2, Equation 4, and Equation 5. Functional form (2.12) developed by Nelson (1964) is employed in Equation 3. The form (2.12) leads to an estimate of annual rate of technological progress embodied in capital, while form (2.15) results in an empirical relationship between the average age of capital and the embodied technology. Both estimates are interesting and desirable. Equation 1 is more inclusive with many insignificant variables included. In comparison, other equations only include relatively significant variables. Equation 4 tests the hypothesized constant return to scale with respect to producer internal inputs, imposing a restriction of constant return to producer *internal physical inputs*. Equation 5 tests the hypothesized constant return to scale with respect to *producer internal inputs and regional factors*.

**Table 5.2 Parameter Estimates of Production
Growth Equations of Textile-Apparel**
(Dependent Variable: Annual Growth Rate of Value Added)

Variable	Equat.1	Equat.2	Equat.3	Equat.4	Equat.5
INTERCEPT	-0.2796	0.6588	0.6959	0.7322	1.2043**
	(1.137)	(0.611)	(0.610)	(0.578)	(0.529)
W-EMPGROW	0.3751**	0.3996**	0.3935**	0.3936**	0.3833**
	(0.070)	(0.066)	(0.066)	(0.064)	(0.066)
W-EDGROW	0.3120	------	------	------	------
	(0.194)				
W-EXPGROW	-0.0977	------	------	------	------
	(0.066)				
P-EMPGROW	0.0802*	0.0815*	0.0804*	0.0811*	0.0783*
	(0.048)	(0.046)	(0.046)	(0.046)	(0.046)
P-EDGROW	0.0560	------	------	------	------
	(0.216)				
P-EXPGROW	0.2192**	0.1855**	0.1832**	0.1689**	0.1244**
	(0.084)	(0.069)	(0.069)	(0.053)	(0.060)
K-UTLGROW	0.2391**	0.2273**	0.2209**	0.2230**	0.2176**
	(0.053)	(0.051)	(0.051)	(0.050)	(0.051)
K-AGEGROW	-0.0615	-0.0831**	------	-0.0906**	-0.1034**
	(0.041)	(0.038)		(0.032)	(0.036)
K-AGEDELT	------	------	-0.9977**	------	------
			(0.398)		
K-BDGROW	0.1474**	0.1364**	0.1407**	0.1261**	0.1017
	(0.068)	(0.065)	(0.064)	(0.058)	(0.062)
K-R&DGROW	0.0112**	0.0110**	0.0110**	0.0110**	0.0107**
	(0.002)	(0.002)	(0.002)	(0.002)	(0.002)
PTNTGROW	0.0633**	0.0621**	0.0613**	0.0615**	0.0588**
	(0.022)	(0.021)	(0.021)	(0.021)	(0.021)
K-CCGROW	0.0060	------	------	------	------
	(0.009)				
K-MCNGROW	0.0056	------	------	------	------
	(0.004)				
K-MNGGROW	0.0070	------	------	------	------
	(0.009)				
K-TRNGROW	0.0166	0.0261*	0.0248*	0.0254*	0.0244*
	(0.015)	(0.013)	(0.013)	(0.013)	(0.013)
TEXWAGGROW	-0.0127	------	------	------	------
	(0.177)				
APPWAGGROW	0.0647	------	------	------	------
	(0.154)				
TEXEMPGROW	0.0155	------	------	------	------
	(0.081)				
TEXESTGROW	-0.0519	------	------	------	------
	(0.092)				
APPEMPGROW	-0.0609	------	------	------	------
	(0.048)				
APPESTGROW	0.0619	------	------	------	------
	(0.081)				
AIREMPGROW	0.0133	------	------	------	------
	(0.017)				

**Table 5.2 Parameter Estimates of Production
Growth Equations of Textile-Apparel (Con.)**
(Dependent Variable: Annual Growth Rate of Value Added)

Variable	Equat.1	Equat.2	Equat.3	Equat.4	Equat.5
TSVEMPGROW	-0.0028	------	------	------	------
	(0.019)				
CMUEMPGROW	-0.0387	------	------	------	------
	(0.039)				
UTIESTGROW	-0.0501	------	------	------	------
	(0.061)				
FIRESTGROW	0.1882	0.2379**	0.2318**	0.2424**	0.1042
	(0.135)	(0.117)	(0.116)	(0.116)	(0.090)
AMSEMPGROW	-0.0193	------	------	------	------
	(0.030)				
HLTEMPGROW	0.0119	------	------	------	------
	(0.065)				
EDUEMPGROW	-0.0172	------	------	------	------
	(0.017)				
SOCEMPGROW	-0.0203	------	------	------	------
	(0.031)				
R&DEMPGROW	-0.0043	------	------	------	------
	(0.008)				
METRO-APP	1.5056	1.6272**	1.4896*	1.6256**	1.6324**
	(1.203)	(0.762)	(0.756)	(0.760)	(0.765)
RESTRICTION		------	------	105.70	379.80*
				(282.1)	(217.3)
Adj R-sq	0.4592	0.4725	0.4755	0.4742	0.4684

Note: a. Restriction in Equat. 4: Constant return to scale with all producer inputs.
         b. Restriction in Equat. 5: Constant return to scale with all producer inputs
         and regional factor.
         c. * and ** indicate statistically significant at 0.95 and 0.90 levels
         respectively, using two tailed test.

A comparison helps to determine which equation is a better parametric representation of input-output growth relation and reveals to what extent the parameter estimates are reliable. First, most parameter estimates of producer inputs that are statistically significant are quite stable across the equations, although these equations include different numbers of variables and are subject to different restrictions. This signifies the reliability of estimates for the internal inputs. A joint F test was conducted to test the hypothesis that variables included in Equation 1 but not in Equation 2 are all equal to zero. The computed F statistics for textile-apparel and computer-electronics are $F_{21,244}=0.69$ and $F_{21.177}=0.30$ respectively, both much smaller than a critical F at any

**Table 5.3 Parameter Estimates of Production
Growth Equations of Computer-Electronics**
(Dependent Variable: Annual Growth Rate of Value Added)

Variable	Equat. 1	Equat. 2	Equat. 3	Equat. 4	Equat. 5
INTERCEPT	0.7912	-0.3443	-0.4004	-0.1663	1.6709
	(1.818)	(1.068)	(1.085)	(1.042)	(0.689)
W-EMPGROW	0.1868**	0.1915**	0.2035**	0.1901**	0.1848**
	(0.042)	(0.040)	(0.040)	(0.040)	(0.040)
W-EDGROW	-0.2601	------	------	------	------
	(0.267)				
W-EXPGROW	-0.0987	------	------	------	------
	(0.090)				
P-EMPGROW	0.2085**	0.2347**	0.2425**	0.2283**	0.2252**
	(0.052)	(0.050)	(0.050)	(0.049)	(0.050)
P-EDGROW	0.1977**	0.2397**	0.2367**	0.2073**	0.1832**
	(0.070)	(0.064)	(0.065)	(0.049)	(0.060)
P-EXPGROW	-0.1090	------	------	------	------
	(0.099)				
K-UTLGROW	0.2100**	0.2031**	0.1957**	0.2000**	0.1957**
	(0.050)	(0.047)	(0.048)	(0.046)	(0.047)
K-AGEGROW	-0.0932**	-0.0645**	------	-0.0712**	-0.0781**
	(0.028)	(0.024)		(0.022)	(0.023)
K-AGEDELT	------	------	-0.7011*	------	------
			(0.415)		
K-BDGROW	0.1650**	0.1836**	0.1812**	0.1515**	0.1184
	(0.079)	(0.076)	(0.077)	(0.064)	(0.072)
K-R&DGROW	0.0859	0.1113*	0.1015	0.0938	0.0813
	(0.067)	(0.063)	(0.064)	(0.059)	(0.063)
PTNTGROW	-0.0086	------	------	------	------
	(0.011)				
K-CCGROW	-0.0023	------	------	------	------
	(0.012)				
K-MCNGROW	0.0046	------	------	------	------
	(0.013)				
K-MNGGROW	-0.0187	------	------	------	------
	(0.021)				
K-TRNGROW	0.0102*	------	------	------	------
	(0.006)				
CMPEMPGROW	-0.1066**	-0.0893**	-0.0884**	-0.0892**	-0.0913**
	(0.050)	(0.029)	(0.029)	(0.029)	(0.029)
CMPESTGROW	0.0166	------	------	------	------
	(0.065)				
ELEEMPGROW	0.2055**	------	------	------	------
	(0.081)				
ELEESTGROW	-0.1606	------	------	------	------
	(0.139)				
CMPWAGGROW	0.0773	------	------	------	------
	(0.115)				
ELEWAGGROW	0.0203	------	------	------	------
	(0.115)				
AIREMPGROW	0.0416*	------	------	------	------
	(0.024)				

Table 5.3 Parameter Estimates of Production
Growth Equations of Computer-Electronics (Con.)
(Dependent Variable: Annual Growth Rate of Value Added)

Variable	Equat. 1	Equat. 2	Equat. 3	Equat. 4	Equat. 5
TSVEMPGROW	-0.0304 (0.051)	------	------	------	------
CMUEMPGROW	0.0344 (0.086)	------	------	------	------
UTIESTGROW	-0.0754 (0.128)	------	------	------	------
FIRESTGROW	-0.4093 (0.255)	------	------	------	------
AMSEMPGROW	0.1260 (0.086)	0.1314* (0.072)	0.1346* (0.072)	0.1345* (0.071)	0.1116 (0.072)
HLTEMPGROW	0.3728* (0.193)	0.2920* (0.176)	0.3260* (0.177)	0.2687 (0.173)	-0.0412 (0.112)
EDUEMPGROW	0.0293 (0.054)	------	------	------	------
SOCEMPGROW	0.2213** (0.088)	0.1718** (0.081)	0.1685** (0.081)	0.1711** (0.080)	0.1105 (0.077)
R&DEMPGROW	-0.0244 (0.015)	------	------	------	------
METRO	1.2834 (1.849)	------	------	------	------
RESTRICTION		------	------	275.89 (347.9)	433.96** (179.3)
Adj R-sq	0.5681	0.5627	0.5527	0.5635	0.5517

Note: a. Restriction in Equat. 4: Constant return to scale with all producer inputs.
b. Restriction in Equat. 5: Constant return to scale with all producer inputs and regional factors.
c. * and ** indicate statistically significant at 0.90 and 0.95 levels respectively, using two tailed test.

commonly used significance level. Although this does not prove that the hypothesis is true[1], the parameter estimates in Equation 2 can be treated as the same as or similar to their counterparts in Equation 1. Moreover, Equation 2 for the textile-apparel group has an adjusted R squared of 0.4725, comparing favorably with 0.4592 of Equation 1. This is an important sign of inclusion of irrelevant variables, which explain no more variation in the production growth but only result in inefficiency of the estimates. Equation 1 and 2 for the computer-electronics group have similar adjusted R squared values, 0.5681 vs. 0.5627--no notable explanatory power is generated by the 21 additional variables. By comparison, Equation 2 is likely to be a better representation of the relationship examined for both groups.

Second, the restriction of constant return to scale with respect to producer internal inputs is imposed in Equation 2. The estimates are labeled as Equation 4. The restriction made no difference in the estimated input-output growth relationship. This is indicated by the insignificant estimates of Lagrangian multiplier for the restriction and essentially unchanged estimates of other variables in Equation 4. The estimates provide evidence that return to scale with respect to producer inputs can be considered constant for both industry groups.

Third, the restriction of constant return to scale with respect to producer internal inputs and significant regional factors is also imposed to Equation 2. The estimates are presented as Equation 5. Statistically, the estimates of restriction are significant, and the restriction made a significant difference in parameter estimates of other variables for both industry groups. This indicates that Equation 5 cannot be considered the same as Equation 2. Based on this evidence, the return to scale with respect to producer internal inputs and regional factors cannot be treated as constant.

The overall comparison strongly suggests that Equation 2, 3, and 4 are better models. The following interpretation is largely based on the estimates of Equation 2. However, using significant estimates in Equation 1, one could reach a similar interpretation due to the similarity of the two sets of estimates. Based on Equation 2, the average value of marginal products of producer inputs, technological factors, and regional factors can all be estimated using the average levels of the output and the inputs over the 1985-90 period. The estimates are presented in Table 5.4. Furthermore, given the estimate of output elasticity of each factor input and the average growth rates of relevant factors over 1985-90 period in the sample, the contribution of a factor to growth is the product of the elasticity and the growth rate of the factor input, $(\partial Q/\partial X)(X/Q)(dX/Xdt)$. Absolute and relative measures of the contributions of producer inputs and regional factors to production growth are shown in Table 5.5.

5.1.2. Production Growth and Contributors

According to production theory and growth theory, producer physical inputs and regional complemental and substitutive factors should all positively contribute to production growth, while regional diseconomies and disamenities should negatively contribute to production and growth. Some regional factors may have positive as well as negative impacts at the same time on production growth. For example, amount of workers employed in the same industry is an important indicator of localization economies or technological externalities that have positive influence on growth. However, if labor is not perfectly mobile, the industry in this area can face an inelastic labor supply curve. Consequently, the industry is characterized by increasing average cost to expansion. Theory itself cannot tell in balance which impact is greater. Only empirical estimation and testing

Table 5.4 Output Elasticities, Average Level of Input, and Average Value of Marginal Product (VMP) of Inputs in Two Groups

	Textile & Apparel			Computer & Electronics		
	(1)	(2)	(3)	(1)	(2)	(3)
	Output	Average	Average	Output	Average	Average
Variable	Elastic.	Input	VMP	Elastic.	Input	VMP
(I)						
W-EMPGROW	0.3996	301	17.9	0.1915	136	22.0
P-EMPGROW	0.0815	41	26.8	0.2347	64	57.4
K-UTLGROW	0.2273	4483	0.68	0.2031	3400	0.93
K-BDGROW	0.1364	4169	0.44	0.1836	4320	0.66
(II)						
P-EDGROW	------	----	----	0.2397	14.9	252
P-EXPGROW	0.1855	13.3	188	------	----	----
K-AGEGROW	-0.0831	10.9	----	-0.0645	9.5	----
K-AGEDELT*	-0.9977	----	----	-0.7011	----	----
(III)						
K-R&DGROW	0.0110	141	1.0	0.1113	790	2.20
PTNTGROW	0.0621	145	5.7	------	----	----
K-TRNGROW	0.0261	158	2.2	------	----	----
(IV)						
FIRESTGROW	0.2379	4676	0.66	------	----	----
METRO-APP	1.6272	----	----	------	----	----
CMPEMPGROW	------	----	----	-0.0893	7271	0.19
AMSEMPGROW	------	----	----	0.1314	9118	0.22
HLTEMPGROW	------	----	----	0.2920	69566	0.06
SOCEMPGROW	------	----	----	0.1718	14083	0.19

Note: a. Average input is the average annual input level in 1985-90 period; average input of labor (production worker and technic/professional) are measured in person year; capital in equipment, buildings, and R & D are all measured in thousand dollars; spending on patent purchase and worker training are also in thousand dollars.

b. Sample means of value added are $13.5 Million and $15.6 million for textile-apparel and computer-electronics companies respectively.

Table 5.5 Contribution of Each Factor and Each Group of Factors to Production Growth
Textile-Apparel

Variable	(1) Elasticity	(2) Growth Rate	(3)a (1)*(2)	(4)b % of Growth
W-EMPGROW	0.3996	-0.967	-0.3864	
P-EMPGROW	0.0815	-0.065	-0.0053	
K-UTLGROW	0.2273	1.351	0.3080	
K-BDGROW	0.1364	2.480	0.3383	
Group total			0.2546	9.1%
P-EXPGROW	0.1855	2.235	0.4146	
K-AGEGROW	-0.0831	1.033	-0.0858	
K-AGEDELTc	-0.9977	0.082	-0.0818	
Group total			0.3288	11.8%
K-R&DGROW	0.0110	1.051	0.0116	
PTNTGROW	0.0621	3.959	0.2458	
K-TRNGROW	0.0261	15.261	0.3983	
Group total			0.6557	23.5%
FIRESTGROW	0.2379	3.462	0.8236	29.5%
METRO-APP	1.6272		1.6272	58.3%d
Total			2.1231	73.9%e
Actual Growth			2.7884	100.0%

Computer-Electronics

Variable	(1) Elasticity	(2) Growth Rate	(3)a (1)*(2)	(4)b % of Growth
W-EMPGROW	0.1915	-1.057	-0.2024	
P-EMPGROW	0.2347	0.759	0.1781	
K-UTLGROW	0.2031	2.064	0.4192	
K-BDGROW	0.1836	2.541	0.4665	
Group total			0.8614	20.6%
P-EDGROW	0.2397	1.142	0.2737	
K-AGEGROW	-0.0645	-3.423	0.2208	
K-AGEDELTc	-0.7011	-0.436	0.3056	
Group total			0.4945	11.9%
K-R&DGROW	0.1113	2.700	0.3005	7.2%
CMPEMPGROW	-0.0893	-0.459	0.0410	
AMSEMPGROW	0.1314	5.447	0.7157	
HLTEMPGROW	0.2920	4.205	1.2278	
SOCEMPGROW	0.1718	6.257	1.0749	
Group total			3.0594	73.3%
Total			5.0214	112.9%
Actual Growth			4.1729	100.0%

Note: a. Contribution of each factor to production growth is measured as the annual growth rate of value added.

b. Contribution of each group of factors to production growth is measured as percent of annual growth of value added.

c. Variable K-AGEDELT is real, not percent, change in age of capital stock.

d. The estimate only pertains to apparel companies.

e. The total figure does not include contribution of metro location.

can settle the contention. Growth theory also points out that embodied technological progress should contribute to production and productivity growth. It is true, however, only when the embodied technology would positively exert its force in production. Practically, technology embodied in labor input affects production and productivity not only by its level but also by its motivation. In comparison, technology in capital is not affected by any self-consciousness and the efficiency of capital is exclusively determined by the level of the embodied technology. If a measure of technology embodied in labor is systematically associated with workers' attributes, the empirical estimate is subject to an alternative interpretation.

Table 5.2 and Table 5.3 in conjunction with Table 3.6 provide a large amount of information. To discuss the findings in an orderly manner, we need to examine the estimates group by group.

5.1.2.1. Conventional Inputs: Capital and Labor

As suggested in virtually all earlier research, conventional inputs are the most significant factors in production growth. Growths of production workers (W-EMPGROW), technical/ professional/ managerial employees (P-EMPGROW), capital stock in equipment adjusted to utilization (K-UTLGROW), and capital in buildings (K-BDGROW) are all statistically significant for both textile-apparel and computer-electronics groups.

Table 5.4 shows that the parameter estimate for labor input, lumping production workers and professionals together, is about 0.48 for textile-apparel and 0.43 for computer-electronics, and the estimate for capital input, adding equipment and structure together, is 0.36 for textile-apparel and 0.39 for computer-electronics. Given the average levels of output and inputs in both groups, implied annual average values of marginal product of production workers and professionals are $17.9K and $26.8K for textile-apparel and $22.0K and $57.4K for computer-electronics with weighted average wage rates of $18,973 for textile-apparel and $33,600 for computer-electronics. The wage rates computed using published data for the sample areas are available only for all employees as a whole. In 1988 the average annual wage rates in textile, apparel, computer, telecommunication equipment, and electronics are respectively $17.7K, $13.6K, $31.7K, $29.3K, and $24.6K (CBP 1988) with weighted average wage rates of $15,607 for textile-apparel and $28,578 for computer-electronics. The estimated figures seem to go with actual wage rates very well if some fringe benefit is taken into account. These estimates furnish interesting information which deserves further inquiry: given the additional variables measuring educational attainment and professional experience, the estimates for physical labor input should be the same for all kinds of labor in all industries if the labor market functions perfectly. The estimated occupational difference, and the inter-industrial difference in the wage rates should result from causes other than the difference in labor quality. This inquiry, however, is beyond the scope of this research.

The estimated average value of marginal product of capital is 0.44 and 0.66 in structure and 0.68 and 0.93 in equipment for textile-apparel and computer-electronics industries respectively. Considering the capital utilization of 80.3% in the sampled textile-apparel group and 66.6% in the computer-electronics group, the marginal product of total equipment or gross rate of return is 0.54 for textile-apparel and 0.61 for computer-electronics. Griliches' estimates of output elasticity of all assets implies a similar gross rate of return to capital, 0.52 (see Griliches 1986; his Table 1 and Table 2 show that output elasticity is 0.291 and average levels of capital input and output are $124 millions and $223 millions respectively), but he did not explicitly interpret these terms. To estimate net return to capital, depreciation should be deducted from gross return. Using the Accelerated Cost Recovery System (ACRS), the estimated return to equipment and buildings are 0.34-0.41 and 0.34-0.56 respectively, with computer-electronics industries having return higher than textile-apparel by 0.07 for equipment and 0.22 for structure. Measured by any standard, the returns seem to be very high. One reason is the missing variable to measure the value of land. As a result, return to capital, especially return to buildings, must be overestimated. There may also be other reasons that make estimated return to capital so high. First, the respondents in the research (and maybe in Griliches' research as well) represent a group that are successful. Many other companies that have gone out of business cannot appear in the sample data. Return to capital for the whole industry can be much lower than estimated here if the unsuccessful companies are taken into account. Second, rental cost on input such as buildings in certain areas can be very high, especially in technological advanced industries like computer and electronics located in urban areas. Third, net return to capital in some industries may be indeed much higher than interest rates due to their overvalued products.

Table 5.5 presents estimated contribution of conventional producer inputs to output growth. The estimates are surprising: magnitude is much smaller than one could imagine either in absolute terms or in relative terms. In combination, all labor and capital inputs can only account for a 0.2546 percent annual growth for textile-apparel companies and a 0.8614 percent for computer-electronics. The corresponding share of the actual growth of the production that can be accounted for by the changes in the conventional inputs is 9.1% and 20.6% in the two groups respectively. Most macro growth theorists may be very unfamiliar with this picture. The estimated, very limited contribution is largely due to low and even negative growth of inputs. Notably, input of production workers in the two industry groups and input of technical/ professionals in textile-apparel companies have negative growth rates, contributing negatively to production growth. Capital inputs including equipment and structure did not grow as fast as production in both industry groups.

In short, returns to conventional factor inputs at the company level are different from those at the more aggregate level. Similarly, production growth at the micro level must be very different from growth at the national aggregate level. Micro production growth must be profoundly affected by many factors not included in macro growth models. Without introducing other relevant internal and external input variables, the contribution of conventional inputs to growth could be exaggerated and growth left unexplained could be much larger.

5.1.2.2. Producer Technological Inputs

Technological inputs show up as significant contributors to production growth. Surprisingly, in the computer-electronics industries only R & D (K-R&DGROW) is statistically significant, while in textile-apparel industries, in addition to R & D, value of patent and technology purchase (PTNTGROW) and spending on employee training (K-TRNGROW) are also related to growth. The reason may be the difference in technological stability between the two groups. Textile-apparel's products and technology of production are stable and the technological inputs can improve product and process technology with greater certainty in a longer period. In contrast, computer-electronics production is subject to constant change in products; growth in the industries is more dependent on breakthrough than on improvement on routine production process or technique. Therefore, only R & D seems to matter in computer-electronics' production growth.

Estimated output elasticity of R & D capital varies in a wide range. It is 0.0110 in textile-apparel and 0.1113 in computer-electronics, bracketing Griliches' estimate of 0.089 using 1977 company level data from all kinds manufacture sectors. Estimated average values of the marginal product of R & D capital are extraordinarily high, 1.0 in textile-apparel and 2.2 in computer-electronics, although the estimates are not as high as Griliches' estimate (In his sample, means of value added and R & D input are $223 millions and $3.4 millions, implying a gross return of 5.8 to R & D). As discussed in chapter 2 and expressed in equation (2.32), these estimates seem consistent with the hypothesized non-linear relationship between R & D input and output in production function. Yet this is not a complete picture of return to R & D capital because of the difference of depreciation and obsolescence rate between production capital and R & D capital. Since data on capital life are not available, the researcher can only compare average age with one another. Average age of production capital in both industry groups is about 10 years, and average age of R & D capital is only about 5 years. This suggests that the service life of R & D capital is only about one half of that of production capital. Approximately, gross rate of return to R & D capital should be twice as high as to production capital if the producers are in equilibrium (i.e., the rates of return to all inputs are the same). The estimates for the textile-apparel industries seem to agree with each other in this respect, while in the computer-electronics group return to R & D is about 3 times as high as that to production capital. Therefore, the researcher concludes that the net return to R & D investment in the textile-apparel industries is about the same as to production capital, but in the computer-electronics industries R & D investment is more rewarding than investment in production capital. This partly explains why the computer-electronics companies have invested in R & D heavily. Another reason for the intensive R & D input in the computer-electronics industries is the technological nature of the industries: unlike many other industries, the computer-electronics industries are characterized by constant emergence of new technologies and obsolescence of old ones, and R & D is not a luxury. A company must conduct R & D to make its products competitive in order to stay in business. If this interpretation is credible, those companies who do not conduct R & D will sooner than later go out of business.

The estimates of the contribution of R & D to output growth, 0.0116 percent for the textile-apparel and 0.3005 for the computer-electronics, indicate that the textile-apparel manufacturers did not benefit from R & D activity nearly as much as the computer-electronics companies. The reason is the combination of lower input level and lower growth rate of R & D capital in the textile-apparel industries. Sample data show that in 1990 a capital stock of $155k was designated to R & D in an average textile-apparel company as opposed to $864k in a typical computer-electronics company. Moreover, average annual growth rate of R & D capital in the computer-electronics group is more than 2.5 times as high as in the textile-apparel group. These two factors made R & D activity in the textile-apparel industries a less important contributor to growth than in the computer-electronics group.

Patent purchase in the textile-apparel group is significant with an estimated output elasticity of 0.0621. The implied average value of return to the input is 5.7. The high reward to patent purchase is due to the non rival nature of technology in standardized production: once a producer bought a patent /technology, he could use the new technology over and over in a fairly stable process without incurring great expense.

Only when market changes or new technology emerges, will return to the investment diminish. There is a great technical difficulty in estimating the total return to the input of patent purchase accurately, but a NSF granted research (Pakes and Schankerman 1984) estimates that the average rate of obsolescence of patent is 0.25. Since textile-apparel industries are technologically more stable than most other manufacturing sectors, one can reasonably assume that patent life in the industry group is not shorter than five years. Due to the difficulty of collecting the data on patent purchase over a long period, this study only gathered and employed crude data on overall expenditure in patent purchase before and after 1985. Because patents purchased three or four years ago can become less productive than new patents, the computed growth rate of input level tends to be lower than the actual rate. Consequently, the output elasticity and return to patent purchase can be overestimated. Although it is difficult to know how much the estimates may be inflated, the significant large size of estimate does suggest the importance of this input to production growth.

Employee training in textile-apparel also appears to be highly rewarding with an output elasticity of 0.0261 and a rate of gross return of 2.2. It is similarly difficult to estimate the net return. No information is available about how often an employee needs to be retrained to keep up with general pace of technological progress in the industry. Nevertheless, the estimate provides very useful information: reward to the investment in textile-apparel industries is at least double as much as input if employees need to be trained once a year and about four times if they need to be trained every other year.

The two technological inputs, patent purchase and employee training, account for a 0.64 percent annual growth in the textile-apparel industries. Compared with textile-apparel manufacturers, the computer-electronics producers did not benefit from patent purchase and worker training, although these producers also made some investment in those technological inputs. The results suggest that the computer-electronics producers rely heavily on developing their own new technology through R & D activities but not on introducing other firms' technology or on routinely training workers. The reason may be the intensive technological competition between producers in the industries: most computer-electronics producers are not willing to sell or patent their most profitable technology; thus, outsiders can only purchase the less profitable patent/technology at an affordable price. Another reason related to the technological competition is the high price of the patents. As documented (Anderla and Dunning 1987), the cost for licensing patent has risen from about 2 to 15 percent of licensees' sales up to the mid-1980s. The high cost makes parent purchase/license a less viable approach for many companies to promote production growth.

5.1.2.3. Embodied Technology

Technology embodied in capital has long been a research interest in growth literature. The embodied technological progress measured by the reduction of the average age of capital jelly (K-AGEGROW or DELTAGE) is found to have significantly contributed to production growth. It should be stressed that the parameter estimates for the average age of capital stock are likely to represent the excess impact of embodied technology to production growth, because the capital in equipment is measured by current value of the asset which takes into consideration the level of technology embodied. Due to this double counting of embodied technology, the parameter estimate tends to be smaller than it should be. Thus, the estimated impact of the average age on production is very conservative. In the following discussion, the focus is on: (1) estimates of the age-technology relationship and the rate of technological progress; and (2) importance of embodied technology to sustained growth.

First, the estimated parameters of technological progress in capital appear small but significant. The estimates can be used to compute the age-technology relationship and the rate of technological progress embodied in capital. Recalling functional specifications of growth rate (2.12) and (2.15) and the relationship between the parameter estimates of the growth equation, the rate of technological progress embodied in new capital, λ_k, and exponential parameter describing age-technology relationship, α_k, can be computed. The parameter estimates in Equation 2 of Table 5.2 and Table 5.3 imply that $\lambda_k = 4.5\%$ and $\alpha_k = 0.36$ for textile-apparel manufacturers and $\lambda_k = 3.6\%$ and $\alpha_k = 0.32$ for computer-electronics companies. Thus, the age-technology relationship for the two industry groups are $T_k = a_0 e^{4.5t} A^{-.36}$ and $T_k = a_0 e^{3.6t} A^{-.32}$ respectively. The technological progress embodied in capital goods looks much the same for the two technologically very different industry groups. The reasons may reside in the equipment used by the two industry groups and the technological progress made by the capital goods industry, remembering that embodied technological advance is made by the machine goods industry rather than by user industries. Although products of the computer-electronics industries are much more sophisticated than those of the textile-apparel industries, the majority of the equipment used in the production process need not be much more sophisticated than those in textile-apparel. Put differently, nowadays textile-apparel industries employ process technology that can be as advanced as used in the computer-electronics industries. In fact, Table 3.6 shows that the textile-apparel companies invest proportionally no less than the computer-electronics producers in computer and numerical control system, in equipment upgrading, and in management system improvement. Even if the equipment is made by different equipment manufacturers, these machine tool manufacturers tend to be at a similar technological level.

Second, the importance of the embodied technology is examined. Table 5.5 shows that the reduction in the average age of equipment in computer-electronics accounts for a growth of 0.2-0.3 percent per year, a relatively unimportant figure. The contribution to growth is negative in textile-apparel industries due to a slight increase in the average age. Given the sample average age of equipment, 10.9 years in textile-apparel group and 9.5 in computer-electronics, a one-year reduction in the average age could raise growth rate by 0.76 percent in textile-apparel and 0.68 percent in computer-electronics. The significant estimates suggest that if the average age of capital is in the current range, the average age of capital is a useful proxy of technology embodied in capital. However, some researchers argue that it is not feasible to constantly make capital younger after capital becomes relatively new. Denison (1964) contends that embodied technological progress is unimportant because over a ten-year period a one-year reduction in average age is a big achievement and sustained changes in average age are hard to obtain. This proposition, however, is implicitly based on an age-technology equivalent assumption and is not entirely consistent with a more complete analysis and general experience. As demonstrated in chapter 2, part effect of technological progress on growth is under-identified because embodied technological change actually contributes to production growth in two terms, λ_k and $\lambda_k dA/dt$, in equation (2.12) and equation (2.15). Term λ_k has the same coefficient as $dK_x/K_x dt$ but incorporated into the intercept, and only term $\lambda_k dA/dt$ or $-\alpha_k dA_x/A_x dt$ can be explicitly estimated. Given the parameter estimates for capital input, the researcher can estimate the part of the intercept that should be separately termed as $\beta_k \lambda_k$. In both industry groups the estimated additional contribution of embodied technology to production growth is about 0.7-0.8 percent per year, given estimates of β_k equal to 0.20 to 0.22 and λ_k equal to 0.32-0.36. Technological change over time is more influential than simple reduction of the average age at any given time to production growth. In combination the technological progress in new capital appears to be responsible for a growth of about 1 percent per annum in computer-electronics industries and about 0.7 percent per year in textile-apparel. Although these estimates are obtained very indirectly, the message the estimate conveys is clear: embodied technology is a very important factor contributing to production growth even when average age of capital stock becomes constant. Practically, it is for a company's own benefit to keep its production facilities in the industry's average age, if not younger.

The embodied technology in labor behaves differently across industries. Unexpectedly, the increase in educational attainment of technical/ professional employees (P-EDGROW) made no difference in the output growth rate across textile-apparel producers and the increase in work experience of technical/ professionals (P-EXPGROW) did not promote the growth in computer-electronics. The results reflect the nature of technological progress in each industry group. Knowledge in textile-apparel industries is quite standardized and less dynamic than in computer-electronics industries. Once an individual completes professional study in a formal education institute, a marginal increase in education does not significantly widen or deepen his/her professional knowledge. Additional quality is more like art: experience, skill, and even innate sense rather than formal knowledge. This may particularly pertain to the apparel industry. Stable technology makes work experience valuable. In contrast, the computer-electronics industry is characterized by a high rate of technological obsolescence. Work experience in a technologically very dynamic industry is less important because the experience of working with certain technique or a piece of particular equipment can soon become irrelevant when new technology emerges (Our experience with computer software may intuitively confirm this point. Just think about the numerous software packages which were widely used but no longer exist in our computers). Educational attainment in this field may be far more crucial than experience, because advanced fundamental knowledge provides the individual with potential in developing application skills.

Estimated output elasticities of technological progress embodied in professional employees are substantial: 0.1855 for professional experience in textile-apparel industries and 0.2397 for professional educational attainment in computer-electronics. Considering the average years of experience of professional employees in textile-apparel companies, 13.3, a one-year increase in experience tends to raise the growth rate by 1.4 percent, and there is plenty of room for further increase in work experience. Similarly, a one-year increase in educational attainment of professional employees in computer-electronics leads to a 1.6 percent increase in growth. Since increase in formal education can soon meet a ceiling, say 18 or 19 years of formal education including 2-3 years graduate education, educational attainment as a source of increase in production seems to have only a limited impact on long run growth. However, this is not a complete picture. Actual educational attainment also depends on what one learns during the period. A 4-year college education in this decade can be very different from that in the early twentieth century, especially in technologically dynamic fields. Using years of formal education, one can only capture part of the impact of educational attainment on growth. As shown in equation (2.18) and (2.25), part of the educational effect on labor quality, average annual growth rate of quality of education (λ_L), is dependent on enlargement and enrichment of the general knowledge base, and the effect cannot be separated from the intercept in the empirical estimate. A full appreciation of the contribution of educational attainment must take both quantity and quality of education into account.

Table 5.5 shows that the increased experience of technical and professional employees accounts for a 0.41 percent annual growth in textile-apparel production; the increased educational attainment of technical and professional employees contributes to a growth of 0.27 percent per annum in computer-electronics. The technology in capital contributes to growth of textile-apparel production negatively due to aging of the equipment in the industry group; but the same factor is responsible for a growth of 0.2208-0.3056 percent per year in computer-electronics production. As a group, the embodied technology accounts for a growth of 0.3288 percent per year in textile-apparel production and 0.4945 percent in computer-electronics. Equivalently, the share of production growth attributable to embodied technological progress is 11.8% and 11.9% for textile-apparel and computer-electronics industries respectively. This is only a part of the contribution of embodied technology to output growth. The contribution incorporated in the intercept is under-identified.

A disturbing finding is the unimportance of educational attainment and work experience of production workers to production growth for both textile-apparel and computer-electronics companies. The insignificance of educational attainment and experience of production workers can be attributable to workers' position in production. Many production workers are not much more than machine operators or assemblers. Even in a technologically advanced industry, a machine operator or assembler needs to learn just a little about a specific task to work efficiently. As a result, educational attainment and work experience of production workers are far less important than those of technical and professional employees to production growth.

5.1.2.4. Regional Factors

Depending on technological natures of industries, a regional factor may or may not have obvious influence on production growth. Table 5.2 shows that two specific regional variables, growth rate of finance-securities-insurance-real estate sectors measured by establishment (FIRSGROW) and metro area location for apparel companies (METRO-APP), have significant parameter estimates. Theory and earlier studies did not provide any causal explanation of positive relation between this sector and company production growth. Probably, using these services incurs a significant cost to textile-apparel producers and increasing the number of establishments in the sector results in a lower cost to textile-apparel producers. An alternative, and conservative, interpretation may only relate a higher growth rate of textile-apparel production to the areas where this service sector also grew faster in an earlier period. This is the least the researcher can claim. Metro area location for apparel manufacturers, computed as a product of the metro dummy and the apparel dummy, appears to be an important factor contributing to the growth of apparel production. Perhaps this is the biggest difference between textile and apparel industries, although the two industries share many common technological features. This statistical result confirms early findings (Moomaw 1985) that apparel production relies heavily on urban location. This urban oriented growth in the apparel industry is largely due to the nature of the product market: most high value added products of this industry have their markets concentrated in major cities and demand for the products varies widely with respect to seasons and fashions. Only those producers who can timely meet the change in demand can successfully grow. Obviously, these producers must be located close to their market in order to do so.

Consistent with early justification that technologically more advanced production such as computer-electronics depends more on regional complemental or substitutive factors, Table 5.3 shows that more regional factors are significant to production growth. The important regional factors include size of computer industry in each area (CMPMGROW), recreation and amusement services (AMSMGROW), health services (HLTMGROW), and social services (SSVMGROW), all measured by the growth rate of employment in the sectors in each area. The most significant regional factor is the growth of the size of computer industry, with a negative sign. This variable is included to measure the contribution of technological spillovers and localization economies. The negative sign may well suggest that more and more companies of the industry concentrated in the same area have bid against each other for the same inputs, e.g., skilled labor and business services, causing a contraction of individual companies' production, holding other things constant. In balance the cost of the competition outweighs the benefit of technological spillovers from growth of the whole industry in the same local market. Regional factors measured by health services, social services, and recreation and amusement services all contribute positively to production growth not only because the services sectors have a positive influence on computer-electronics production but also because these sectors have very high growth rate, from 4.2 to 6.2 percent per year.

All the significant regional factors, except employment in the computer industry, are more or less related to consumer services and amenities. Functions of recreation and amusement, health care, and social services are considered to serve employees to maintain and even upgrade their quality and productivity. These findings suggest that variation of consumer services and amenities in these areas are more important than variation of producer services. One reason may be that computer-electronics companies depend more on highly skilled professionals and these well paid skilled employees tend to choose a place with a convenient and comfortable environment. On the other hand, insignificant estimates for all producer services variables do not necessarily mean that these services are not important. It is very likely that most sampled areas have furnished producers with sufficient services. Therefore, further increase in the size of these services sectors will not significantly influence production. The significant estimates of output elasticities of the regional factors suggest that the regional factors can directly account for a part of the growth in computer-electronics industries.

If the estimates of the regional factors are interpreted literally, the estimates of average value of the marginal product of each relevant regional factor also can be computed: one more finance, insurance, security, and real estate establishment emerging in an average area could lead to a $660 increase in value added for an average textile-apparel company, one more health care employee in an average area could raise value added by $60 for an average computer-electronics company, and so on. A question may arise from the estimates: why these establishments and employees in other sectors cannot claim the return from textile-apparel or computer-electronics firms if they indeed contribute to production and growth. Since most of these regional variables are measured by employment, one can directly relate labor input to output in any relevant industries. Employees in all industries tend to be paid the value of their marginal product; otherwise, labor input tends to be reallocated among different industries. With competitive rate of return to labor input or, equivalently, without loss of private return, the positive effect of these employees on the production of other industries is what economic externalities refer to. The estimates show that growths in these services sectors generate externalities favorable to production growth in computer-electronics industries, and to a much less extent, in textile-apparel industries.

Metro area location for apparel manufacturers is an important contributor to the growth of apparel production. An average apparel factory located in a metro area is likely to have a growth rate higher than its counterparts located in non metro areas by 1.627 percent per year. In relative terms, this single factor can account for more than one half of total growth in apparel production.

Regional factors seem less important to growth in textile production, but the contribution of the finance-insurance-real estate service sector to textile production growth is not trivial. This sector appears to have the same relation with textile and apparel companies. A growth of 0.82 percent per year in both textile and apparel companies is related to the growth in the number of establishment in this sector.

In the computer-electronics group, regional factors jointly contributed to a growth of 3.0594 percent per annum, the biggest contributor of the four groups of input factors. Without the positive contribution of regional factors, production growth in computer-electronics could be cut back more than one half. According to the estimates, total growth add up to more than 100%. This implies that some factors such as diseconomies and disamenities are missing in the model. As a result, there is a negative unexplained growth incorporated in the intercept. Similarly, some factors positively contributing to growth are not identified in textile-apparel industries and their impact is also absorbed into the intercept. Nevertheless, with the regional variables included, the unexplained residual of growth has substantially reduced, compared with all macro growth models.

Statistically, the majority of producers in both groups are in equilibrium in a conventional sense: a proportional increase in all internal inputs leads to the same proportional increase in output, holding other things constant. On the other hand, viewing regional factors as a part of inputs, most producers are not in equilibrium. Individual productions have a strong tendency to grow as regional services sectors grow.

5.2. LABOR PRODUCTIVITY GROWTH

This section estimates the labor productivity growth equation developed earlier. The equation, (2.35'), is copied from section 2.3 and labeled as (5.2) for convenience,

$$(5.2) \qquad \dot{Q}_t = \alpha_0 + \alpha_1 \dot{K}_t - \alpha_2 \dot{A}_k + \alpha_3 \dot{L}_t + \alpha_4 \dot{E}_{st} + \alpha_5 \dot{E}_{et} + \alpha_6 \dot{Z}_t + \alpha_7 \dot{R}_t ,$$

Subject to $\qquad \alpha_1 + \alpha_3 + \alpha_6 = 1 .$

The equation has a similar functional specification as production growth equation. The only difference is the restriction arising from per worker input measures and imposed on the parameter estimates of all physical inputs. If the market mechanism functions well, production growth and productivity growth should go hand in hand, since low productivity can hold back production growth and high productivity can induce expansion of production. There should appear no systematic divergence between the two. The estimates of the growth equations confirms that markets for textile-apparel and computer-electronics did function well: both groups show a strong tendency of a constant return to scale with producer inputs and estimated marginal products are reasonable.

Table 5.6 presents the parameter estimates of the labor productivity growth equations for textile-apparel and computer-electronics industries. The three functional specifications are essentially the same as the first three equations in Table 5.2 and Table 5.3. A comparison between Table 5.2, Table 5.3 and Table 5.6 shows that estimated labor productivity growth equations closely resemble production growth equations for both industry groups. Given the relationship between production growth (5.1) and labor productivity growth (5.2) as well as the estimated constant return to scale with producer inputs (refer to Table 5.2 and Table 5.3), the results seem not surprising. Factors that contribute to production growth also contribute to productivity growth. Since labor productivity grew faster than production for both industry groups, contribution of many factors to productivity growth is slightly larger. Table 5.7 shows the contribution each factor made to productivity growth. All interpretations in the preceding section for production growth qualitatively pertain to productivity growth.

Table 5.6 shows that none of the restrictions imposed on the productivity growth is statistically significant. This implies that all the interpretations for production growth are also basically quantitatively appropriate for labor productivity growth. The average growth rate of labor productivity is the average growth rate of value added minus the average growth rate of labor input times its restricted parameter estimate, dQ/Qdt-$\beta_{L1}dL_1/L_1 1dt$-$\beta_{L2}dL_2/L_2 dt$, where L_1 and L_2 represent production workers and technical/ professional employees respectively. The average growth rates are on the bottom of Table 5.7. The rates are slightly lower than presented in Table 3.6, where the estimates are 5-year annualized growth rate of output per worker calculated directly from original data. The minor discrepancy arises from the different estimation processes. The following are highlighted findings about the sources of labor productivity growth in the U.S. textile-apparel and computer-electronics industries.

First, capital deepening was an important factor to labor productivity growth at a micro level: the more capital available to an average worker, the higher was labor productivity. Capital growth is estimated to contribute to labor productivity growth by about 0.7 (0.3195+0.4083) percent per year for textile-apparel and 1.0 (0.4277+0.5410) percent per year for computer-electronics companies.

**Table 5.6(A) Estimates of Labor Productivity Growth Equations
Textile and Apparel**

	Equation 1		Equation 2		Equation 3	
Variable	Estimate	Std Err	Estimate	Std Err	Estimate	Std Err
INTERCEPT	-0.3191	1.133	0.5749	0.599	0.5931	0.598
W-EMPGROW	0.3905**	0.065	0.4171**	0.061	0.4149**	0.061
W-EDGROW	0.3092	0.194	------	-----	------	-----
W-EXPGROW	-0.0990	0.066	------	-----	------	-----
P-EMPGROW	0.0789*	0.048	0.0796*	0.046	0.0783*	0.046
P-EDGROW	0.0561	0.216	------	-----	------	-----
P-EXPGROW	0.2216**	0.083	0.1884**	0.069	0.1868**	0.069
K-UTLGROW	0.2471**	0.052	0.2365**	0.050	0.2323**	0.050
K-AGEGROW	-0.0555	0.039	-0.0768**	0.037	------	-----
K-AGEDELT	------	-----	------	-----	-0.9104**	0.384
K-BDGROW	0.1713**	0.054	0.1646**	0.051	0.1739**	0.051
K-R&DGROW	0.0113**	0.002	0.0111**	0.002	0.0112**	0.002
PTNTGROW	0.0646**	0.022	0.0637**	0.021	0.0633**	0.021
K-CCGROW	0.0056	0.009	------	-----	------	-----
K-MCNGROW	0.0054	0.004	------	-----	------	-----
K-MNGGROW	0.0074	0.009	------	-----	------	-----
K-TRNGROW	0.0175	0.014	0.0273**	0.013	0.0262*	0.013
TEXWAGGROW	-0.0185	0.177	------	-----	------	-----
APPWAGGROW	0.0702	0.154	------	-----	------	-----
TEXEMPGROW	0.0180	0.081	------	-----	------	-----
TEXESTGROW	-0.0549	0.092	------	-----	------	-----
APPEMPGROW	-0.0586	0.048	------	-----	------	-----
APPESTGROW	0.0625	0.081	------	-----	------	-----
AIREMPGROW	0.0135	0.017	------	-----	------	-----
TSVEMPGROW	-0.0036	0.019	------	-----	------	-----
CMUEMPGROW	-0.0392	0.039	------	-----	------	-----
UTIESTGROW	-0.0537	0.060	------	-----	------	-----
FIRESTGROW	0.1822	0.134	0.2290*	0.116	0.2218*	0.116
AMSEMPGROW	-0.0199	0.030	------	-----	------	-----
HLTEMPGROW	0.0111	0.065	------	-----	------	-----
EDUEMPGROW	-0.0174	0.017	------	-----	------	-----
SOCEMPGROW	-0.0210	0.031	------	-----	------	-----
R&DEMPGROW	-0.0041	0.008	------	-----	------	-----
METRO-APP	1.7694	1.200	1.6384**	0.761	1.5153**	0.755
RESTRICTION	-249.35	431.1	-308.52	439.4	-366.50	435.4
Adj R-sq	0.4607		0.4735		0.4760	

Note: * and ** indicate statistically significant at 90% and 95% levels respectively.

In relative terms, they account for about 23% (10.0% + 12.7% in Table 5.7(A) and 10.0% + 13.6% in Table 5.7(B)) of total growth in labor productivity for both industry groups.

Second, technology/knowledge embodied in capital and labor account for a labor productivity growth of 0.34 (0.4210-0.0793) percent per year in textile-apparel and 0.49 (0.2837+0.2067) in computer-electronics. Aging of capital in textile-apparel industries lowered labor productivity by 0.079 percent per year, whereas reduction of the average age of capital in computer-electronics raised

**Table 5.6(B) Estimates of Labor Productivity Growth Equation
Computer and Electronics**

Variable	Equation 1 Estimate	Std Err	Equation 2 Estimate	Std Err	Equation 3 Estimate	Std Err
INTERCEPT	0.3790	1.809	-0.7634	1.022	-0.6423	1.055
W-EMPGROW	0.1911**	0.043	0.1878**	0.040	0.2044**	0.040
W-EDGROW	-0.2813	0.268	------	-----	------	-----
W-EXPGROW	-0.1010	0.090	------	-----	------	-----
P-EMPGROW	0.2268**	0.051	0.2377**	0.048	0.2488**	0.049
P-EDGROW	0.2248**	0.068	0.2593**	0.064	0.2571**	0.066
P-EXPGROW	-0.0832	0.098	------	-----	------	-----
K-UTLGROW	0.2173**	0.050	0.2044**	0.046	0.2002**	0.047
K-AGEGROW	-0.0800**	0.027	-0.0848**	0.025		
K-AGEDELT	------	-----	------	-----	-0.5962	0.393
K-BDGROW	0.2481**	0.062	0.2327**	0.058	0.2210**	0.059
K-R&DGROW	0.1282**	0.062	0.1371**	0.057	0.1253**	0.059
PTNTGROW	-0.0060	0.011	------	-----	------	-----
K-CCGROW	-0.0024	0.012	------	-----	------	-----
K-MCNGROW	0.0061	0.013	------	-----	------	-----
K-MNGGROW	-0.0179	0.021	------	-----	------	-----
K-TRNGROW	0.0085	0.006	------	-----	------	-----
CMPWAGGROW	0.0736	0.116	------	-----	------	-----
ELEWAGGROW	0.0259	0.115	------	-----	------	-----
CMPEMPGROW	-0.1113**	0.050	-0.0916**	0.029	-0.0886**	0.029
CMPESTGROW	0.0254	0.065	------	-----	------	-----
ELEEMPGROW	0.1862**	0.081	------	-----	------	-----
ELEESTGROW	-0.1694	0.140	------	-----	------	-----
AIREMPGROW	0.0382	0.024	------	-----	------	-----
TSVEMPGROW	-0.0294	0.051	------	-----	------	-----
CMUEMPGROW	0.0380	0.086	------	-----	------	-----
UTIESTGROW	-0.0753	0.128	------	-----	------	-----
FIRESTGROW	-0.3999	0.256	------	-----	------	-----
AMSEMPGROW	0.1222	0.086	0.1326*	0.070	0.1303*	0.072
HLTEMPGROW	0.4304**	0.191	0.3187*	0.170	0.3545**	0.174
EDUEMPGROW	0.0251	0.055	------	-----	------	-----
SOCEMPGROW	0.2217**	0.088	0.1781**	0.080	0.1684**	0.081
R&DEMPGROW	-0.0263*	0.015	------	-----	------	-----
METRO	1.1766	1.857	------	-----	------	-----
RESTRICTION	-740.87	451.5	-513.15	473.1	-361.03	472.4
Adj R-sq	0.5639		0.5722		0.5543	

Note: * and ** indicate statistically significant at 90% and 95% levels respectively.

labor productivity by about 0.2 percent per year. In textile-apparel
industries, professional experience, but not professional education,
contributed positively to labor productivity growth, while in computer-
electronics the pattern is exactly reversed--professional educational
attainment, not professional experience, was the significant contributor
to labor productivity growth. In combination, the relative contribution
of the technologies embodied in capital and labor inputs to labor
productivity growth was about 11 % (13.2%-2.4% in Table 5.7(A) and
6.8% +4.9% in Table 5.7(B)) percent for both industry groups. Taking

Table 5.7 Absolute and Relative Contribution of Each Factor to Labor Productivity Growth

Textile and Apparel

Variable	(1)	(2)	(3) (1)*(2)	(4) % of Growth
W-EMPGROW	0.4171	-0.967	-0.4033	
P-EMPGROW	0.0796	-0.065	-0.0052	
K-UTLGROW	0.2365	1.351	0.3195	10.0%
K-BDGROW	0.1646	2.480	0.4082	12.7%
Group total			0.7277	22.7%
P-EXPGROW	0.1884	2.235	0.4210	13.2%
K-AGEGROW	-0.0768	1.033	-0.0793	-2.4%
K-AGEDELT	-0.9104	0.082	-0.0746	-2.3%
Group total			0.3417a	10.8%
K-R&DGROW	0.0111	1.051	0.0117	0.3%
PTNTGROW	0.0637	3.959	0.2522	7.9%
K-TRNGROW	0.0273	15.261	0.4166	13.0%
Group total			0.6805	21.2%
FIRESTGROW	0.2290	3.462	0.7928	24.8%
METRO-APP	1.6384		1.6384	51.2%b
Total				79.5%c
Actual Growth			3.1969	100.0%

Computer and Electronics

Variable	(1)	(2)	(3) (1)*(2)	(4) % of Growth
W-EMPGROW	0.1927	-1.057	-0.2037	
P-EMPGROW	0.2434	0.759	0.1840	
K-UTLGROW	0.2072	2.064	0.4277	10.0%
K-BDGROW	0.2247	2.541	0.5710	13.6%
Group total			0.9987	23.6%
P-EDGROW	0.2485	1.142	0.2838	6.8%
K-AGEGROW	-0.0604	-3.423	0.2067	4.9%
K-AGEDELT	-0.5954	-0.436	0.2596	6.2%
Group total			0.4905a	11.7%
K-R&DGROW	0.1320	2.700	0.8640	20.6%
CMPEMPGROW	-0.0897	-0.459	0.0412	1.0%
AMSEMPGROW	0.1266	5.447	0.6896	16.4%
HLTEMPGROW	0.3201	4.205	1.3460	32.1%
SOCEMPGROW	0.1713	6.257	1.0718	25.5%
Group total			3.1486	75.0%
Total				130.9%
Actual Growth			4.1926	100.0%

Note: a. The estimate of K-AGEDELT is not included to avoid double-counting.
  b. The estimate only pertains to apparel companies.
  c. The estimate does not include the contribution metro area location made.

into account the estimated rate of technological progress embodied in capital, 3.9 in textile-apparel and 3.0 in the computer-electronics group[2], and its impact absorbed by the intercept, 0.9 percent per year in textile-apparel and 0.6 in computer-electronics, embodied technologies were responsible for a productivity growth of 1.2 percent per annum in textile-apparel and 1.1 percent per annum in computer-electronics, equivalently, 37% of labor productivity growth in textile-apparel and 26% in computer-electronics. Considering the under-identified contribution to labor productivity of knowledge in technical and professional labor input (λ_L in (2.17) which is absorbed into the intercept in the empirical estimate), as a whole category the embodied technology contributed even more to labor productivity growth.

Third, other technological inputs accounted for an annual labor productivity growth of 0.68 percent for the textile-apparel group and 0.86 for computer-electronics. Of six other technological inputs, R & D was the only contributor to productivity growth in computer-electronics, while investments in patent purchase and employee training made sizable contribution to productivity growth in textile-apparel. Relatively, the producer technological inputs account for about 21% of labor productivity growth in both industry groups.

Fourth, regional factors that are irrelevant at the macro level were responsible for a large part of productivity growth in both industry groups. Computer-electronics companies benefitted more from regional factors than did textile companies. Compared with the textile-apparel industry group, computer-electronics companies were more sensitive to competition over the same type of labor and rely more on a variety of social services and regional amenities. Metro area location was crucial to labor productivity growth in the apparel industry. Apparel companies located in metro areas are likely to have productivity growth rate 50 percent higher than their counterparts located in non metro areas.

Finally, in real terms, all factors, except patent purchase and employee training, contributed more to labor productivity growth in computer-electronics than in textile-apparel. In relative terms, however, the importance of each group of factors to productivity growth is very similar for the two industry groups.

5.3. DISCUSSION OF THE FINDINGS

The empirical study generated a large volume of information. To stress major points and support industrial and regional policy consideration, this section summarizes the findings and addresses the implications from both theoretical and practical points of view.

In general, capital input in both textile-apparel and computer-electronics industries can increase production and labor productivity.

Estimated return to capital input is much higher than the market interest rate. In the estimation, three estimates are related to capital input: (1) the coefficient of capital input growth, (2) the coefficient of technology embodied in capital, and (3) a term as indicated by λ_k in equation (2.12) and (2.15) and under-identified from the intercept of the growth equation. All the three estimates are statistically significant. Thus, the contribution of capital to production and productivity growth can be well beyond the single parameter estimate of capital input growth. In the real world, capital is a physical carrier of technology, but only new capital investment can incorporate advanced technology and realize the profitability of the newly developed technology. Therefore, the contribution of embodied technology to production and productivity growth actually depends on the new capital input.

Denison questioned the importance of embodied technology as a contributor to production growth (Denison 1964). He contends that a one year reduction in average age of capital over a ten-year period is a significant change, but this reduction in capital age can only result in marginal gain of production growth. The contribution of embodied technology to production and productivity growth has remained as one of the most intuitively appealing and empirically elusive hypothesis in economics (Mchugh and Lane 1983, 1987). Conceptual development and empirical estimates presented in this book shed some light on the more complete picture of the contribution of embodied technology to production and productivity growth. The paradox Denison addressed is basically due to the limitation of using average age as a proxy of embodied technology. The complete estimate of the contribution of embodied technology also must take into account the part not directly identifiable in a normal estimation. At least this study has developed an indirect estimate. If the rate of technological progress embodied in new capital is about 4 percent per year as estimated here, embodied technological progress can make a growth of 0.8 percent per annum in production and labor productivity even if average age of capital remains unchanged.

The empirical evidence from this study has important bearings on industrial development policy. Specifically, new investment contributes to production and productivity growths along two lines: increase in capital intensity and introduction of up-to-date technology. A policy encouraging new investment should be considered as a positive effort to promote production and productivity growth. However, social cost-benefit analysis must be conducted to reveal the subsequent impact on redistribution of social wealth. Even without any policy incentive, industrial developers should see new investment worthwhile because of the estimated high private return to capital, not to mention the return to embodied technology. At the macro level, importance of new investment to growth can be further appreciated in conjunction with other empirical research. De Long and Summers

(1991) estimate that high rates of investment in machinery, 12.2 percent of GDP per year, explain nearly all of Japan's extraordinary 5.4 percent per year growth in real productivity and that each additional percentage point of GDP invested in equipment is associated with an increase in GDP growth of 0.3 percent per year. If this estimate is credible, neoclassic growth theory is faced with a strong challenge as that theory contends that permanent rate of growth of labor productivity is not affected by investment level.

Technology/knowledge carried by highly skilled technical and professional employees is an important factor to production and labor productivity growth. Educational attainment and experience of production workers have no significant influence on production and productivity growth. Evidently, technical/ professional/ managerial employees play a crucial role in modern production. Thus, the society is more and more dependent on highly educated and experienced professionals as technology advances. In addition to the positive impact on efficiency, social division of labor is associated with a divergence of opportunity to contribute to economic development, resulting in more inequality in all other related fields, especially in earnings. After controlling for education and experience, value of marginal product of physical labor in technical/ professional position is systematically higher than that in production lines. This disturbing finding may suggest a very big issue for a technologically advanced society to resolve.

Since increase in professional education and improvement on education quality can significantly contributes to productivity growth in the two industry groups, investment in public higher education is rewarding, particularly in technologically very dynamic fields. At the producer level, the research findings suggest that computer-electronics manufacturers invest more in professional training, including on-job and off-job additional formal education to update their technological capability. To textile-apparel companies, maintaining a stable professional crews and increasing their experience are beneficial to production and productivity growth.

Industrial developers may want to exploit the higher return to R & D investment. Based on the conservative calculation without considering social return, R & D on the average can generate profit higher than all other inputs, especially for the producers in technologically advanced industries. Considering the spillover effect, R & D activities are even more encouraging. It has been shown in chapter 4 that state and local R & D investment credit policies have positive influence on investment in R & D for both industry groups. The same policies also induce inputs in establishing computer and numerical control systems, upgrading equipment, improving management, and training employees in textile-apparel industries. Thus, state and local R & D policies are effective in promoting technological progress and productivity growth through inducing R & D and other technological inputs. Unlike production capital, R & D only accounts for a small proportion of total capital input, so redistribution of social wealth caused by a R & D credit policy should be minor.

Production and productivity growth is found to benefit substantially from regional factors. The findings have apparent location meaning: computer and electronics production should select localities which can provide better consumer services and amenities in order to maintain and upgrade their work force, while the apparel industry may want to locate its production in metro areas where they can get timely access to markets and get feedback from them. It may be important for regional developers and policy makers to build their strength in service sectors in order to attract technologically advanced industry and foster the growth.

However, the findings and the interpretations about regional influence are only tentative for at least two reasons. First, the areas, where sample data were drawn, must have provided a certain level of producer services which exceeded the threshold and determined companies' location decision at the beginning. Once a company located in such an area, further improvement of regional business services merely has marginal effect on existing production. In the sample of computer-electronics group, 27 companies are located in non metro areas. More regional variation is needed to generate significant estimates for producer services variables. A better sample may be collected in a disproportional method--proportionally more cases can be drawn from non metro areas.

Second, the measurement of regional variables may have large room to improve. For example, the level of transportation services by air is measured by employment in establishments engaged in furnishing domestic and foreign transportation by air and those operating airports and flying fields and furnishing terminal services. This measure may not be as adequate as the operation number of commercial flights to capture the influence of air transportation services on production and productivity growth. Similarly, communication services may be better measured by technology used in the communication services sector than by employment number. An important regional variable, change in educational attainment of regional population, was not available when the analysis was done. As expected, educational attainment of population has positive influence on production and productivity growth in computer-electronics industries, but the influence may not be very strong given the two variables measuring educational attainment of actual labor inputs.

Compared with estimates for producer inputs, parameter estimates for regional factors are less stable. This can be observed from Table 5.2 and Table 5.3 when different restrictions are imposed. Should a more complete set of variables and more appropriate measures be used in an empirical study, the results can be improved.

It should be noted that all the estimates presented in this chapter are direct contributions of technology-related inputs and regional factors to production and productivity growth. Yet variations of technology-related inputs and regional factors may induce additional producer inputs and affect marginal products of all producer inputs. Only after these indirect influences are examined, can one draw a full picture of technological inputs-regional factors-production and productivity growth relationships. The indirect contribution of regional factors to production and productivity growth is examined in the next two chapters.

Notes

1. To firmly claim that the omitted variables are all equal to zero, a rigorous hypothesis test is like this,

H_0: At least one omitted variable is not equal to zero,

H_a: Omitted variables are all equal to zero.

The structure of the hypothesis is obviously different from those usually used. Conducting a joint F test as specified above requires a lower point of critical F value as opposed to upper point of critical F published in virtually all F tables. However, as discussed in the text, the comparison of adjusted R squared signifies inclusion of irrelevant variables. Moreover, significant parameter estimates in Equation 1 and Equation 2 differ only by negligible margins. Therefore, all estimates and interpretations based on Equation 2 are empirically valid.

2. Production growth and labor productivity growth equations are very similar, as derived in chapter 2. However, due to the restriction imposed in labor productivity growth equations, estimated rate of technological progress embodied in capital using labor productivity growth equations are slightly lower than those from production growth equations.

6 Technological Efficiency
and the Determinants

The preceding chapter examined the direct contribution of technology-related variables and regional factors to production and labor productivity growth. To draw a whole picture, the researcher also must examine the contribution of these inputs and regional factors to productivity growth from different angles. Production and labor productivity growth results from the changes in (1) levels of internal inputs and regional factors and (2) technological efficiency of using these inputs--the amount of increase in output for a given increase in inputs. A traditional measure of efficiency is output elasticity. Output elasticity may change as the level and quality of the input and other variables change. Therefore, technological inputs and regional factors can contribute to production and productivity growth by affecting the output elasticities of producer inputs.

Each producer input or regional factor has a unique output elasticity. The large number of input variables prevents a researcher from using these measures in an empirical study. To show an overall picture, a set of aggregate measures can be created and examined. In fact, these measures have been used for a long time without explicitly making the connection to output elasticities of inputs by most users. The frequently used measures of technological efficiency are total factor productivity (TFP), economies of scale, and neutral technological progress, that can all be derived from output elasticities. Since these measures are often referred to as productivity in literature, the researcher follows the convention and uses productivity to mean technological efficiency of using inputs.

This chapter investigates technological and regional determinants of three efficiency or productivity measures. Figure 6.1, which is a part of Figure 2.1, shows conceptual relationships and the major groups of variables being examined in this chapter.

159

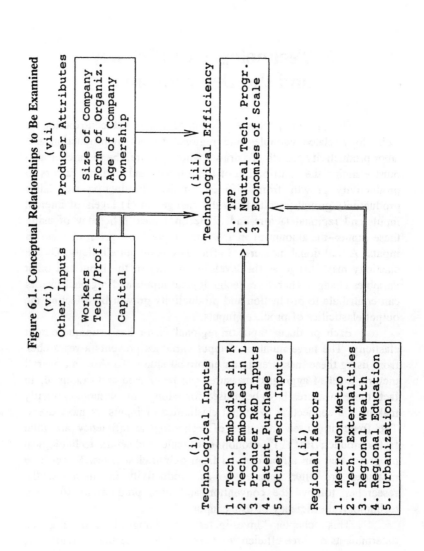

Figure 6.1. Conceptual Relationships to Be Examined

(vii)
Producer Attributes

Size of Company
Form of Organiz.
Age of Company
Ownership

(vi)
Other Inputs

Workers
Tech./Prof.
Capital

(iii)
Technological Efficiency

1. TFP
2. Neutral Tech. Progr.
3. Economies of Scale

(i)
Technological Inputs

1. Tech. Embodied in K
2. Tech. Embodied in L
3. Producer R&D Inputs
4. Patent Purchase
5. Other Tech. Inputs

(ii)
Regional factors

1. Metro-Non Metro
2. Tech. Externalities
3. Regional Wealth
4. Regional Education
5. Urbanization

6.1. EARLIER RESEARCH

There are two branches of literature on productivity and correspondingly two approaches to assess the determinants of productivity. The first branch is represented by the mainstream economists' works (e.g., Griliches 1980, 1984, 1986, Mansfield 1980, and Terleckyj 1982, 1983). Usually, a Cobb-Douglas (C-D) production function with constant return to scale is assumed to develop a TFP equation with TFP growth as the dependent variable and the growth rate of technological input, R & D in particular, as the explanatory variable. TFP is defined as growth rate of output less contribution of conventional producer inputs to the growth. Depending on the assumptions imposed or the data available, researchers either use a TFP equation of output elasticity form or an equation of marginal product form to estimate the impact of R & D on TFP growth or return on R & D.

Applying several variants of a TFP growth equation derived from a general C-D functional form to time-series data (1959-76) for twenty seven industries, Griliches and Lichtenberg (1984) conducted several sophisticated analyses to estimate how much R & D capital input, defined as capital stock designated for R & D, contributed to TFP growth in the U.S. industries. Their findings suggest a strong relationship between the TFP and privately-funded R & D input but no relationship between the TFP and government-financed R & D. Their study only included R & D, capital, and labor as input variables. As a commentator points out, 'The authors include only the conventional inputs and R & D in their model,... However, apart from the transitory, cyclical, and noise factors, there may be certain long-term structural characteristics of industries...' (Terleckyj 1984). As a result, some specification error may be involved in the estimates.

Mansfield (1980) also adopted a C-D function to develop a TFP equation of marginal product form. Two single TFP equations were applied to 20 industries 1958's data and 16 petroleum and chemical firms respectively to estimate the impact of basic and applied research on productivity growth in manufacturing. As defined by NSF, basic research is 'original investigation for the advancement of scientific knowledge... which do not have immediate commercial objectives.' By applied research, the author means the research with clear commercial objectives. The estimates show that both basic and applied research inputs significantly contributed to TFP growth both at the industry and firm levels; the estimated return on basic research was greater than 150% in many cases. Mansfield also includes a unionization variable in the TFP equation. He estimated that the labor organization of the industries was significantly negatively related to total factor productivity. Because the sample was small (20 observations for cross sectional industry TFP growth model and 16 observations for cross sectional firm level TFP growth model), the author recognized the roughness and likely error of the sample and the results as well.

Griliches (1980, 1984, and 1986) published a series of empirical studies on the impact of private R & D and capital inputs on firms' TFP and labor productivity. All models were essentially developed from a C-D function. In most cases, a single equation OLS technique was adopted, while he also explored the simultaneous estimates (Griliches 1980, 1984). The empirical test indicated that two stage least square (2SLS) estimates were less significant than OLS estimates--the coefficient for R & D became insignificant in four out of six industry groups in his 1980 study[1]. In his 1984 study, Griliches estimated a system of semireduced production function and labor demand function equations with all input and output variables measured in growth rates. The estimates showed a substantial decrease in the returns to scale--about 0.5-0.9, depending on equations estimated. Most of his studies identified R & D as a significant contributor to TFP growth. This set of Griliches' studies sheds important light on the research of this kind--his methodology and his empirical estimates can all serve as the most important references. On the other hand, due to the inherent difficulty of collecting data from firms, his studies have apparent limits. First, his sample consisted only of large R & D intensive firms. Second, in some of his estimations (e.g., in his 1984 and 1986 studies), firms in all different industries were combined in the same data set and the same production function was implicitly assumed. Third, as Mansfield (1980) commented, the data Griliches used were well behind the time when his study was conducted, and were inappropriate with respect to the latest change in return to R & D.

Goto and Suzuki (1989) developed a TFP equation of marginal product form from a C-D function with growth of R & D capital as the only independent variable. They applied this model to time series data of 40 Japanese firms in seven industries. Their estimates revealed that R & D capital was a significant and substantial contributor to TFP growth and that the rate of return on R & D capital was from 0.20 to

0.80 across the seven industries. They interpreted the estimate as 'excess rates' because in their survey the R & D input was difficult to separate from conventional input, resulting in double-counting of R & D capital input. No attempt is made to include and estimate the impact of other inputs on the TFP growth. Therefore, a related problem in their empirical work is specification error.

Spatial variation and determinants are usually not of concern to mainstream economists. In addition to R & D input, very limited industrial characteristic variables can be found in the literature.

A few notable economists deviated from the mainstream tradition by explicitly addressing the regional variation of production and productivity. Perroux (1950, 1955) and Myrdal (1957) both emphasized an unbalanced regional growth with the former focusing on the propulsive industries and growth poles and the latter stressing historical accident and the cumulative effect of circular causation. Perroux and Myrdal also described a 'trickle down' or 'spread' effect resulting from increased demand for raw and intermediate inputs and from diffusions of technology and standardized production. Their theories imply that economic growth due to new industries' emergence and expansion can only occur in developed areas.

Several recent studies followed this line of argument in developing new models. Arthur (1989) emphasized a result of lock-in by historical small events in economic activities due to increasing returns to earlier adopted technology. He argued that increasing returns arise mainly from coordination externalities of the adopted technology that may or may not be potentially superior to competing technologies. Adopting historical accident and circular causation, Krugman (1991a, 1991b) developed a model of increasing returns to developed areas. The increasing returns were attributed to an interaction between transportation cost and economies of scale. A prominent feature of these studies is appreciation of economies of scale and technological spillovers within early established economic core areas. These models are relatively new and highly abstract, and many important regional factors thought important by economic geographers and regional scientists are not incorporated.

The second branch of the research can be found in regional science literature. The approach is largely based on empirical evidence and intuitive argument regarding operational form and relevant variables. The evidence on the relationship between productivity and industries' attributes or regional factors are used to justify the inclusion of relevant variables in productivity equations. The promising feature of this approach is the direct estimation of the influence of external factors on productivity growth.

Sveikauskas (1977) developed a variant of the CES production function to evaluate the relationship between urbanization economies (measured in city size) and labor productivity. His findings indicate that a doubling of city size is typically associated with a 6 percent increase in labor productivity. He interpreted the positive impact of city size as a result of the static advantage of specialization and the dynamic advantage of emergence of new ideas and constant rearrangement and recombination of new elements. In practice, however, size of a city is a result of combination of many social economic sectors. These sectors contribute to productivity gain differently. The highly aggregated measure of city size cannot help to find which sectors play the key role. Practitioners are left with no choice but that of moving to large cities. A measure of mass like city size should be included to capture the impact of unknown local and regional factors only if a researcher has no choice about specific regional factors.

Hulten and Schwab (1984) investigated the regional productivity growth in U.S. manufacturing for the period 1951-1978. They estimated that during this period total factor productivity in U.S. manufacturing grew 1.4-2.5 percent annually across the census divisions. Among other findings, they found there was no apparent regional variation in the growth of total factor productivity and that regional variation in output growth was largely determined by the variation in the growth rate of factor inputs across regions. Unlike many other researches dealing with regional variation of production or productivity, their study did not examine any specific regional variable.

Testing the relationship between agglomeration economies and TFP growth, Beeson (1987) applied a truncated Translog production function--Translog without quadratic terms-- to state level manufacturing time series data to construct variable output elasticities and a variable TFP growth. The TFP was then broken down to economies of scale and neutral technological change. The three measures of technological efficiency were considered to depend on several agglomeration variables: accessibility measured by a potential index, age and industry mix of each region, and educational attainment of the regional labor force. The findings are interesting. While both the economies of scale and the neutral technological change were related to urbanization characteristics such as share of metro area population and accessibility, the effects tended to be offsetting when TFP growth was used as a dependent variable. The author contended that productivity was related to agglomeration economies, but the relation was 'clouded' by the measure of TFP. Beeson's work is the only one that examined regional determinants of the three technological efficiency measures jointly.

In a recent study, Moomaw and Williams (1991) readdressed the issue of the determinants of growth of TFP of manufacturing at the state level. They used educational attainment of manufacturing workers, highway density, proportion of technical/ professional employees in manufacturing work force, change in wage rate, change in local tax, TFP, and production growth in a system of two equations with TFP and production growth as two endogenous variables. Impacts of the regional variables on TFP and production growth were estimated in the simultaneous equation system. Their findings were mixed: educational attainment appeared as a positive contributor to TFP; highway had no significant relationship with TFP; surprisingly, the proportion of technical and professional employees was negatively related to production growth. The authors interpreted the negative estimate for proportion of technical and professional employees as a result of the current cost incurred by R & D labor input that could result in increase in output growth only in the future. Their approach is a useful addition to the literature, because they tried to explicitly identify the regional factors that may affect productivity growth and can also be manipulated by policy. However, since TFP is defined as output growth less contribution made by conventional inputs, TFP is always measured as a part of output growth. In their study, Moomaw and Williams created a measure for TFP using the same definition and formula. Thus, adding output growth as an independent variable in TFP growth equation, as they did, cannot be justified on both theoretical and statistical bases. As a result, regressing one variable on a part of itself can only yield conceptually ambiguous and statistically inflated estimates.

By comparison, the empirical research approach used by the first group to examine the impacts of producer inputs on TFP growth is theoretically more rigorous and technically more standardized. Therefore, this study employs the same approach to estimate determinants of TFP, economies of scale, and neutral technological change. To make findings comparable with earlier research in regional science, this study includes a set of regional variables to assess the influence of regional factors on the technological efficiency measures.

6.2. THE MODEL AND OPERATIONAL FORMS

Conventionally, TFP growth is defined as the growth rate of output less the constant returns to scale-weighted growth of capital and labor inputs

(6.1)
$$TFP = \dot{Q} - \frac{\sum_i \beta_i \dot{X}_i}{\sum_i \beta_i} \ ,$$

where dotted Q and X_i are the growth rates of output and the ith input respectively, and $\Sigma \beta_i$ is the sum of output elasticities of the inputs.

Following the tradition in growth literature, NTP is defined as the residual of production growth not explained by the growth of producer inputs,

(6.2)
$$NTP = \dot{Q} - \sum_i \beta_i \dot{X}_i \ .$$

If conventional inputs alone make all contributions to production growth and if production is characterized by constant returns to scale, TFP is identical to neutral technological progress. Because at the national aggregate level return to scale is always assumed to be constant, little attention is paid to the difference between TFP and NTP. They are indifferently termed 'technological progress'. Growth literature (Denison 1985, Solow 1988) suggests that technological progress can be attributed to overall improvements of factor quality, better allocation of resources, advance of knowledge base, and evolution of social organization. At the producer level, however, the quality and combination of factor inputs, technology of production, and many regional services differ from area to area. Moreover, many companies may frequently experience change in scale of production through expansions or contractions. Therefore, returns to scale with a company's conventional inputs may not be constant, resulting in divergence between TFP and NTP.

Scale economies refer to large-scale production at lower per unit cost. Scale economies are determined by technology of production and scale of operation. However, there co-exist many different, profitable technologies to produce the same or similar output. These alternative technologies require different combinations of inputs and external conditions, while also permitting different optimal scales of production. To study productivity, the only meaningful measure of scale economies is the scale of production relative to the optimal scale of the given production technology. So far there is no operational measure for different technologies and no reference point of optimal scale for each production technology readily available. Fortunately, in most empirical studies, the researcher only needs to examine the relative scales of production for given technologies. Considering constant returns to scale as the optimal level of operation, scale economies are the difference between actual return and the constant returns to scale weighted growth of inputs

$$(6.3) \qquad SCALE = \left(1 - \frac{1}{\sum_i \beta_i}\right) \times \sum_i \beta_i \dot{X}_i \ .$$

This is the conventional measure of scale economies and used in earlier research (e.g., Beeson 1987). This measure is used in this study for comparison.

For any given technology, scale economies are very likely to increase with the scale of production and then, after reaching some peak, decrease as scale continues to rise. When a producer operates at the range of diminishing returns to scale, the scale of production may be too large for the given technology. On the other hand, when factors other than conventional inputs also contribute to production, production may be characterized by diminishing returns to scale with respect to the conventional inputs. This may be the case for the production that substantially demands, and benefits from, external factors supported by the regional economy.

To construct the operational measures of TFP, NTP, and scale economies, this study adopts a very general production function

$$(6.4) \qquad Q_t = a_t F\left(L_{wt}, L_{pt}, K_{et}, K_{bt}\right) ,$$

where Q_t is output, a_t a parameter to capture neutral technological change, L_{wt}, L_{pt}, K_{et}, and K_{bt}, respectively, production workers, professional employees, equipment, and buildings. Differentiating the function with respect to time and then dividing both sides by output yield

(6.5)
$$\frac{dQ_t}{Q_t dt} = \frac{\partial Q_t}{\partial a_t} \frac{da_t}{a_t dt} + \frac{\partial Q_t}{\partial L_{wt}} \frac{L_{wt}}{Q_t} \frac{dL_{wt}}{L_{wt} dt} + \frac{\partial Q_t}{\partial L_{pt}} \frac{L_{pt}}{Q_t} \frac{dL_{pt}}{L_{pt} dt}$$
$$+ \frac{\partial Q_t}{\partial K_{et}} \frac{K_{et}}{Q_t} \frac{dK_{et}}{K_{et} dt} + \frac{\partial Q_{bt}}{\partial L_{bt}} \frac{K_{bt}}{Q_t} \frac{dK_{bt}}{K_{bt} dt}.$$

Using simple notations $\beta_X = (\partial Q_t/\partial X_t)(X_t/Q_t)$ and dotted $\dot{X}_t = dX_t/(X_t dt)$ and rearranging the terms yield

(6.6)
$$\dot{Q}_t - \beta_w \dot{L}_{wt} - \beta_p \dot{L}_{pt} - \beta_e \dot{K}_{et} - \beta_b \dot{K}_{bt} = \dot{a}_{0t},$$

or

(6.7)
$$\left(\dot{Q}_t - \beta_w \dot{L}_{wt} - \beta_p \dot{L}_{pt} - \beta_e \dot{K}_{et} - \beta_b \dot{K}_{bt} \right)$$
$$= \left(\dot{Q}_t - \frac{\beta_w \dot{L}_{wt} + \beta_p \dot{L}_{pt} + \beta_e \dot{K}_{et} + \beta_b \dot{K}_{bt}}{\beta_w + \beta_p + \beta_e + \beta_b} \right) -$$
$$\left(\beta_w \dot{L}_{wt} + \beta_p \dot{L}_{pt} + \beta_e \dot{K}_{et} + \beta_b \dot{K}_{bt} - \frac{\beta_w \dot{L}_{wt} + \beta_p \dot{L}_{pt} + \beta_e \dot{K}_{et} + \beta_b \dot{K}_{bt}}{\beta_w + \beta_p + \beta_e + \beta_b} \right)$$
$$= \dot{a}_{0t}.$$

It is immediately apparent that the relation NTP=TFP-SCALE or TFP=NTP+SCALE holds. NTP or dotted a_0 is the average contribution to productivity growth of all factors not included in the production function. An external factor that contributes to NTP and TFP may actually lower a producer's scale economies because the external factor may have pushed production to the range of diminishing returns to scale with respect to internal inputs. Specifically, if a regional factor can more or less substitute for a conventional input at no or negligible cost, the producer is not likely to cut his inputs; instead, he is more likely to expand his production using constant conventional input levels and the external factor. Following this logic, a researcher may expect to observe a positive relationship between an external factor and NTP/TFP and a negative relationship between the factor and scale economies as measured.

To derive operational equations, a production function with embodied technology, derived in chapter 2, is used. The function is presented in (6.8) for convenience,

$$(6.8) \qquad Q_t = a_t F\left(J_t, M_t, Z_t, R_t\right),$$

where Q_t, J_t, M_t, and Z_t are respectively the output, the capital stock, the labor input, and the R & D and other technological inputs; and R_t is a vector of regional factors. A growth equation the same as (2.25) in chapter 2 can be derived and written in a neater form

$$(6.9) \qquad \dot{Q}_t = \beta_0 + \beta_1 \dot{K}_t - \beta_2 \dot{A}_t + \beta_3 \dot{L}_t + \beta_4 \dot{E}_{st} + \beta_5 \dot{E}_{et} + \beta_6 \dot{Z}_t + \beta_7 \dot{R}_t,$$

where dotted inputs and output represent growth rates. β_0 is made of three terms since λ_k and λ_L are not directly measurable and, therefore, absorbed into the intercept. Making a slight rearrangement of terms yields,

$$(6.10) \qquad \dot{Q}_t - \left(\beta_1 \dot{K}_t + \beta_3 \dot{L}_t\right) = \beta_0 - \beta_2 \dot{A}_t + \beta_4 \dot{E}_{st} + \beta_5 \dot{E}_{et} + \beta_6 \dot{Z}_t + \beta_7 \dot{R}_t,$$

or

$$(6.10') \qquad \left| \dot{Q}_t - \frac{\beta_1 \dot{K}_t + \beta_3 \dot{L}_t}{\beta_1 + \beta_3} \right| - \left| \beta_1 \dot{K}_t + \beta_3 \dot{L}_t - \frac{\beta_1 \dot{K}_t + \beta_3 \dot{L}_t}{\beta_1 + \beta_3} \right|$$

$$= \beta_0 - \beta_2 \dot{A}_t + \beta_4 \dot{E}_{st} + \beta_5 \dot{E}_{et} + \beta_6 \dot{Z}_t + \beta_7 \dot{R}_t.$$

The left hand side of equation (6.10) is NTP or TFP-SCALE, and the right hand side are terms of technological inputs and regional factors. It is the primary objective of this chapter, and many earlier studies, to investigate how much the producer internal and external, especially regional, factors are responsible for the technological efficiency of production.

6.3. DETERMINANTS OF TECHNOLOGICAL EFFICIENCY

6.3.1. Empirical Measures of Technological Efficiency
Applying equation (6.5) to the sample data yields the output elasticities of conventional inputs. Table 6.1 presents the estimates.

Table 6.1 Estimates of Output Elasticities of Inputs
(Dependent Variable: Annual Growth Rate of Output Value)

TEXTILE-APPAREL (N=279)			COMPUTER-ELECTRONICS (N=210)		
Dep Mean 2.77219			Dep Mean 4.17291		
Variable	Estimate	St. Err.	Variable	Estimate	St. Err.
INTERCEPT	2.5638**	0.4176	INTERCEPT	3.0731**	0.5388
W-EMPGROW	0.4504**	0.0591	W-EMPGROW	0.2288**	0.0406
P-EMPGROW	0.1103**	0.0469	P-EMPGROW	0.2644**	0.0518
K-BDGROW	0.1469**	0.0567	K-BDGROW	0.1035*	0.0613
K-UTLGROW	0.2509**	0.0582	K-UTLGROW	0.2963**	0.0552
R-square	0.4049		R-square	0.5176	
Adj R-sq	0.3962		Adj R-sq	0.5082	

Note: (1) All dependent and independent variables are measured by annual percentage growth rates.
(2) * and ** indicate statistically significant at 90% and 95% levels respectively.

Applying formula (6.1), (6.2), and (6.3) to the estimates and to individual company growth data yields empirical measures of TFP, NTP, and economies of scale. Table 6.2 shows the means and standard deviations of the derived measures of NTP. TFP, and economies of scale.

Table 6.2 Derived Technological Efficiency Measures

TEXTILE-APPAREL			COMPUTER-ELECTRONICS		
Variable	Mean	St. Dev	Variable	Mean	St. Dev.
NTP	2.5064	6.2996	NTP	3.2048	7.0726
TFP	2.4952	6.3020	TFP	3.0586	7.1346
SCALE	-0.0108	0.2143	SCALE	-0.1462	0.8545

These statistics suggest that much of the productivity growth did not result from the increase in capital and labor inputs, because NTP can account for 2.51 out of 2.77 percent annual output grow in textile-apparel and 3.20 out of 4.17 in computer-electronics. The computer-electronics producers enjoy a higher productivity growth rate measured by NTP and TFP than textile-apparel companies. These rates interestingly bracket, and are reassuringly similar to, Griliches 1984's average figure (2.9% for 133 firms) and higher than most studies that use more aggregated data[2].

It seems strange that scale economies for the computer-electronics group are smaller than for textile-apparel companies. More precisely, a one percent increase in conventional capital and labor inputs yields a 0.99 percent increase in output for an average textile-apparel company, but the same increase in inputs boosts output in a typical computer-electronics producer by only 0.85 percent. The figures imply that: (1) scale economies, as expressed, are not an appropriate single measure of productivity growth; and (2) computer-electronics companies must operate under diminishing returns to scale if they rely solely on conventional inputs (readers may recall that return to scale with producer inputs, including R & D and other technology related inputs, is estimated to be constant in the preceding chapter). A more reasonable hypothesis is that many non-conventional inputs, especially technology related inputs, and regional factors contribute to computer-electronics production. By not accounting for their contribution, a researcher underspecifies the true production function and also detects a diminishing return to scale with respect to capital and labor inputs.

6.3.2. An Overview of Estimates

The three derived measures are used as dependent variables in three operational equations essentially the same as equation (6.10'). Equations with different arrangements of independent variables are extensively tested so that any observed difference in parameter estimates between the pair of companies in each group (i.e., textile and apparel in the first group, computer and electronics in the second group) is represented by an additional interaction term. To illustrate, R & D has a weaker impact (0.0705) on TFP growth in textile than in apparel companies (0.0705 + 0.3179), while professional educational attainment contributes more to computer companies (1.0022) than to electronics producers (1.0022-0.8923). No regional variable is found to have different influence on productivity growth of the industry pairs in both groups. Therefore, other interaction terms are not included in the final equations. Table 6.3 and Table 6.4 report the estimates of the final versions for textile-apparel and computer-electronics groups respectively. Definitions and measures of the producer inputs, company attributes, and regional variables are shown in Table 3.5, Table 4.1, and Table 5.1 respectively.

The overall estimates for TFP and NTP equations are very similar. This is not surprising, given the specification of the two productivity growth measures (if the production is characterized by constant returns to scale with respect to the four capital and labor inputs, the two equation should be identical). The researcher will, therefore, discuss the estimates for TFP and NTP jointly. On the other hand, the equation for scale economies performs very differently, particularly for computer-electronics.

Because the estimates for the two industry groups are very different, the author elects to discuss the two groups separately. The final section of this chapter will make a comparison of these two industry groups while summarizing the findings.

6.3.3. Textile-Apparel Industries
6.3.3.1. Total Factor Productivity (TFP) and Neutral Technical Progress (NTP)

Several technological inputs emerge as significant determinants of productivity growth. The estimates confirm the positive relationship between R & D input and TFP found in earlier research (e.g., Mansfield 1980, Griliches 1980, 1984, and 1986) and the negative relationship between average age of capital stock and productivity growth. In addition, professional experience and patent purchase also contribute to TFP and NTP, consistent with the estimates of chapter 5.

Table 6.3 Estimated Determinants of Technological Efficiency of Textile-Apparel Companies

Dep Variable Mean	TFP 2.4952		NTP 2.5064		SCALE -0.0108	
Variable	Estimate	S.E.	Estimate	S.E.	Estimate	S.E.
INTERCEPT	-2.6118	1.707	-2.6253	1.699	0.0158	0.053
APPAREL	0.7378	0.842	0.6849	0.838	0.0508*	0.026
Technological						
K-AGEGROW	-0.1307*	0.070	-0.1380**	0.070	0.0074**	0.002
K-AGE-APP	0.1361*	0.080	0.1392*	0.082	-0.0031*	0.002
W-EDGROW	0.2722	0.191	0.2794	0.190	-0.0065	0.006
W-EXPGROW	-0.0428	0.065	-0.0414	0.065	-0.0013	0.002
P-EDGROW	0.0484	0.220	0.0493	0.219	-0.0009	0.006
P-EXPGROW	0.2146**	0.084	0.2109**	0.083	0.0036	0.002
K-R&DGROW	0.0705*	0.041	0.0700	0.081	0.0005	0.002
K-R&D-AP	0.3179*	0.183	0.3214*	0.183	-0.0034	0.005
PTNTGROW	0.0539**	0.022	0.0567**	0.022	-0.0028**	0.000
K-CCGROW	0.0047	0.009	0.0055	0.009	-0.0008**	0.000
K-MCNGROW	0.0071	0.004	0.0072	0.004	-0.0001	0.000
K-MNGGROW	0.0129	0.009	0.0127	0.009	0.0002	0.000
K-TRNGROW	0.0091	0.015	0.0095	0.015	-0.0004	0.000
Regional						
AREA-EMP	-0.1119	0.213	-0.1174	0.212	0.0062	0.006
TEXEMPGROW	0.0075	0.020	0.0073	0.019	0.0001	0.000
APPEMPGROW	-0.0465*	0.025	-0.0472*	0.025	0.0007	0.000
TSVEMPGROW	0.0026	0.018	0.0034	0.018	-0.0007	0.000
CMUEMPGROW	-0.0109	0.042	-0.0121	0.042	0.0011	0.001
UTIESTGROW	-0.0232	0.036	-0.0209	0.036	-0.0023**	0.001
FIRESTGROW	0.0494	0.112	0.0465	0.112	0.0023	0.003
BUSEMPGROW	-0.0267	0.023	-0.0269	0.023	0.0001	0.000
AMSEMPGROW	0.0065	0.030	0.0060	0.030	0.0004	0.000
HLTEMPGROW	0.0140	0.061	0.0141	0.061	-0.0003	0.001
EDUEMPGROW	-0.0353**	0.017	-0.0345*	0.017	-0.0007	0.000
ENGEMPGROW	0.0204	0.024	0.0215	0.024	-0.0011	0.000
R&DEMPGROW	0.0070	0.010	0.0066	0.010	0.0004	0.000
METRO	0.8704	0.913	0.9073	0.909	-0.0374	0.028
Company Attribute						
PRIVATE	1.3002	0.974	1.3432	0.969	-0.0417	0.030
HQ-FRGN	0.7084	3.681	1.1087	3.666	-0.4019**	0.116
AGE-CMPNY	-0.0033	0.016	-0.0040	0.016	0.0007	0.000
R-square	0.2299		0.2363		0.2957	
Adj R-sq	0.1270		0.1342		0.2073	

Note: (1) All dependent and independent variables are measured by annual percentage growth rates.
(2) * and ** indicate statistically significant at 90% and 95% levels respectively.

Table 6.4 Estimated Determinants of Technological Efficiency of Computer-Electronics

Dep Variable Mean	TFP 3.0586		NTP 3.2048		SCALE -0.1462	
Variable	Estimate	S.E.	Estimate	S.E.	Estimate	S.E.
INTERCEPT	7.2040**	2.676	7.1148**	2.642	0.0892	0.285
ELECTRON	-2.0293*	1.216	-1.8968	1.201	-0.1324	0.129
Technological						
K-AGEGROW	-0.0402*	0.024	-0.0419*	0.024	0.0262**	0.004
W-EDGROW	-0.3564	0.287	-0.3853	0.283	0.0288	0.030
W-EXPGROW	-0.1197	0.089	-0.1196	0.087	-0.0001	0.009
P-EDGROW	1.0022*	0.539	0.9750*	0.533	0.0272	0.057
P-ED-ELEC	-0.8923*	0.523	-0.8762*	0.516	-0.0162	0.059
P-EXPGROW	-0.0778	0.098	-0.1117	0.097	0.0339**	0.010
K-R&DGROW	0.0541*	0.031	0.0760*	0.042	-0.0219**	0.006
PTNTGROW	0.0026	0.011	0.0025	0.011	0.0001	0.001
K-CCGROW	-0.0059	0.013	-0.0038	0.012	-0.0021	0.001
K-MCNGROW	0.0111	0.014	0.0106	0.013	0.0005	0.001
K-MNGGROW	-0.0369	0.029	-0.0294	0.021	-0.0075**	0.002
K-TRNGROW	0.0046	0.006	0.0048	0.006	-0.0002	0.000
Regional						
AREA-EMP	-0.1500	0.364	-0.0979	0.360	-0.0520	0.038
CMPMGROW	-0.0089	0.020	-0.0093	0.019	0.0004	0.002
ELEMGROW	-0.0163	0.069	-0.0037	0.068	-0.0126*	0.007
TSVEMPGROW	0.0442	0.049	0.0442	0.048	0.0001	0.005
CMUEMPGROW	0.0026	0.082	0.0236	0.081	-0.0210**	0.008
UTIESTGROW	-0.2489**	0.064	-0.2581**	0.063	0.0092	0.006
FIRESTGROW	-0.2297	0.204	-0.2565	0.202	0.0267	0.021
BUSEMPGROW	0.0462	0.057	0.0411	0.056	0.0051	0.006
AMSEMPGROW	0.2126**	0.085	0.2108**	0.084	0.0017	0.009
HLTEMPGROW	0.4826**	0.200	0.4125**	0.197	-0.0701**	0.021
EDUEMPGROW	-0.0556	0.060	-0.0424	0.060	-0.0132**	0.006
ENGEMPGROW	-0.0760	0.058	-0.0752	0.058	-0.0008	0.006
R&DEMPGROW	-0.0275*	0.015	-0.0260*	0.015	-0.0016*	0.001
METRO	-1.0266	1.745	-1.0946	1.723	0.0680	0.186
Company Attribute						
PRIVATE	0.0242	1.029	-0.1628	1.016	0.1871*	0.109
HQ_FRGN	1.4819	2.782	1.9153	2.747	-0.4333	0.297
CUSTOMIZE	1.1005	1.184	1.3108	1.169	-0.2103**	0.126
AGE-CMPNY	-0.0552*	0.031	-0.0547*	0.031	-0.0004	0.003
R-square	0.2688		0.2746		0.4387	
Adj R-sq	0.1415		0.1483		0.3375	

Note: (1) All dependent and independent variables are measured by annual percentage growth rates.

(2) * and ** indicate statistically significant at 90% and 95% levels respectively.

A reduction in the average age of capital raises TFP and NTP for capital-intensive textile mills, but not for apparel companies. The two significant estimates of the capital age for apparel producers, K-AGEGROW and K-AGE-APP, are canceled. The findings are also consistent with earlier research. As an earlier comprehensive study noted (Cline 1990), since 1970s, new equipment in the textile industry has raised productivity many times that of earlier machines, while in the apparel industry little equipment innovation has emerged, and the most important assembly process has remained almost strictly manual, largely because economies of scale in a fashion-driven industry are less important.

The influence of R & D input on TFP and NTP also differs between textile and apparel producers. For the same percent increase in R & D capital, TFP in the design-sensitive apparel industry grows much more than in the standardized textile industry. R & D in the apparel industry is related to process and product technology such as computer-aided fashion design. The return on R & D is likely much higher than that in the textile industry. This difference also results, because the textile industry R & D tends to improve the appearance and quality of products, but hardly changes the fundamentally fixed product, thereby resulting in a small marginal increase in value-added.

Most regional factors appear irrelevant to TFP and NTP with two exceptions: growth in size of the regional apparel industry and growth of the education sector. Growth of the nearby apparel industry tends to lower the TFP and NTP of individual apparel companies; this means regional competition for factors and product markets outweighs the positive localization effects generally claimed for external scale economies and technological externalities of the same industry. The negative effect of competition is likely to result from higher labor prices of scarce professional inputs[3] and stable or even lower prices of product.

Growth of education services is also negatively related to TFP and NTP. This could suggest that better education services increases the stock of human capital which then demands a higher price for its labor inputs. An alternative interpretation may be more optimistic-- policy makers and general public in the areas with low productivity growth have recognized the weakness of their areas and have made efforts to enhance their education sector to upgrade their labor force. The alternative interpretation will be sustainable if a positive impact of education expansion on company productivity growth appears in the future. This finding appears to coincide with Moomaw and Williams' (1991) study concerning the empirically negative relationship between productivity growth and quality of the work force. The estimate of exact time lag between education expansion and company productivity growth requires special investigation beyond the scope of this study.

The irrelevance of all other regional factors indicates that standardized textile-apparel production does not depend on sophisticated regional infrastructure and services. This finding is consistent with all known economic geography and regional literature.

The company attribute variables are included primarily as controls. The attribute variables have no perceptible impact on productivity growth.

6.3.3.2. Economies of Scale (SCALE)

The operational form of the economies of scale measures the rate of joint return on conventional inputs. Several technology-related and regional variables appear significant.

Technology embodied in capital, measured as the average age of equipment, has a significant positive sign. This means that the older (or younger) the equipment, the greater the economies (or diseconomies) of scale at observed production levels. Following the logic described earlier, technological improvements drastically reduce the level of scale-efficient production below current operation levels. This supports the general proposition that the factors that can improve the quality of conventional inputs tend to push current production beyond optimal scale, measured by constant returns to scale with respect to the conventional inputs.

A dummy variable for apparel companies is included in the equation of economies of scale to distinguish textile from apparel producers. The significant positive estimate indicates that apparel companies operate at a range of slightly increasing return to scale, while textile mills are in a range of slightly diminishing return to scale, given the mean of SCALE equal to -0.01 and the parameter estimate for the apparel dummy variable equal to 0.05. This estimate makes a clear distinction between the two subgroups--textile mills are driven by non-conventional inputs significantly more than are apparel companies. Since regional factors have the same estimates for the two subgroups, the variables that are responsible for the difference are very likely to be technology-related. More specifically, technology embodied in capital measured by change in average age of production capital is the major cause of the difference in economies of scale between the two subgroups.

In the equation only one regional variable, utilities services, is significant. Based on the earlier conceptual argument, the negative sign suggests that utilities services tend to bring textile-apparel production to a scale beyond otherwise constant-return-to-scale level, assuming return to scale is bell shaped with the scale of operation. In other words, textile-apparel production relies on and benefits from utilities services and expands production accordingly.

Economies of scale of textile-apparel are much more affected by technological than regional input, particularly patent purchase and acquisition of more computer and numeric control systems, each of which acts to reduce economies of scale. First, these technological inputs can partly substitute for capital and labor and have higher rates of return. Based on the logic discussed earlier, producers may not proportionally downsize the conventional inputs while making the technological inputs, leading to an increase in total inputs relative to output. Second, the negative estimates may indicate that technological inputs have made firms more flexible and profitable at lower production levels. In either case, the traditional measure of economies of scale may no longer be an appropriate indicator of productivity. This is especially true for modern technology-intensive industries, because in these industries scale of input is largely determined by the amount of technology-related inputs. This is also increasingly true for large-scale producers whose investments during the 1980s were intended to help 'downsize' the firms, tighten quality standards, secure more inputs from high-quality suppliers, and compete profitably at lower output levels. The data of this study appear to reflect this trend in all respects.

The only significant company attribute variable is the dummy variable to distinguish headquarters located in foreign countries from those located elsewhere. The negative estimate means smaller economies of scale which corresponds to the levels of operation scale either smaller or larger than a constant-return-to-scale level. This is an interesting sign that foreign controlled companies are less stable. The foreign controlled companies may experience more expansion or contraction in the period ahead.

In summary, textile-apparel companies can be characterized by constant returns to scale. Three technology-related variables tend to push current production level into a range beyond constant-return-to-scale. Most regional factors have no impact on the economies of scale.

6.3.4. Computer-Electronics Industries

6.3.4.1. Total Factor Productivity (TFP) and Neutral Technical Progress (NTP)
Several technological input variables have significant parameter estimates. The estimates point to the directions of the relationships between these technology related variables and productivity growth.

Technology embodied in capital measured by average age of production capital is a significant contributor to productivity growth. The contribution to productivity growth is the same for computer and electronics companies--one percent reduction in average age of equipment, equivalent to 0.08 years younger, results in, on the average, a 0.04 percent increase in TFP and NTP.

Growth of professional educational also influences growth of productivity, but the impact is not uniform across industry segments. The impact on TFP and NTP is much stronger for computer companies than for electronics. More precisely, a one percent increase in professional education is associated with about a one percent increase in TFP and NTP growth for an average computer company, but only a 0.1 (i.e., sum of P-EDGROW and P-ED-ELEC) percent increase for an average electronics company. The estimates convey the message that the computer industry depends more on advanced knowledge than does electronics.

Also consistent with all earlier research, an increase in R & D capital leads to higher TFP and NTP due to the innovation of new process or products. R & D capital is estimated to have the same impact on productivity growth of computer and electronics companies. Other inputs that might be expected to facilitate the adoption of existing technology do not show significant influence.

Producer attribute variables are included to reduce the bias of the estimates of technology-related and regional variables. The only significant estimate is the age of companies. The negative sign shows that the younger a company, the higher is the growth rate of productivity.

Findings shown in Table 6.4 indicate that regional factors influence the productivity growth of computer-electronics companies. Recreation services and health services contribute to the productivity growth of these companies, as expected. The estimates confirm the importance of these services in maintaining and upgrading the quality of local employees. Since it is the consumer, not the producer, who pays the cost of recreation and amusement services, computer-electronics companies enjoy net gains in productivity from these services. While the cost of health insurance to an employer is not directly related to the company's location, companies located in the areas with higher growth rate of health services sector benefit more from the quality and availability of the services at the same or similar cost.

Unexpectedly, utilities services and R & D and testing services have negative signs in both TFP and NTP equations. The growth of utilities services is more likely to reflect growth in non-manufacturing business. This pattern of growth creates general pressures on the price of local fixed resources such as land, water, and even electricity. This may, in turn, result in higher production costs. The data seem to support the interpretation--during the 1983-88 period, average employment in total manufacturing and in textile, apparel, computer, and electronics industries all dropped significantly across the sample areas, while total area employment increased by more than ten percent.

The negative effect of growth of R & D and testing services on companies' productivity growth may arise due to competition in both input factor market and output market. Because many computer-electronics companies try to maintain well-staffed R & D and testing capabilities for product development and provide services to outside customers, the growth of independent R & D and testing facilities may siphon off valuable technical workers in the local labor market and undermine the computer-electronics companies' profit in service markets.

6.3.4.2. Economies of scale

Technology related inputs, particularly newer capital, expanded R & D, and more advanced management systems, are estimated to be significant determinants of economies of scale. As expected, each of these investments permits firms to expand production beyond the constant returns to scale level, resulting in the estimated negative relationship between the technological input variables and economies of scale. These estimates jointly confirm the view that typical production in this industry group involves a wide range of technological inputs and that technological inputs are partially substitutable for conventional capital and labor. Therefore, the measure of economies of scale should include these technological inputs[4].

Regional factors influence economies of scale of computer-electronics producers more than those of textile-apparel producers. Localization measured by the size of the area's electronics industry, communication services, health services, and education services all appear to reduce economies of scale of production. As discussed earlier, external factors that facilitate production growth without imposing full costs on individual producers tend to push scale of production to pass constant-return-to-scale level with respect to capital and labor. The empirical estimates are consistent with the logic.

Localization economies are negatively associated with the internal economies of scale. A cluster of a large number of similar producers means competition both for factor inputs and product market. This competition tends to push costs of inputs up and profits of output down. However, the estimate suggests that localization or technological externalities of electronics production outweighs the adverse influence of competition for factor inputs. The communication services sector is a regional factor statistically more significant and numerically more substantial than localization; companies located in the areas with better communication services are very likely to expand far beyond optimal scale. Both localization and communication services improve a firm's access to important technology and information. The findings indicate that as an information industry, the computer-electronics group is itself very sensitive to information about technologies and markets. The location and productivity of these industries are crucially dependent on regional spillovers of technology. Unlike the textile-apparel group that depends very little on regional factors for its productivity, computer-electronics producers are vitally dependent upon their regional economies and are far less likely to become footloose.

Health services and education services clearly contribute to the improvement of labor force quality. Estimated negative signs for the two service sectors indicate that the scale of computer-electronics production expands substantially with growth of health services and education services, resulting in a diminishing returns to scale with conventional capital and labor. The reason that production can be sustained at this scale appears to hinge on the improvement of labor inputs. Without the support of these services, computer-electronics production could not operate at the current scale.

Overall, technology-related inputs and regional factors have considerably stronger influence on the economies of scale of computer-electronics production than on those of textile-apparel production.

Textile-apparel production is more heavily dependent on conventional inputs, while computer-electronics production relies more on technological inputs and regional services. Given the significant estimates of several technological inputs and the conceptual argument for their inclusion in a measure of economies of scale, one is led to conclude that traditionally measured economies of scale is not a good single indicator of productivity growth, especially for technology intensive industries like computer-electronics.

6.4. SUMMARY AND CONCLUSION

This chapter examines technological and regional determinants of the technological efficiency of company production by testing the relationship between technology-related inputs / regional variables and the three technological efficiency measures, i.e., total factor productivity, neutral technological progress, and economies of scale. Several concluding points emerge from the empirical analysis.

First, there are substantial differences in the determinants of technological efficiency between industries. This means that research results obtained from aggregate data cannot provide reliable guides for practical measures that improve productivity growth in particular industries or at state and local levels.

Second, the results of empirical tests suggest acceptance of the hypothesis that educational attainment and experience of employees, local communication services, R & D services, utilities services, health services, recreation services, and localization economies all affect productivity growth and that the regional impact on productivity growth is stronger for the computer-electronics industries than for the textile-apparel industries. However, the impact is much more complicated than first hypothesized, with some factors facilitating firms' technological efficiency growth and some others adversely influencing the growth.

Third, educational attainment and experience of employees, technology embodied in new equipment, and other technology related inputs are important contributors to companies' productivity. Technological inputs contribute more to efficiency growth in computer-electronics than in textile-apparel. The picture is further complicated by the difference of contribution each single input makes to different producer groups.

Fourth, TFP and NTP are similar to each other in concept and in measure, but very different from economies of scale. TFP and NTP are far more straightforward than economies of scale in empirical measures and interpretations. These features are reflected in the estimates of the determinants for technological efficiency. The estimates of the economies of scale equation sometimes remain provocative and leave sufficient room for more thought and conjecture. At least, they cast serious doubt on the appropriateness of economies of scale as a suitable indicator of technological efficiency or, as more commonly referred to, productivity growth. Empirical researchers concerned with productivity growth will find their estimates easier to understand and interpret when the most suitable measures are used to guide practical works.

Notes

1. It seems that Griliches overlooked those insignificant estimates and discussed the estimates as if they were all significant. Mansfield (1980) pointed out that two thirds of the 2SLS estimates have a t ratio below 1.6, insignificant at the 90% level. Although neither of the economists discussed the reasons for the insignificant 2SLS estimates, it is easy to infer from an econometric technical point of view that substitution of instruments for original variables is responsible for the poorer fit. In general, if variables used to create instruments are not closely related to the instruments or to the dependent variable, instrument variable methods including 2SLS cannot yield a good fit of the estimates. In this case, loss due to specification error may be greater than gain from reduction in simultaneous bias.

2. Hulten and Schwab (1984) estimate that the TFP growth rate is around 1.4%-2.0% for census divisions for the period of 1951-78 and Moomaw and Williams (1991) estimate that the TFP growth rate varies across the 48 states from 0.3% to 3.0% with a mean of about 1% for the period 1954-76.

3. The author indirectly tested this interpretation by including wage rate in the equations, because wage rate is normally affected by supply and demand of labor input. The estimates for apparel employment growth became insignificant once wage rate was included, the estimate for wage rate was itself insignificant though. This partly supports the interpretation. Economic theory and standard practice do not support inclusion of wage rate in a production function and a growth equation. Therefore, the wage rate was not included in the final version of the equations.

4. An additional statistical test shows that return to scale with respect to all producer inputs, including technological inputs, was constant both for textile-apparel and computer-electronics industry groups.

7 Determinants of Technological Inputs

According to earlier research findings, embodied technology, R & D capital, and other technology related inputs all contribute to production and productivity growth. Logically, one ought to further investigate the factors that determine the types and the levels of technology related inputs. However, this has been largely a neglected research topic, especially when the unit of analysis is an individual producer. A small branch of earlier research suggests that investment in adoption of advanced technologies varies with manufacturers' characteristics and regional or location factors. Taking this evidence into account and employing a theoretically more rigorous method, this chapter examines the determinants of the technology related inputs.

The influences of embodied technology, producer attributes, and regional factors on technological inputs are part of indirect contributions of these factors to production and productivity growth. The conceptual relationship being examined is illustrated in Figure 7.1., which is a part of Figure 2.1. Microeconomic producer theory serves as the theoretical basis to develop operational equations. The standard producer factor demand function is the basic functional form derived in this chapter. A simultaneous equation method is employed in the estimation. A set of input intensity functions is also estimated to reveal the influential factors to intensities of technological inputs. The estimates and discussion are presented in the appendix to this chapter.

This chapter is organized as follows. Section 7.1 reviews earlier studies. Section 7.2 develops a theoretical model and its operational forms. Section 7.3 presents and discusses empirical estimates of the technological input demand functions. The final section summarizes and concludes this chapter.

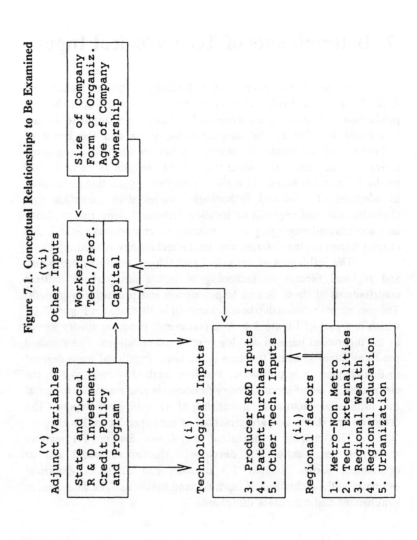

Figure 7.1. Conceptual Relationships to Be Examined

7.1. EARLIER RESEARCH

A limited number of earlier studies provides sketchy evidence about the determinants of technology related inputs. The Office of Technology Assessment (1984) examined new business formation and employment growth for high-tech and other industries over the 1976-80 period, reporting that size of city was positively related to business formation and employment growth, while wage rates and energy costs were negatively associated with the growth. That study also suggested that the percentage of local employment as scientific, technical, and professional employees affected the growth of high-tech industries positively, whereas local tax was negatively related to the growth in non high-tech sectors.

Rees and Stafford (1983) used two survey data sets--one is collected by the authors, the other is from the Congress' Joint Economic Committee--to examine the location factors that influence high-technology industries. The locational variables included those related to the friction of distance as well as those related to the attributes of areas: labor availability, quality, and cost; quality of life and other amenity variables; access to markets, materials, and various transportation networks; access to development capital; and so on. Among these variables, labor skills and availability, transportation availability, quality of life, market access, utilities supply, and tax climate within region emerged to be the most important locational factors in location decisions of high-tech plants. Depending on the data sets used, the ranks of the importance of these variables were somewhat different.

In another study, Rees, Briggs, and Oakey (1984) applied a descriptive statistical analysis to the survey data of more than 600 manufacturing plants in the machinery and electronics industries (SIC 35 and 36) to examine the rates of the adoption of new process technology such as computerized numerical control technology. Since adoption of the new technology is the purpose and the consequence of investment in this input, their research is equivalent to examination of process technology related inputs and its variation across different plants and locations. They found that new technologies were more likely to be adopted by multi-plant firms, larger plants, and older plants, although the rates of adoption of these technologies are different. They also examined the interactive effect of plant characteristics and location on the adoption rates of advanced technologies. Their findings showed that small, single plant firms in the manufacturing heartland had higher adoption rates for machine control technology than similar companies in the South and West and that the use of microprocessors was more prevalent among small firms in California and Massachusetts than elsewhere. However, in many occasions their findings were mixed and inconclusive, suggesting the complex nature of inputs in adoption of advanced technologies.

Markusen, Hall, and Glasmeier (1983, 1986) conducted empirical research on locational determinants of high-tech industry inputs for about 100 4-digit SIC sectors using a linear regression method. Since the locational pattern of the high-tech industries is a direct result of spatial variation of producer inputs, the estimated relationship between regional contextual factors and locational pattern is similar to the relationship between the regional factors and induced producer inputs. Their findings (1983) indicated that percent of black population discouraged high-tech input, while defense spending contributed the high-tech input. They also estimated (1986) that amenities, business services, and accessibility were positively related to high-tech input. Unexpectedly, their estimates showed a peculiar negative relationship between university R & D input and private high-tech inputs.

Examining the effects of factor cost and externalities on induced adoption of information technology in Italian manufacturing, Antonelli (1990) employed a common assumption of producer optimization behavior to justify the importance of wage rates and externalities to the adoption of advanced technology and applied a simple linear function to Italian provincial level (similar to US county level) data. In Antonelli's research, input in advanced information technology was measured by fax machine and modem in manufacturing. Externalities were measured by (1) city population as a percentage of total area population, (2) share of employment accounted for by large firms, (3) share of employment accounted for by firms with headquarters located in the same province, and (4) the ratio of workers in advanced services sectors (mainly engineering services, R & D, consulting, and advertising) to the labor force in each province. The estimates showed that the wage rates and externalities all had significant positive influence on the adoption of the information technology. The author concluded that the regions most endowed with human and fixed capital and higher wages were more likely to search for new technologies and to adopt technological and organizational innovations and later exploit their advantages. Unfortunately, the author does not follow an appropriate process in deriving an operational form of equation, as there is no functional relation between his theoretical model and operational form. As a result, the simplified linear equation suffers from specification error. The omission of input factors in his empirical estimation may seriously bias his estimates.

The Census Bureau (1991) conducted a large scale survey on the adoption of seventeen advanced manufacturing technologies of more than 10,000 establishments in five major capital goods industries (SIC 34 through 38). The seventeen advanced technologies are used either for production (e.g., computer aided design, numerically controlled or computer numerically controlled machines, pick and place robots and other robots) or for management (e.g., local area network for technical data, local area network for factory use, and intercompany computer network linking plant to subcontractors, suppliers, and customers). Such manufacturing characteristics as establishment size, age of plant, manufacturing process, market orientation, and market price for major products were evaluated to reveal their impacts on the rates of adoption of the advanced technology. The descriptive statistical analysis of the survey data resulted in the following conclusions: most plants used at least one of the 17 advanced technologies; larger plants tend to adopt all the technologies more rapidly than smaller ones; establishments certified as suppliers for government and military customers used more advanced technologies; establishments whose market prices of major products exceed $10,000 per piece employed more advanced technologies; and older plants were likely to adopt computer control technology. These findings, however, are crude since this Census Bureau's study only employed simple frequency distributions without any statistical control and statistical tests.

In an early part of the current study, descriptive statistical methods are also used to take a first look at the relationship between a variety of technological inputs and companies characteristics as well as locational variables using textile-apparel and computer-electronics companies sample data. The statistical results to a large extent are consistent with the findings of earlier survey studies.

As a starting point of the current research, these earlier survey studies are informative and very interesting. Nevertheless, these findings are far from robust and systematic. This is not only because the data collected from earlier surveys are largely qualitative in nature (most questions in earlier surveys are answered by yes or no) but also because the methods analyzing the data are largely descriptive without controlling for the influence of other factors. Moreover, most earlier studies did not base their research on well established theory regarding factor inputs. Production theory suggests that investment decisions are primarily affected by producer internal factors, including the current levels of inputs and technology of production. Without inclusion of these important internal input variables, any estimated relationship between locational variables and technological input can be seriously biased. The current study is designed not only to build upon earlier findings, but also to overcome these weaknesses by using a more systematic approach based on production theory and a more advanced statistical method.

7.2. FACTOR INPUT DEMAND FUNCTIONS

Inputs in R & D and in adoption of advanced manufacturing technologies correspond to the demand of firms for new technologies to optimize production. The determinants of the technological inputs can be examined in a producer demand function frame. The part of the inputs related to an average company's practice can be considered as 'normal' inputs, while the other part of the inputs can be considered as 'induced inputs'--inputs related to companies' characteristics and regional environmental factors.

A demand function is derived from a production function. However, only when the production function is explicitly specified, can an explicit factor demand function be derived and estimated. Some assumption must be made in order to specify a production function. Given a well specified production function, a system of simultaneous equations of demand functions resulting from the first order condition of a producer optimization behavior may be solved. An alternative to the reduced form of the demand function is to estimate the structure form of the demand function(s) directly. In this case, with other endogenous variables present, two stage least square or other instrument variable methods should be used to develop consistent estimates[1]. Because this study examines the relationship between technology related inputs and internal / external influential factors, the structural form of the demand function is more appropriate than the reduced form. Arguably, not all producer inputs are strictly endogenous. This empirical study treats only a few technological inputs as endogenous. Four technological input demand functions, demand for capital input[2], demand for technical and professional employees, demand for R & D, and demand for other technology related inputs combined, are specified. Induced impact on the technological inputs of regional factors and other exogenous variables are estimated.

Christenson, Jorgenson, and Lau (1973) proposed that transcendental logarithmic production function (Translog) is the most general functional form that can provide a non-linear local fit to any production frontier. Both Cobb-Douglas (C-D) and constant elasticity of substitution (CES) production functions are special cases of the Translog production function. The Translog function requires the least economic and technical assumptions compared with other functional forms. More and more empirical studies employ this technique to examine input-output technological relationship. Nevertheless, few have ever mentioned any shortcomings of the Translog function in practice.

An empirical weakness of the Translog function results from a large number of quadratic and cross terms. For instance, if a production requires five different inputs, the Translog production function has five quadratic terms and ten cross terms in addition to the five individual input variables. In general, the number of variables in the function is $2K + K*(K-1)/2$ if K different inputs are included in a production function. Consequently, multicollinearity is almost an inevitable problem in an empirical research. In most earlier studies employing the Translog function, the shortcoming is not apparent since only two or three input variables are used. In this study, the model includes two labor inputs, two capital inputs, four variables for knowledge and skill embodied in labor input, one for technology embodied in capital, and five other technological inputs, not to mention many regional factors and producer attribute variables. The large number of additional quadratic and cross terms makes empirical estimates very unstable.

Another weakness or inconvenience of using the Translog in practice is that the individual parameter estimates of the function are not directly interpretable. Any meaningful economic or technical indicators (such as output elasticities) have to be further computed using several estimated parameters and sample data. For instance, to estimate output elasticity of capital, not only should the parameter estimate of capital be considered, but also parameters of all cross terms with capital as a factor must be included. The estimated output elasticity is a variable whose value is dependent on all other input variables appearing in the cross terms as factors.

This study pretested a Translog function with 5 inputs. The results show that (1) there appears severe collinearity due to inclusion of 15 quadratic and cross terms and (2) some parameter estimates of producer inputs have signs that conflict theory and common sense. The test also shows that elimination of these quadratic and cross terms, leading to Cobb-Douglas specification, results in much more reasonable parameter estimates. Based on the general argument and the particular test, a general C-D production function is adopted. Using the C-D production function form also makes this study comparable with the most relevant earlier research on firms' production (e.g., Griliches 1980, 1984 and 1986)[3].

A general C-D production function with regional factors and producer attributes can be written as

(7.1)
$$Q = A \prod_{i=1}^{k_1} X_i^{\beta_i} \prod_{j=1}^{k_2} R_j^{\alpha_j},$$

where Q is the output level, A the neutral technological efficiency, X_i the ith producer input, R_j the jth pure exogenous variable, and β_i and α_j are the output elasticities of input X_i and variable R_j respectively. A company's profit can be written as a standard form (7.2)

(7.2)
$$pQ - \sum_{i=1}^{k_1} W_i X_i,$$

where p is the price of the output, Q the output level, X_i and w_i the level and the price of the ith input respectively. The optimization behavior is characterized by maximizing profit and being subjected to production technology. The mathematic form can be written as (7.3)

(7.3)
$$\max_{X_1, X_2, \dots X_k} \left[pQ - \sum_{i=1}^{k_1} W_i X_i \right],$$

subject to
$$Q = A \prod_{i=1}^{k_1} X_i^{\beta_i} \prod_{j=1}^{k_2} R_j^{\alpha_j} .$$

The first order condition is

(7.4)
$$pA\beta_i X_i^{\beta_i-1} \prod_{k \neq i}^{k_1} X_k^{\beta_k} \prod_{j=1}^{k_2} R_j^{\alpha_j} - w_i = 0, \quad i = 1,2,3,\ldots$$

Instead of solving the demands as functions of a price vector alone, we can write the demand function for input X_i as equation (7.5)

(7.5)
$$X_i = \left[\frac{w_i}{pA\beta_i}\right]^{\frac{1}{\beta_i-1}} \left[\prod_{k \neq i}^{k_1} X_k^{\beta_k} \prod_{j=1}^{k_2} R_j^{\alpha_j}\right]^{\frac{1}{1-\beta_i}}, \quad i = 1,2,3,\ldots$$

The input demand functions are of a general C-D form. Taking logarithms on both sides yields log linear factor demand functions

(7.6)
$$LnX_i = \frac{1}{1-\beta_i} Ln(A\beta_i) + \frac{1}{1-\beta_i} Lnp + \frac{1}{\beta_i-1} Lnw_i + \sum_{k \neq i}^{k_1} \left[\frac{\beta_k}{1-\beta_i} LnX_k\right]$$
$$+ \sum_{j=1}^{k_2} \left[\frac{\alpha_j}{1-\beta_i} LnR_j\right], \quad i = 1,2,3,\ldots$$

The price of output cannot be meaningfully included in an empirical analysis because of the wide array of different products in each industry. As a result, the price of output becomes a part of the intercept in the econometric model. Notations in function (7.6) can be simplified so the function can be rewritten as

(7.7)
$$LnX_i = b_0 + b_1 Lnw_i + \sum_{k \neq i}^{k_1} b_k LnX_k + \sum_{j=1}^{k_2} a_j LnR_j, \quad i = 1,2,3,\ldots$$

where b_0, b_1, b_k, and a_j are, respectively, $(1/(1-\beta_i))Ln(A\beta_i) + (1/(1-$

β_i))Lnp, $1/(\beta_i-1)$, $\beta_k/(1-\beta_i)$, and $\alpha_j/(1-\beta_i)$. Since β_i, i$=1,2,3,...$, is positive and less than unity, it is expected that Lnw_i has a negative coefficient $(b_1 < 0)$, while LnX_k has a positive sign $(b_k > 0$, for $k=1,2,...$ and $k \neq i)$, meaning that input X_i is negatively related to its price and positively related to the levels of other producer inputs. The sign of a_j is unknown. If regional factor R_j is strictly substitutive for producer input X_i, a_j should have a negative sign. If the regional factor R_j is strictly complementary to X_i, a_j should be positive. Because many regional factors can be either substitutive for or complementary to producer inputs, the sign of a_j is a matter of an empirical test. Moreover, many regional factors may not be directly substitutable for or complementary to a specified input, but may influence production cost in general. Therefore, these regional factors can be considered as part of the determinants of the levels of producer inputs.

If all producer inputs X_k, $k \neq i$, in function (7.7) are considered as endogenous variables, equation (7.1) and (7.7) will constitute a large system of simultaneous equations. Consequently, estimation can involve technical difficulties and, especially, noise arising from substitution of instrument variables for the presumed endogenous variables will be inevitably overwhelming. In this study only four technology related variables, capital in equipment, technical and professional labor input, R & D input, and other technology related inputs, are used as endogenous variables in the demand functions. Other producer inputs (production workers and capital stock in buildings) are treated exogenously in the estimates.

To specify the input demand function, a researcher also must take embodied technologies into consideration. The embodied technologies may substitute for physical inputs or may stimulate more physical inputs. In either case, embodied technology can be considered as a set of distinctive determinants of technology related physical inputs.

Following earlier chapters modeling embodied technology, equipment input is conceptualized as capital jelly--capital with embodied technology, while labor input is labor 'jelly'--labor with embodied knowledge and skills. Therefore, capital and labor inputs are both expressed as inputs with embodied technologies. Using earlier developed empirical relationship between the weighted average age of capital and embodied technology and the relationship between the weighted years of schooling or experience of employees and embodied knowledge/ skill in labor, capital jelly and labor jelly can be written as

$$(7.8) \qquad J=a_0 e^{\lambda_J t} A^{-\alpha_k} K, \qquad M=r_0 e^{\lambda_L t} E_s^{\alpha_s} E_e^{\alpha_e} L \ .$$

Making substitution of the capital and labor jellies for capital and labor inputs and including the R & D input, D, and other technology related inputs, Z, in the production function results in a specific factor demand function for production capital comparable with (7.7) and numbered as (7.9),

$$(7.9) \qquad LnK=(b_0+b_J Lna_0+b_J \lambda_K t+b_M Lnr_0+b_M \lambda_L t)+b_1 Lnr_K-b_J \alpha_K LnA$$
$$+b_M LnL+b_M \alpha_s LnE_s+b_M \alpha a_e LnE_e+b_D LnD+b_Z LnZ+\sum_{j=1}^{k_2} a_j LnR_j \ ,$$
$$i=1,2,3,...$$

where the terms in parentheses cannot be individually estimated, and therefore, will be incorporated in the intercept; $-b_J\alpha_K LnA$, $b_M\alpha_s LnE_s$, and $b_M\alpha_e LnE_e$ are terms to estimate the effects on the demand for capital input of average age of equipment, average years of schooling, and the average years of experience respectively; $b_D LnD$ and $b_Z LnZ$ indicates the terms of the impacts on the demand for capital of R & D input and other technology related input (patent purchase, inputs in computer control device/system, machine upgrading, management system improvement, and worker training) respectively. Similarly, all other three demand functions can be derived with embodied technologies as independent variables.

7.3. DETERMINANTS OF PRODUCER TECHNOLOGY RELATED INPUTS

7.3.1. An Overview of the Estimates
Four demand functions of the same form as (7.9) are estimated for capital input in equipment, technical and professional labor input, R & D capital input, and input in adoption of advanced technologies using the 2SLS method. Definitions and measures of producer inputs,

company attributes, and regional variables are shown in Table 3.5, Table 4.1, and Table 5.1 respectively. The estimates of the four factor input demand functions are presented in Table 7.1, Table 7.2, Table 7.3, and Table 7.4. Since the dependent variable, K-TECH90, is the sum of five inputs (i.e., patent, computer and numerical control system, machine upgrading, management technology, and employee training) aiming at adoption of existing technologies, the function with K-TECH90 as the dependent variable is equivalent to a function of demand for adoption of advanced technology. As components of the combined dependent variable, the five input variables are no longer included in this function as right-hand-side variables. Those company characteristics and regional variables that make no contribution to explanatory power (i.e., whose inclusion lowers adjusted R squared) are dropped from the equations. However, all technology related variables, significant or not, are retained in the equations. The unequal treatment of the two types of variables is due to the fact that our understanding about the relationship between external factors and internal variables is rudimental and empirical, while our knowledge about producer internal input-output relationship is based on the well established production theory. Logically, the investigation into the relationship between internal and external factors is exploratory in nature, while the study on the relationship between internal variables is to further test the relationship quantitatively.

Several general findings can be addressed. First, the three groups of variables--producer inputs, company characteristics, and regional factors--all have significant estimates in the four technological inputs functions for both industry groups. Second, most producer inputs have either complemental or substitutive effect on technological inputs, but estimates appear mixed and deserve careful discussion. Third, each company characteristic or regional variable has different parameter estimates for the two industry groups and sometimes different signs. Fourth, regional factors can be roughly divided into two groups: (1) producer services (i.e., air transportation, transportation services other than air traffic, communication services, utilities, business services, engineering and management services other than R & D and testing, and R & D and testing services) and (2) consumer services/ quality of life/ amenity (i.e., recreation and amusement services, health services, education services, finance-insurance-real estate, and social services); the producer services seem to have greater impact on the demand for capital input and other technology related capital inputs than on the

Table 7.1 2SLS Estimates of Demand Functions for Capital and Technical/Professional Inputs
Textile-Apparel

Variable	K-UTLZ90 Estimate	K-UTLZ90 Std Err	P-EMP90 Estimate	P-EMP90 Std Err
INTERCEPT	-0.7462	1.8184	1.6612	1.2641
Conventional Inputs				
K-UTLZ90	------	------	0.1262**	0.0375
K-BD90	0.4747**	0.0661	-0.0128	0.0473
W-EMP90	0.1967	0.1299	0.5552**	0.0778
P-EMP90	0.3030**	0.0919	------	------
Embodied Technology/Knowledge				
K-AGE90	-0.4142**	0.1560	0.1073	0.1030
W-EDUC90	-0.3802	0.4531	0.0940	0.3104
W-EXP90	0.0787	0.1277	0.1750**	0.0847
P-EDUC90	1.3614	0.9436	-1.9817**	0.6331
P-EXP90	-0.0080	0.1278	-0.0759	0.0850
Physical Technological Inputs				
K-R&D90	0.0461	0.0334	0.0397*	0.0214
PATENT90	-0.0142	0.0519	0.0588*	0.0350
K-CC8590	-0.0020	0.0383	0.0567**	0.0241
K-MCN8590	0.0007	0.0360	-0.0266	0.0242
K-MNG8590	-0.0072	0.0468	0.0087	0.0313
K-TRN8590	0.0210	0.0524	0.0143	0.0379
Company Attributes				
APPAREL	-0.3230**	0.0725	------	------
PRIVATE	-0.2781	1.0941	-0.1332	0.7352
PUBLIC	-0.2617	1.2177	-0.1771	0.8089
HQ-STATE	0.1548	0.1025	-0.1796**	0.0672
HQ-US	0.1695**	0.0814	-0.2392**	0.0559
HQ-FRGN	------	------	0.2057	0.1943
AGE-CMPNY	-0.3019**	0.1094	------	------
BUYCRTF	------	------	------	------
SALECRTF	------	------	------	------
Regional Variables				
TXTLEW88	0.1783	0.3853	-0.6094**	0.2578
APPLW88	------	------	0.5823**	0.2469
R&DCRDT	-0.0929	0.0962	------	------
COLLEGE	------	------	------	------
METRO	------	------	------	------
POP86	-0.2841**	0.0778	-0.0735*	0.0428
URBANPOP	0.2021**	0.1018	------	------
TOTEMP88	------	------	-0.2458	0.2976
TOTEST88	------	------	0.4096	0.3200
TXTLEE88	0.1115**	0.0478	-0.0106	0.0306

Table 7.1 2SLS Estimates of Demand Functions for
Capital and Technical/Professional Inputs(Con.)
Textile-Apparel

Variable	K-UTLZ90		P-EMP90	
	Estimate	Std Err	Estimate	Std Err
Regional Variables (Con.)				
APPLE88	-0.1357*	0.0818	-0.0342	0.0596
AIR88	-0.0755	0.0777	------	------
TRNSVC88	0.1826*	0.1029	------	------
CMMNCT88	------	------	-0.0947	0.0936
UTILIT88	------	------	-0.0836	0.0631
ENGNRG88	------	------	------	------
R&DTSVC88	0.1338**	0.0678	0.0357	0.0418
BUSSVC88	0.2943**	0.1153	------	------
FIRE88	------	------	------	------
PCMINC85	0.3546**	0.1063	------	------
AMUSE88	------	------	------	------
HEALTH88	0.1502	0.1735	------	------
EDUCAT88	-0.2039**	0.0804	0.1027*	0.0583
SCLSVC88	------	------	------	------
PHYSIC85	------	------	------	------
HOSPIT85	------	------	-0.1175*	0.0608
R-square	0.6928		0.7181	
Adj R-Sq	0.6486		0.6775	

Note: * and ** indicate statistically significant at 90% and 95% levels respectively.

demand for technical and professional labor input. The estimates
provide evidence that the two industry groups have substantially
different production functions and technological inputs in the two
industry groups are respectively dependent on two sets of internal and
external factors.

7.3.2. Determinants of Technological Inputs
7.3.2.1. Conventional Inputs
          Production capital input is significantly related to technical and
professional input and R & D input for textile-apparel producers. To
be specific, textile-apparel companies with more capital in equipment
are more likely to hire more technical and professional employees and
conduct more R & D. In this survey, several respondents in the textile-
apparel industries explicitly described a joint mission of part of their
capital stock for production and R & D. This provides an alternative

Table 7.2 2SLS Estimates of Demand Functions for R & D and Other Technological Inputs
Textile-Apparel

Variable	K-R&D90 Estimate	Std Err	K-TECH90 Estimate	Std Err
INTERCEPT	-3.5770	2.4686	5.0843**	2.4087
Conventional Inputs				
K-UTLZ90	0.1681*	0.0976	0.1024	0.0734
K-BD90	0.0632	0.1236	0.2305**	0.0823
W-EMP90	-0.5273**	0.1936	0.3715**	0.1664
P-EMP90	0.2618*	0.1547	0.1167	0.1141
Embodied Technology/Knowledge				
K-AGE90	0.1729	0.2692	-0.7757**	0.1868
W-EDUC90	0.5393	0.7735	-0.4518	0.5357
W-EXP90	0.2000	0.2074	-0.0494	0.1717
P-EDUC90	1.1260	1.6964	-1.9686*	1.1420
P-EXP90	-0.2313	0.2246	0.4063**	0.1598
Physical Technological Inputs				
K-R&D90	------	------	0.1745**	0.0376
PATENT90	-0.0448	0.0903	------	------
K-CC8590	0.1354**	0.0614	------	------
K-MCN8590	0.1617**	0.0536	------	------
K-MNG8590	0.1972**	0.0748	------	------
K-TRN8590	0.1894**	0.0799	------	------
Company Attributes				
APPAREL	------	------	-0.3489**	0.0883
PRIVATE	------	------	-0.9755	1.5251
PUBLIC	------	------	------	------
HQ-CNTY	------	------	-0.0908	0.0896
HQ-STATE	------	------	------	------
HQ-US	-0.1669	0.1347	------	------
HQ-FRGN	------	------	------	------
AGE-CMPNY	------	------	0.0912	0.1391
BUYCRTF	------	------	------	------
SALECRTF	------	------	------	------
Regional Variables				
TXTLEW88	0.3074	0.6622	1.0411**	0.4926
APPLW88	-0.5081	0.6395	-0.7177	0.4665
R&DCRDT	0.6666**	0.1563	0.0815	0.1139
COLLEGE	1.0093*	0.5891	------	------
METRO	------	------	-0.3338**	0.1580
POP86	-0.1486	0.1167	0.2367**	0.0826
URBANPOP	-0.5162**	0.2135	------	------
TOTEMP88	0.2534	0.1792	-1.0805*	0.5713
TOTEST88	------	------	1.0320*	0.6263
TXTLEE88	-0.0986	0.0773	-0.2388	0.0586

**Table 7.2 2SLS Estimates of Demand Functions for
R & D and Other Technological Inputs(Con.)**
Textile-Apparel

	K-R&D90		K-TECH90	
Variable	Estimate	Std Err	Estimate	Std Err
Regional Variables (Con.)				
APPLE88	0.0291	0.1413	0.0328	0.1046
AIR88	------	------	------	------
TRNSVC88	-0.2246	0.1584	------	------
CMMNCT88	------	------	-0.3292*	0.1720
UTILIT88	------	------	0.2697**	0.1077
ENGNRG88	-0.2193	0.2735	------	------
RDTSVC88	------	------	-0.2398**	0.0850
BUSSVC88	-0.2604	0.2431	------	------
FIRE88	0.2781	0.3438	-0.1557	0.2842
PCMINC85	------	------	------	------
AMUSE88	------	------	------	------
HEALTH88	------	------	------	------
EDUCAT88	------	------	------	------
SCLSVC88	-0.7835**	0.2345	0.2607	0.1711
PHYSIC85	------	------	0.5283*	0.2715
HOSPIT85	-0.1488	0.1689	0.2326**	0.1121
R-square	0.4135		0.6487	
Adj R-Sq	0.3399		0.5998	

Note: * and ** indicate statistically significant at 90% and 95% levels respectively.

explanation for the estimated positive relationship between production capital and R & D input: value of R & D input is proportionally related to the value of production equipment. Conceptually, one would expect a complemental effect of production capital on most other producer inputs. Empirically, production capital and most other inputs can all partially measure scale of production in the same direction. In any sense, a positive relationship between producer inputs is consistent with expectation. The insignificant estimate of production capital in K-TECH90 demand function, however, indicates the difference between inputs in adoption of existing technologies and other inputs. The value of K-TECH90 in textile-apparel production is dependent on other factors that will be discussed shortly.

**Table 7.3 2SLS Estimates of Demand Functions for
Capital and Technical/Professional Inputs**
Computer-Electronics

Variable	K-UTLZ90		P-EMP90	
	Estimate	Std Err	Estimate	Std Err
INTERCEPT	-0.3251	1.8466	-1.9447**	0.9919
Conventional Inputs				
K-UTLZ90	------	------	0.0149	0.0321
K-BD90	-0.0457	0.1014	0.1435**	0.0473
W-EMP90	0.7327*	0.1134	0.3040**	0.0621
P-EMP90	0.0511	0.1395	------	------
Embodied Technology/Knowledge				
K-AGE90	-0.4964**	0.2154	0.0222	0.1074
W-EDUC90	-0.6445	0.3754	-0.2124	0.1774
W-EXP90	-0.1567	0.1892	0.1916**	0.0903
P-EDUC90	0.0930	0.7980	0.4362	0.3898
P-EXP90	0.0037	0.2174	-0.1836*	0.1048
Physical Technological Inputs				
K-R&D90	0.0464	0.0388	0.0190	0.0186
PATENT90	-0.0457	0.0535	-0.0214	0.0263
K-CC8590	-0.0572	0.0474	0.0283	0.0229
K-MCN8590	-0.0141	0.0462	-0.0200	0.0223
K-MNG8590	0.0588	0.0587	0.0694**	0.0279
K-TRN8590	0.0025	0.0701	0.0712**	0.0350
Company Attributes				
ELECTRON	------	------	-0.1062**	0.0469
PRIVATE	------	------	------	------
PUBLIC	0.1684*	0.1013	0.1412**	0.0484
HQ-STATE	-0.5301**	0.1790	-0.1535*	0.0861
HQ-FRGN	-0.3009	0.2500	------	------
BATCH	-0.2978**	0.0862	------	------
STANDARD	------	------	-0.0963**	0.0483
AGE-CMPNY	------	------	------	------
BUYCRTF	------	------	------	------
SALECRTF	------	------	------	------
Regional Variables				
CMPTRW88	0.6284	0.6615	-0.1333	0.3261
ELECW88	------	------	-0.0645	0.3352
R&DCRDT	------	------	------	------
COLLEGE	------	------	-0.4881**	0.2214
METRO	------	------	------	------
POP86	------	------	------	------
URBANPOP	-1.0191*	0.6135	0.5090	0.3206
TOTEMP88	1.5623**	0.6922	------	------
TOTEST88	-1.6407**	0.7792	------	------

Table 7.3 2SLS Estimates of Demand Functions for Capital and Technical/Professional Inputs(Con.)
Computer-Electronics

Variable	K-UTLZ90 Estimate	Std Err	P-EMP90 Estimate	Std Err
Regional Variables (Con.)				
CMPTRE88	------	------	0.0595*	0.0350
ELECE88	------	------	-0.0200	0.0526
AIR88	------	------	-0.0521	0.0526
TRNSVC88	0.3702*	0.2200	------	------
CMMNCT88	------	------	-0.0762	0.1077
UTILIT88	------	------	-0.1002	0.0978
ENGNRG88	-0.4921	0.3389	------	------
RDTSVC88	------	------	0.0691	0.0558
BUSSVC88	0.4136	0.3975	0.2499	0.1757
FIRE88	0.6091	0.4448	------	------
PCMINC85	------	------	------	------
AMUSE88	------	------	------	------
HEALTH88	------	------	0.4633**	0.2121
EDUCAT88	-0.3368**	0.1583	------	------
SCLSVC88	0.3489	0.3131	------	------
PHYSIC85	------	------	-0.2732**	0.1167
HOSPIT85	0.0595	0.0802	------	------
R-square	0.5641		0.7839	
Adj R-Sq	0.4911		0.7463	

Note: * and ** indicate statistically significant at 90% and 95% levels respectively.

In contrast, technical and professional labor input and R & D input are not dependent on production capital in computer-electronics, but inputs in adoption of advanced technologies is positively related to production capital. The findings suggest that R & D capital and technical and professional personnel are designated to innovation and separated from routine production outlay in the computer-electronics industries. Therefore, the level of production capital input has no influence on technical and professional labor input and R & D capital input. Unlike textile-apparel companies, computer-electronics producers invested significantly more in computer and numerical control systems, management systems, and machine upgrading as more input was committed in production.

Capital in structures is estimated to be complemental to capital in equipment and to inputs in adoption of advanced technologies in textile-apparel industry groups. The positive relationship between

Table 7.4 2SLS Estimates of Demand Functions for R & D and Other Technological Inputs
Computer-Electronics

Variable	K-R&D90		K-TECH90	
	Estimate	Std Err	Estimate	Std Err
INTERCEPT	-2.1238	2.9298	2.2885	1.8029
Conventional Inputs				
K-UTLZ90	0.1066	0.1136	0.1443**	0.0682
K-BD90	-0.2987*	0.1716	-0.0302	0.0994
W-EMP90	-0.1136	0.2217	0.1813	0.1307
P-EMP90	0.1065	0.2321	0.2045	0.1416
Embodied Technology/Knowledge				
K-AGE90	0.7115*	0.3707	-0.8045**	0.2219
W-EDUC90	-0.0633	0.6226	-0.6905*	0.3736
W-EXP90	0.2309	0.3203	0.0860	0.1923
P-EDUC90	1.4527	1.3576	-1.3789*	0.8109
P-EXP90	-0.8360**	0.3638	0.2424	0.2225
Physical Technological Inputs				
K-R&D90	------	------	0.2034**	0.0359
PATENT90	0.2542**	0.9162	------	------
K-CC8590	0.2881**	0.7804	------	------
K-MCN8590	0.1647**	0.7783	------	------
K-MNG8590	0.1015	0.9966	------	------
K-TRN8590	0.1210	0.8987	------	------
Company Attributes				
ELECTRON	-0.3225*	0.1650	0.2500**	0.0982
PRIVATE	-0.2077	0.1645	-0.1150	0.0933
PUBLIC	------	------	------	------
HQ-CNTY	0.2463	0.1768	------	------
HQ-STATE	------	------	0.2356	0.1819
BATCH	0.2171	0.1509	------	------
STANDARD	0.1698	0.1674	------	------
AGE-CMPNY	------	------	0.3589**	0.1576
BUYCRTF	------	------	------	------
SALECRTF	------	------	------	------
Regional Variables				
CMPTRW88	------	------	1.3073*	0.7031
ELECW88	------	------	------	------
R&DCRDT	0.5115**	0.1943	------	------
COLLEGE	------	------	------	------
METRO	------	------	------	------
POP86	0.1144	0.7458	-0.3217**	0.0995
URBANPOP	------	------	------	------
TOTEMP88	------	------	------	------
TOTEST88	------	------	------	------

**Table 7.4 2SLS Estimates of Demand Functions for
R & D and Other Technological Inputs(Con.)**
Computer-Electronics

Variable	K-R&D90		K-TECH90	
	Estimate	Std Err	Estimate	Std Err
Regional Variables (Con.)				
CMPTRE88	------	------	-0.1332*	0.0736
ELECE88	------	------	------	------
AIR88	-0.3647*	0.1905	0.3464**	0.1166
TRNSVC88	0.8637**	0.3309	------	------
CMMNCT88	------	------	------	------
UTILIT88	-0.4284	0.3181	0.2556	0.2007
ENGNRG88	------	------	------	------
RDTSVC88	------	------	0.0684	0.1135
BUSSVC88	------	------	0.8750**	0.2762
FIRE88	------	------	-1.4300**	0.4264
PCMINC85	------	------	0.3297**	0.1381
AMUSE88	------	------	------	------
HEALTH88	------	------	------	------
EDUCAT88	-0.2860	0.2491	------	------
SCLSVC88	-0.5905	0.5107	------	------
PHYSIC85	0.4646	0.3703	------	------
HOSPIT85	------	------	------	------
R-square	0.4274		0.5495	
Adj R-Sq	0.3276		0.4855	

Note: * and ** indicate statistically significant at 90% and 95% levels respectively.

structure and equipment is expected: machines need buildings to be
deployed. Adoption of advanced technologies, including computer and
numerical control production, machine upgrading, and management
system improvement, usually results in rerouting production. Large or
modern structures are more likely to furnish the advanced technologies
with required space. On the other hand, the insignificant estimates of
K-BD90 in P-EMP90 and K-R&D90 functions suggest that technical
and professional employees and R & D facilities do not require more
input in structures to be accommodated.

The estimates for computer-electronics companies show a very
different picture: structure is empirically irrelevant to inputs in
equipment and adoption of advanced technologies. The two insignificant
estimates indicate that capital in structure is neither necessarily
complemental to nor strongly substitutive for capital in equipment. In
other words, routine production in computer-electronics does not

require inputs in equipment and structure proportional to each other. This can happen only if production equipment is not standardized among the producers. The findings may reflect a constant change in product and process technologies in this very dynamic industry group. The input in structure is significant in another two input functions. The value of structure is positively related to technical and professional labor input: companies with more or better buildings hire more technical and professional employees. Regardless of causal direction, the positive sign is reasonable. However, the structure is negatively related to R & D input: companies with more or better buildings have less R & D capital. This negative estimate implies that companies with large amounts of fixed input in structures tend to be production, not R & D, oriented. Moreover, the two significant estimates imply that a majority of technical and professional employees are involved in production but, surprisingly, not R & D. Since this industry group is characterized by intensive technical and professional labor input, the estimates further suggest that in this industry group production itself needs constant modification and improvement which require sophisticated labor input.

Parameter estimates of production worker input is significant in three of the four demand functions for textile-apparel. Production worker input is positively related to technical and professional input and inputs in adoption of advanced technologies. This confirms an expected complemental effect of labor input to the other two inputs: to utilize production workers efficiently, the textile-apparel companies with large production worker input rely on additional technical and professional personnel and adoption of advanced technology. The estimate of production worker input in the R & D input function is negative: companies with more production workers are less likely to conduct R & D. The estimate of production worker input is significant and positive in the K-TECH90 function for textile-apparel: companies with more production workers invest more in adoption of advanced technologies. Because R & D aims at invention and innovation and K-TECH90 is a combination of adoption of existing product and process technologies, the findings imply that the more labor intensive the textile-apparel companies, the more likely the companies are to be recipients of advanced technologies and the less likely the companies are to be inventors or innovators.

In the computer-electronics industries, the level of labor input is positively associated with input in equipment and with technical and professional labor input, but not related to R & D and adoption of existing technologies. The two significant estimates suggest a complemental role production workers play: for a one percent increase in production worker labor input, a typical computer-electronics producer would increase production equipment by 0.7327 percent and technical-professional labor input by 0.1435 percent. On the other hand, production worker input is not proportionally related to R & D and adoption of technologies: computer-electronics companies with large production labor input are not necessarily the major R & D players or adopters of existing technologies. This may add a vivid piece to the dynamic picture of the industry group: many smaller computer-electronics companies are busy in developing, adopting, and testing many different new technologies, while some larger manufacturers hire many production workers to assemble final products.

The influence of technical and professional employees on other inputs appears to be very different in the two industry groups. In the textile-apparel industries, technical and professional input is complemental to production equipment input and R & D input: the more technical/ professional employees a company hires, the more likely the company is to conduct R & D. The insignificant estimate of technical and professional input in the input function for adoption of advanced technology can reflect a combined effect of complementarity and substitutability between the input of professionals and adoption of new technologies in the textile-apparel industries.

The technical and professional input is insignificant in all the input demand functions for the computer-electronics industries. Apparently, technical and professional input needs not to be proportional to other technological inputs in this industry group. Thus, technical and professional input in computer-electronics is relatively independent from other inputs, or this input is not only complementary to other technological inputs but also substitutable for other technological inputs. Compared with the textile-apparel industry group, the computer-electronics group has a more complex underlying production function in which producer inputs are less likely to be simply complemental to or substitutive for each other.

7.3.2.2. Embodied Technologies

Technology embodied in production capital, measured by the weighted average age of utilized equipment in 1990, is significantly related to equipment input and inputs in adoption of advanced technologies for both industry groups. Statistically, a one percent reduction in average age of equipment is related to a 0.4142 percent increase in equipment input and a 0.7757 percent increase in adoption of advanced technologies for a typical textile-apparel company and a 0.4964 percent increase in equipment and a 0.8045 increase in adoption of technologies for a typical computer-electronics company. These estimates appear to confirm a strong complementarity, stressed by Nelson (1964), of embodied technologies and physical capital input. Apparently, companies with newer equipment enjoy higher return to capital; this in turn results in more input in equipment. Embodied technologies also lead companies to adopt more advanced technologies. The interaction of embodied technologies and physical input is likely to make advanced producers even more competitive, which is bad news for companies with older production capital. On the other hand, average age of capital is positively related to R & D input in computer-electronics. The positive estimate suggests that computer-electronics companies with older production capital are more likely to be R & D, not production, oriented.

Knowledge and skills embodied in labor input are estimated to be partially responsible for the variation in the level of other technology related inputs. However, the empirical findings are mixed.

Educational attainment of production workers is significant only for computer-electronics companies. The negative estimate signifies a substitution of education of production workers for input in employee training, which is part of integrated measure of adoption of technologies, and any other production process related technological inputs. Therefore, educational attainment of production workers is an indirect contributor to production and productivity growth of the computer-electronics industries, although, as estimated in production and productivity growth equations, this factor is not a direct contributor to production and productivity growth. Experience of production workers is positively associated with technical and professional labor input in both industry groups: companies with a more experienced work force usually have more technical and professional employees. Consequently, these companies can reinforce their advantage of advanced human capital stock. Like educational attainment, experience of production workers is not a significant direct contributor to production and productivity growth, but the skills carried by production workers may indirectly contribute to production and productivity growth.

Educational attainment of technical and professional employees is significantly and negatively related to technical and professional input of textile-apparel companies, signifying a strong substitution effect of the embodied knowledge for the physical units of professional labor input. Educational attainment of technical and professional employees is also negatively associated with adoption of advanced technologies in both industry groups, a substitution effect between knowledge of technical/professionals and investment in adoption of new technologies. Professional experience in computer-electronics is estimated to be substitutable for technical and professional personnel input and R & D capital: companies with more experienced professional crews hire fewer technical and professionals and spend less in R & D capital, other things being equal. Although professional experience is not a direct contributor to production and productivity growth for computer-electronics companies (see chapter 5), this same factor appears to contribute indirectly to production and productivity growth. In contrast, in the textile-apparel industries experience of technical and professional employees is positively related to inputs in adoption of advanced technologies--experienced professionals encourage the adoption of the advanced technologies in the textile-apparel industries.

In short, embodied technologies, knowledge, and skills are more or less related to producer technological inputs. Some factors appear to be indirect contributors to production and productivity growth, because they can partly influence the inputs that contribute directly to production and productivity growth of the two industry groups.

7.3.2.3. Technology Related Physical Inputs

R & D is significant in two K-TECH90 functions, while several components of K-TECH90, i.e., PATENT90, K-CC8590, K-MCN8590, K-MNG8590, and K-TRN8590, are significant in at least one R & D input function. This indicates that R & D activities require other technological inputs to be effective and vice versa. Evidently, a company either does all or does nothing in developing and pursuing advanced technologies.

Although R & D and K-TECH90 are complementary to each other, the components in adoption of advanced technologies in the two industry groups are different. Patent purchase is a significant factor for computer-electronics companies but not for textile-apparel. The estimates suggest that patents in the textile-apparel industries can be directly used in production without additional input in R & D to digest or modify the technologies. In the computer-electronics industries, however, the more patents purchased or licensed, the more R & D input is induced to digest or further advance the technologies. On the other hand, inputs in management systems and employee training tend to induce R & D input in textile-apparel group but not in computer-electronics. Textile-apparel companies that make efforts to improve management and employee skills are likely to see the importance of R & D and conduct more R & D at the same time.

R & D capital is also positively related to technical and professional input in the textile-apparel group. One would expect such a positive relationship if technical and professional employees are largely devoted to R & D activities. It is interesting that only textile-apparel companies hire technical and professional employees proportional to R & D input. The insignificant estimate for the computer-electronics group implies a different story: R & D activities in this group are more heterogeneous and do not need proportional technical and professional labor input.

Inputs in computer and numerical control technology and in machine upgrading have positive estimates in R & D input functions for both industry groups. Together with the significant positive estimate of R & D input in the adoption of advanced technologies, the findings suggest that companies that make any type of technological inputs are well aware of the benefit of advanced technologies adopted from outside or developed in-house. The findings confirm and extend the conceptual argument made in an earlier research that the adoption of technology rarely takes place in isolation from other changes (Dewar 1988). One would expect that the technologically advanced companies will gain further competitive edge and the technologically less active companies will either catch up with the technological leaders by involving in a wide scope of technological activities or give up their market position completely.

7.3.2.4. Company' Characteristics
Ownership, headquarters location, age of company, state and local R & D credit policies, mode of production, and certification practice are all statistically significant in at least one of the input demand functions. However, the estimates are mixed.

Ownership is a significant characteristic in the computer-electronics industries but not in the textile-apparel industries: public corporations in computer-electronics industries (PUBLIC) have larger capital stock and hire more technical and professional employees. Companies with headquarters located in a different county tend to hire fewer technical and professional employees, signifying the nature of standardized production carried out in branch companies. Moreover, the estimates also show that textile-apparel companies with headquarters in a different state (HQ-US) have larger capital stock, while computer-electronics companies with headquarters in a different county (HQ-STATE) have smaller capital stock. These estimates reflect different natures of standardized production technologies in the two industry groups. As sample statistics show (chapter 3), the average age of equipment of computer-electronics makers is 8.2 years as opposed to 10.8 years of textile-apparel companies. Obviously, stable production technologies in textile-apparel allow heavy inputs in standardized production without causing a rapid depreciation and technological obsolescence. On the other hand, constantly changing product and process technologies in the computer-electronics industries lead branch companies to instal production equipment which only meets current needs and can be replaced in the near future with more advanced technologies.

As expected, different modes of operation require different combinations of inputs. Computer-electronics companies conducting batch production have significantly smaller capital stock, while companies carrying out standardized mass production have significantly fewer technical and professional employees.

Statistically, the age of companies makes a difference in production capital input in the textile-apparel industries: new textile-apparel plants are more capital intensive and, consequently, more technologically advanced, allowing them to take advantage of embodied technologies and avoid the comparative disadvantage of higher labor cost. The age of computer-electronics companies, on the other hand, is positively related to adoption of advanced technologies. This finding is consistent with earlier research (e.g., Rees et al 1986).

Textile-apparel companies that are certified suppliers have larger R & D capital stock. The mode of the transaction and the requirement for the quality and the reliability of products may explain the larger R & D input of certified producers. The market for the product of certified suppliers is less uncertain and the quality and reliability of the certified products must be high. These incentives and requirements both make certified suppliers commit more R & D input to improve their products. The insignificant estimate for the computer-electronics group indicates that companies make R & D input according to conditions other than product certification.

The two subgroups in each industry group show notable differences in technological inputs. Compared with textile companies, apparel companies invest less in production capital and in adoption of advanced technologies. Because most components in the aggregate measure, K-TECH90, are associated with process technologies and because most textile mills conduct mass production, the estimates imply that the adoption of advanced process technologies is more important to large volume production than to batch production. There also exists notable differences between computer and electronics producers: relative to computer companies, electronics components producers can be characterized by fewer professional employees, less R & D capital outlay, but more input in adoption of advanced technologies. Electronics components companies employ more outside technological sources to conduct standardized mass production, while computer companies depend more on their own innovation to produce numerous varieties of new products. The findings support the argument that technological competition in the computer industry is more intensive than in electronics and that the rate of technological obsolescence in the computer industry is higher than in electronics.

7.3.2.5. Regional Factors

Because of the diverse influences of individual regional factors on technological inputs, it is useful to estimate a combined effect of regional contextual variables on the technology related inputs. Since the parameter estimates measure the elasticities of technological inputs with respect to exogenous variables, the sum of the parameter estimates of regional factors which are statistically significant is an indicator of the combined effect. The estimates of overall influence of the significant regional factors on each of the four industries are reported in Table 7.5[4]. The summarized estimates show the percentage changes in the four technological inputs that can be expected for a one percent increase in all significant regional factors. The findings are highlighted as follows.

**Table 7.5   Overall Influence of Regional Factors on
Technology Related Inputs**

Tech. Input	Textile	Apparel	Computer	Electronics
K-UTLZ90	0.5328	0.2856	-1.0641	-1.0641
P-EMP90	-0.6977	0.4940	-0.2385	-0.2980
K-R&D90	-0.2904	-0.2904	0.5000	0.5000
K-TECH90	1.3571	0.3160	0.9735	-0.2006

First, production capital inputs in the computer-electronics group are negatively elastic with respect to regional factors-- regional factors are substitutable for capital input. Second, inputs in adoption of existing technologies (K-TECH90) in the textile industry is positively elastic--regional factors have complemental influences on textile mills' inputs. Third, all other technological inputs in all the four industries tend to be inelastic with respect to regional environment. A careful comparison reveals that regional factors together tend to be complemental to production capital and substitutive for R & D input in textile-apparel, but the pattern for computer-electronics is reversed: complemental to R & D and substitutive for production capital. These estimates convey the message that as a regional economy grows, computer-electronics companies are likely to be more R & D intensive and, consequently, more innovation oriented, while textile-apparel manufacturers tend to focus more on standardized production.

There are many statistically significant estimates of regional variables, but the impact of each regional variable varies across the input demand functions and across the industries. Therefore, a detailed discussion on each significant regional variable is presented.

Textile-Apparel Industry Group

Factor cost measured by the wage rates is significant in the professional input function. Consistent with production theory, the estimate of the wage rate in textile has a negative sign--a higher labor cost leads to a lower level of labor input. However, the estimate of the wage rate in the apparel industry has a positive sign, contradicting the standard production theory. The positive estimate of the wage rate in the apparel industry can be interpreted only by the efficiency wage theory. As Katz (1986) proposed, the productivity of workers is a positive function of the wage rate; profit maximizing behavior may result in wage payments above market clearing levels so as to increase productivity by reducing turnover, shirking, adverse selection, or to increase worker morale. The two estimates of wage rates indicate a difference between the two industries' technical and professional labor markets: the competition for qualified technical and professional employees in the apparel industry is more intensive than that in the textile industry.

A cross substitution between technical-professional input and adoption of advanced technologies is observed in the sample data, but only for textile: local wage rates in the textile industry are positively related to input levels of adoption of advanced technologies (K-TECH90). Textile companies located in areas with high textile wage rates almost certainly spend more on adoption of advanced technologies, including patent purchase, computer and numerical control, machine upgrading, management improvement, and employee training. Statistically, a one percent increase in textile wage rate is related to a 1.0411 percent increase in input in adoption of advanced technologies.

State and local R & D credit policy is significantly and positively related to R & D input. However, the estimates alone cannot tell us the efficiency and social cost-benefit of the resource reallocation induced by the credit policies. Since the credit policies do not show up as a significant factor in technological efficiency equations (TFP, neutral technological progress, and economies of scale), one may be skeptical about the desirability of the government intervention into market activities. More investigation on social cost-benefit of the policies are required to fully justify the policy device.

Accessibility to qualified labor, measured by percent of labor force with a college degree, is estimated to be complemental to R & D input in textile-apparel. Textile-apparel companies located in areas with more college graduates are willing to do more in R & D, taking the advantage of the readily available human resource.

Population size has mixed effects on technological inputs. The estimate is negative in capital input and technical-professional input functions, positive in the K-TECH90 function, and is not significant in the R & D input function for the textile-apparel group. It can be inferred that textile-apparel companies in large metro areas tend to be faced with intensive competition for resources and higher prices for the resources. As a result, these companies are likely to make less investment in production capital and hire fewer employees. On the other hand, many producers who cluster in large areas exert a demonstration effect in applying advanced technology, resulting in more input in adoption of advanced technologies.

To be comparable with earlier research (e.g., Moomaw 1985), two additional variables are used to measure agglomeration economies: urbanization and localization economies, with the former measured by urban population percentage and the latter by industry percentage of total area employment. In this study textile and apparel industries' percentages are measured separately, and the variables are arranged such that each variable can only affect the observations which belong to its industry. The variables measuring urbanization and localization also have mixed relationships with technological inputs. For textile-apparel, the urbanization variable is positively related to capital input and negatively related to R & D input. According to the estimates, urbanization economies can foster the scale of production by inducing more production capital and, in the meantime, urbanization discourages private R & D activities probably due to the spillover effect. Notably, in empirical studies all agglomeration variables are composite and relatively vague measures which can pick up in a densely crowded area everything not explained by other clearly specified factors. Therefore, one should not put too much faith in the estimates of these mass variables.

The parameter estimate of localization economies differs between textile and apparel: localization stimulates capital input in textile but discourages capital input in apparel. The opposite impacts of localization economies on textile and apparel industries seem to be strange, but this is consistent with the estimates of impacts of the wage rates on the two industries. The positive estimate of the size of the textile industry and the negative estimate of the size of the apparel industry reinforce the discussion on the different labor markets for the two industries. The factor input (including technical and professional input) markets for the apparel industry are likely to be subject to more competition than that for the textile industry. The positive effect of externalities is outweighed by the negative effect of increasing costs in the apparel industry. As a result, capital outlays of individual apparel companies are lower in the areas with a large apparel industry.

Producer services are influential factors to capital input and adoption of advanced technologies in the textile-apparel industries. The levels of transportation services, business services, and R & D and testing services are significant variables in the capital input function (K-UTLZ90). These estimates suggest that the producer services are complemental to internal capital input and that better regional producer services induce production capital input. In the K-TECH90 function (i.e., adoption of advanced technologies) the utilities services sector has a positive estimate and the communication and the R & D and testing services sectors have negative estimates for textile-apparel producers. The positive estimate of utilities services is consistent with the expectation of complemental input, while the negative estimates of communication and R & D and testing services seem puzzling. The negative relationships may be interpreted as substitution of external technology for internal input. Better communication services and better R & D and testing services present more opportunities to explore technological externalities generated by other economic agents. As a result, textile-apparel companies that are near these services need not spend as much as companies located elsewhere.

Consumer services and quality of life/amenity measured by per capita money income, health services, education services, and social services are significant in at least one of the input demand functions for textile-apparel. Companies in the areas with high per capita income generally have larger production capital stock. Better education services appear to lead to less capital input but more technical and professional labor input. These estimates indicate that better education services may frequently improve the quality of employees and reduce the demand for capital input, probably due to the substitution of external improvement of employees for capital. More hospitals tend to result in fewer technical and professional employees for an average company. This can be considered as another substitution of improvement of quality of employees for the quantity of the same type of input, assuming that high levels of services contributes to the health and quality of employees. Hospital services also increase input in adoption of advanced technologies. Since better hospital services have a substitution effect for technical and professional labor input, the positive relationship between hospital services and adoption of technologies may be considered as technological activities induced by improved quality of employees. The social services sector is negatively associated with R & D input. There can be at least two different interpretations. The size of social services may be associated with social problems which in turn discourage R & D investment in the same area. On the other hand, one may believe that large social service sectors are found in large areas and, consequently, this variable serves as a proxy of area size. In relatively large areas there are many other investment opportunities competing with the textile-apparel industries, leading to a lower R & D input in textile-apparel. A simple correlation analysis indicated that social services sector is closely related to college graduate percentage, per capita money income, urban population percentage, and area total employment. Furthermore, estimates of population size and urban population percentage are all negative in the same equation. Based on these evidences, the second interpretation may be more appropriate.

Computer-Electronics Industry Group

In contrast with textile-apparel companies, technical and professional input in computer-electronics are not affected by wage rates. Computer-electronics producers are not as sensitive to this factor cost as textile-apparel companies.

A cross substitution between technical-professional input and adoption of advanced technologies is also observed in the computer subgroup: local wage rates in the computer industry are positively related to input in adoption of advanced technologies (K-TECH90). A one percent increase in the computer industry wage rate is related to a 1.3073 percent increase in spending on patent purchase, computer and numerical control, machine upgrading, management improvement, and employee training.

State and local R & D investment credit policy is also significantly and positively related to R & D input. Again, due to the redistribution of social wealth, a comprehensive cost-benefit analysis is required to justify implementation or any expansion of the local policy.

Unlike the estimate for textile-apparel companies, the estimate of accessibility to qualified labor, measured by percent of labor force with a college degree, is negative in the technical and professional input function for the computer-electronics group. The reason may be the substitution of available external sources of consulting and related services for internal technical personnel input.

Area population is negatively related to input level of adoption of advanced technologies (K-TECH90). Unlike the estimate for textile-apparel producers, the significant negative estimate suggests that computer-electronics companies in small areas are likely to be production oriented rather than innovation oriented. Therefore, they tend to spend more on adoption of existing technologies than their counterparts in large areas.

Urban population percentage is negatively related to production capital. The estimate suggests that computer-electronics companies in highly urbanized areas are either smaller or not production oriented. The estimates for the localization variable, the size of the computer industry in an area, also show that computer companies in areas with a large computer industrial sector hire more technical and professional employees (P-EMP90), but spend less in adoption of technologies (K-TECH90). Obviously, strong local computer-electronics industries and spatial concentration of inventors and innovators in the industries are mutually causally related to each other. The negative estimate of localization in the K-TECH90 input function supports the inference that intensive competition in the computer industry leads companies to rely more on their own innovation than on adoption of outside technologies.

Regional producer services are estimated to have influence on technological inputs in the computer-electronics industries. The transportation services sector has significant estimates in the capital input function (K-UTLZ90) and R & D input. Because transportation services are more like necessary inputs in production than facilitators of technological diffusion, the more these services are readily available, the more efficient the internal technological inputs and, as a result, the more production capital and R & D input are induced. Air transportation is negatively related to R & D input and positively related to adoption of advanced technologies. If a positive estimate is considered to reflect a complementary effect and a negative estimate is a substitute, the estimates indicate that air transportation is a substitute for internal R & D input and a complemental factor to adoption of advanced technologies. Because air transportation service itself is not a R & D agent and because air transportation can effectively help a company to reach outside markets, the air transportation sector is likely to play a surrogate role of capturing technological externalities generated by economic agents elsewhere. Meanwhile, the expanded technological externalities due to the air transportation services induces computer-electronics companies to input more in computer and numerical control system, in management, in machine upgrading, in employee training, and etc. The positive relationship between air transportation and input in adoption of technologies also suggests that companies in the areas with higher levels of air transportation services are more likely to be production oriented than innovation oriented, because most components in the composite measure, K-TECH90, are used in production not in R & D.

Business services (BUSSVC88) are estimated to be complemental to adoption of advanced technologies. Companies in

areas with larger business services sectors have spent more in adoption
of existing technologies, because sufficient business services make
adopted technologies more effective.

Finance-insurance-real estate services (FIRE88) was expected
to be a facilitator of producer internal inputs. However, the estimate is
negative. Conceptually, this service sector cannot substitute for
producer inputs in adoption of advanced technologies. A further
investigation reveals a negative relationship between the size of this
service sector and the size of computer-electronics companies,
measured by value added and production worker. This suggests that
companies in areas with larger finance-insurance-real estate sectors are
smaller in manufacturing.

Consumer services and quality of life/amenity variables are
significant for the computer-electronics industries. Computer-electronics
companies in high income areas spend more on adoption of advanced
technologies. Similar to the estimate in the textile-apparel group, better
education services empirically lead to less capital input in the computer-
electronics industries, a possible substitute of external improvement of
employees for the internal capital input. Unlike in the textile-apparel
industries, the number of hospitals has insignificant estimates in the
computer-electronics group. However, number of physicians is
negatively related to technical and professional labor input, a
substitution of improvement of labor quality for the quantity of the
labor input.

In short, regional factors have significant influences on the
technology related inputs for both industry groups. The impacts of the
regional factors on the technological inputs are considered as induced
inputs, an indirect contribution to production and productivity growth.

7.4. SUMMARY AND CONCLUSION

After a detailed discussion of the estimates, a summary helps
to highlight the most important findings. The variables in the demand
functions have been roughly divided into several groups: producer
conventional inputs, embodied technologies, technology related physical
inputs, producer characteristics, agglomeration economies and
externalities, producer services, and consumer services/ quality of life/
amenities. According to the estimates, each group can more or less

influence the level of the technological inputs of both industry groups.

Producer conventional inputs are largely complemental to the technology related inputs, except that production worker input is negatively related to R & D input of textile-apparel companies. Technology related physical inputs are complemental to each other if the estimates are significant. The embodied technologies have fairly consistent substitution effect on the demand of technology related inputs, although in one or two occasions unexpected estimates have been found. These findings suggest that: (1) companies with heavier outlays on conventional inputs demand more inputs in new technologies either developed in-house or purchased from outside; (2) all types of technology-related activities, R & D, or adoption of technologies, are positively related to each other--once a producer makes one technological input (technical and professional labor input, R & D, or adoption of advanced technologies), the producer is likely also to make all other types of technological inputs (especially in the textile-apparel industries); and (3) quality of conventional inputs directly affects efficiency of production, resulting in a difference in demand for the quantity of physical inputs.

The influence of producer characteristics on the demand for technological inputs varies widely across different characteristics, different demand functions, and different industries. There are no general patterns.

Regional contextual factors as a whole influence producer internal technological inputs. Some variables do not show a statistically significant relationship with producer technological inputs. This indicates that some regional factors can play a role more complex than a simple complementary or supplementary role in companies' technological activities. The insignificant estimates can also simply indicate that there is no such relationship in existence, at least in the sample data. Since most individual regional factors can be positively or negatively related to different technological inputs, one cannot expect that improvement or growth of regional services sectors will lead to a consistent growth (or decline in the case of substitution) of all technology related activities. The effect needs to be evaluated case by case. However, the study reveals a possible pattern: growth of a regional economy may lead to adoption of technologies and efficiency of standardized production in the textile-apparel industries, and lead to a smaller scale of production and more innovation activities in the computer-electronics industries. Notably, a complemental or a substitutive effect of a regional factor does not necessarily mean 'good' or 'bad' to a producer. However, a positive relationship does seem to be desirable from a regional point of view, because more economic activities and possible externalities may result from the producer internal inputs. Knowledge of the relationship can help a region exert its influence on private technological inputs according to a region's industrial, technological development goal. It can be further noted that an area without necessities is not attractive to a company and an area that does not provide the advantage of some substitutes for producer internal inputs may not be attractive either. In either case, future research is warranted to provide more concrete evidence.

Appendix 7: Estimates of Technological Input Intensity Functions

Exogenous factors can induce disproportional change in technological inputs: some technological inputs may become more intensive than others due to the change in external condition. The estimates in intensity functions represent excess influence of exogenous factors on the technological inputs.

As a supplement to the estimates of the standard input demand functions, four technological input intensity measures are created, and assumed to be linearly related to company attributes and regional factors. Thus, the influences of company attributes and regional factors on the intensities can be directly estimated. The four intensity measures are capital intensity, technical and professional labor intensity, R & D capital intensity, and intensity of other technology related inputs (i.e., patent purchase or license, computer and numerical control technology, machine upgrading, management system improvement, and employee training). The four measures are constructed using the levels of the four producer inputs divided by number of employees of each company. All company attributes and regional variables are the same as those used in estimating the input demand functions.

A7.1. An Overview of the Estimates

Table A7.1 through Table A7.4 report the estimates of intensity functions for the textile-apparel and the computer-electronics industries. Two equations are estimated for each input intensity function. Equation 1 always includes many company attribute variables and regional factors, while Equation 2 excludes variables whose presence results in a lower adjusted R^2.

An overview of the estimates gives the following impressions. First, there are few significant variables and low R^2s, suggesting that company characteristics and regional contextual factors have less influence on intensities than on levels of the technological inputs. Second, compared with textile-apparel companies, computer-electronics companies are more likely to be influenced by company attributes and regional factors in the intensities of technological inputs. On the other hand, the significant estimates of company attributes and regional factors indicate that exogenous variables do have some excess influence on the technological inputs.

Beyond Capital and Labor

Table A7.1 Estimates of Equipment and Technical/Professional Intensity Functions, Textile-Apparel Companies

	Equipment		Technical/Professional	
Variable	Equat. 1	Equat. 2	Equat. 1	Equat. 2
INTERCEPT	7.4079	-13.0632**	0.0449	0.0190
	(34.052)	(4.290)	(0.071)	(0.057)
PUBLIC	5.5260	------	-0.0160	------
	(7.875)		(0.016)	
HQ-US	-3.1432	------	-0.0341**	-0.0395**
	(6.770)		(0.014)	(0.013)
HQ-FRGN	26.1373	------	0.0464	------
	(25.815)		(0.054)	
AGE-CMPNY	-0.0666	------	0.0001	------
	(0.111)		(0.001)	
R&DCRDT	-0.5127	------	0.0123	------
	(7.991)		(0.016)	
BUYCRTF	6.8157	------	-0.0005	------
	(6.053)		(0.012)	
SALECRTF	-1.2343	------	0.0054	------
	(6.221)		(0.013)	
VALUE90	0.0014	------	0.000008	------
	(0.003)		(0.001)	
P-EDUC90	-0.7905	------	-0.0058	-0.0062*
	(1.826)		(0.003)	(0.003)
P-EXP90	0.4215	------	-0.0001	------
	(0.372)		(0.001)	
METRO	0.1706	------	0.0046	------
	(9.658)		(0.020)	
TXTLEW88	1.2558	1.4932**	0.0043**	0.0045**
	(0.846)	(0.315)	(0.001)	(0.001)
APPLW88	-0.5012	------	0.0028	0.0034*
	(1.001)		(0.002)	(0.001)
URBANPOP	0.1982	------	0.0007	0.0005**
	(0.241)		(0.001)	(0.001)
PCMINC85	-0.0001	-0.0001**	0.0000001	------
	(0.001)	(0.000)	(0.001)	
COLLEGE	-0.3014	------	-0.0022*	------
	(0.616)		(0.001)	
TOTEMP88	0.000012**	0.00001**	0.0000001	------
	(0.000)	(0.000)	(0.001)	
TXTLEE88	-0.4323	------	-0.0001	------
	(0.359)		(0.001)	
APPLE88	-0.4767	------	-0.0003	------
	(0.540)		(0.001)	
TRNSVC88	-0.6986	------	-0.0023	------
	(1.414)		(0.002)	
CMMNCT88	-1.7509	------	-0.0031	------
	(3.380)		(0.007)	
UTILIT88	7.8288	------	0.0306	------
	(8.990)		(0.018)	

Table A7.1 Estimates of Equipment and Technical/Professional
Intensity Functions, Textile-Apparel Companies (Con.)

	Equipment		Technical/Professional	
Variable	Equat. 1	Equat. 2	Equat. 1	Equat. 2
FIRE88	-3.1989	------	-0.0047	------
	(2.385)		(0.005)	
BUSSVC88	4.2524	------	0.0098	------
	(9.430)		(0.019)	
AMUSE88	-1.6916	------	0.0052	------
	(12.746)		(0.026)	
HEALTH88	-7.0787	------	0.0035	------
	(13.395)		(0.028)	
EDUCAT88	-0.7919	------	-0.0045*	-0.0053**
	(1.279)		(0.002)	(0.002)
SCLSVC88	-1.8656	------	-0.0031	------
	(1.362)		(0.002)	
R&DTSVC88	0.1059	------	0.0020	------
	(0.926)		(0.001)	
HOSPIT88	2399.493*	------	2.6913	------
	(1232.45)		(2.601)	
Adj. R-sq.	0.0658	0.1048	0.0806	0.1158

Note: 1. Standard errors are in parentheses.
          2. * and ** indicate statistically significant at 0.90 and 0.95 levels
          respectively.

A7.2. Influential Factors to Input Intensities

A7.2.1. Textile-Apparel Industry Group

Intensity of the equipment input is related to the textile industry wage rate, personal money income, and size of area employment. Faced with higher wage rate, textile companies tend to substitute production capital for the labor, resulting in higher intensity of capital input. Area personal money income has a negative estimate, consistent with a general pattern of industrial location: textile-apparel industries normally cannot gain the upperhand of competition for investment with other businesses in well developed, high income areas. The positive estimate of area total employment indicates that textile-apparel companies in large areas invest proportionally more in production equipment than in labor. This shows a substitution effect of production capital for production labor because labor is usually more expensive in large areas.

Table A7.2 Estimates of Intensity Functions of R & D Input and Other Technological Inputs, Textile-Apparel Companies

	R & D		Inputs in Adoption	
Variable	Equat. 1	Equat. 2	Equat. 1	Equat. 2
INTERCEPT	2.1446	0.7774	5.3740	-2.7863
	(2.625)	(0.588)	(21.604)	(6.072)
PUBLIC	0.2466	------	9.4052*	8.2101*
	(0.607)		(4.996)	(4.446)
HQ-US	0.6416	------	-5.0714	------
	(0.522)		(4.295)	
HQ-FRGN	1.0070	------	0.3227	------
	(1.990)		(16.378)	
AGE-CMPNY	0.0103	------	0.0336	------
	(0.008)		(0.070)	
R&DCRDT	0.8075	------	-0.5204	------
	(0.616)		(5.070)	
BUYCRTF	0.3153	------	5.3868	6.4797**
	(0.466)		(3.840)	(3.104)
SALECRTF	0.9953**	1.1627**	3.5747	------
	(0.479)	(0.385)	(3.947)	
VALUE90	-0.000087	------	-0.0020	------
	(0.000)		(0.002)	
P-EDUC90	-0.0916	------	-0.4407	------
	(0.140)		(1.158)	
P-EXP90	0.0100	------	0.2118	------
	(0.028)		(0.236)	
METRO	-0.4638	------	-0.0078	------
	(0.744)		(6.127)	
TXTLEW88	-0.0252	------	0.4406	0.3819*
	(0.065)		(0.536)	(0.211)
APPLW88	-0.0537	------	0.0238	------
	(0.077)		(0.635)	
URBANPOP	0.0121	------	0.0900	------
	(0.018)		(0.153)	
PCMINC85	-0.0000001	------	-0.0000229	------
	(0.001)		(0.001)	
COLLEGE	-0.0231	------	-0.4177	------
	(0.047)		(0.391)	
TOTEMP88	0.0000002	------	-0.0000007	------
	(0.001)		(0.001)	
TEXTLEMP	0.0101	------	0.0666	------
	(0.027)		(0.227)	
APPLE88	-0.0375	------	-0.0295	------
	(0.041)		(0.342)	
TRNSVC88	0.0441	------	0.6565	------
	(0.109)		(0.897)	
CMMNCT88	-0.3316	------	-1.1609	------
	(0.260)		(2.144)	
UTILIT88	0.0926	------	-2.5698	------
	(0.693)		(5.704)	

Table A7.2 Estimates of Intensity Functions of R & D Input and Other Technological Inputs, Textile-Apparel Companies (Con.)

Variable	R & D		Inputs in Adoption	
	Equat. 1	Equat. 2	Equat. 1	Equat. 2
FIRE88	-0.1885	------	-1.4329	------
	(0.183)		(1.513)	
BUSSVC88	0.3998	------	3.0495	------
	(0.727)		(5.983)	
AMUSE88	0.1675	------	0.1015	------
	(0.982)		(8.086)	
HEALTH88	0.0185	------	-0.2174	------
	(1.032)		(8.498)	
EDUCAT88	-0.1108	------	-0.5384	------
	(0.098)		(0.811)	
SCLSVC88	-0.2064*	-0.1739**	-1.6536*	-1.2459*
	(0.105)	(0.072)	(0.864)	(0.672)
R&DTSVC88	0.0126	------	0.2806	------
	(0.071)		(0.588)	
HOSPIT88	126.8392	------	1667.5866	1111.5360**
	(95.032)		(781.917)	(537.710)
Adj. R-Sq.	0.0076	0.0480	0.0118	0.0660

Note: 1. Standard errors are in parentheses.

              2. * and ** indicate statistically significant at 0.90 and 0.95 levels respectively.

Intensity of technical and professional input is significantly related to company headquarters location, average education level of technical-professional employees, the textile and apparel wage rates, urban population percentage, and area education service. Companies whose headquarters located in different states within the U.S. tend to hire technical and professional employees proportionally fewer than production workers. The other part of the story seems to be proportionally more technical and professional employees hired by companies locally controlled or foreign headquartered. Educational attainment of professional employees is estimated to substitute for physical labor input: the higher is the average educational level of technical and professional employees, the proportionally fewer technical and professional employees are hired. Both the textile and the apparel industries' wage rates are positively related to technical and professional labor input. The positive estimates indicate a substitution of technical and professional labor for production labor input because

Table A7.3 Estimates of Equipment and Technical/Professional Intensity Functions, Computer-Electronics Companies

	Equipment		Technical/Professional	
Variable	Equat. 1	Equat. 2	Equat. 1	Equat. 2
INTERCEPT	-84.2406	-29.3580**	-0.0915	0.0326
	(70.120)	(7.175)	(0.183)	(0.056)
PUBLIC	6.7540	------	0.0847**	0.0865**
	(10.107)		(0.026)	(0.022)
HQ-US	-11.6290	------	-0.0246	------
	(12.715)		(0.033)	
AGE-CMPNY	-0.2874	------	0.0003	------
	(0.290)		(0.001)	
STANDARD	-2.5190	------	-0.0565**	-0.0630**
	(10.031)		(0.026)	(0.023)
R&DCRDT	28.8778**	24.9163**	0.0059	------
	(12.300)	(10.607)	(0.032)	
BUYCRTF	6.9896	------	0.0318	------
	(10.151)		(0.026)	
SALECRTF	-16.1694	------	-0.0714**	-0.0601**
	(10.316)		(0.026)	(0.022)
VALUE90	0.1069	------	0.0002	------
	(0.072)		(0.001)	
P-EDUC90	-1.1327	------	0.0086	------
	(3.321)		(0.008)	
P-EXP90	1.0942	------	-0.0012	------
	(0.742)		(0.001)	
METRO	6.7698	------	-0.0296	------
	(20.048)		(0.052)	
URBANPOP	-0.2956	------	0.0012	0.0019**
	(0.557)		(0.001)	(0.000)
COLLEGE	0.1427	------	-0.0033**	-0.0035**
	(0.646)		(0.001)	(0.001)
PCMINC85	0.0002	0.0003**	-0.0000001	------
	(0.001)	(0.000)	(0.001)	
CMPTRW88	0.8138	------	-0.0009	------
	(1.420)		(0.003)	
ELECW88	1.3553	------	-0.0053	-0.0050**
	(1.763)		(0.004)	(0.000)
CMPTRE88	23.6290	168.0120**	0.5061*	0.3521**
	(110.359)	(38.060)	(0.288)	(0.110)
ELECE88	64.3441	------	-0.1518	------
	(58.902)		(0.154)	
TRNSVC88	0.7780	------	0.0010	------
	(3.156)		(0.008)	
CMMNCT88	9.0955	------	0.0208	------
	(7.615)		(0.019)	
UTILIT88	-3.9843	------	0.0262	------
	(8.441)		(0.022)	
FIRE88	2.1184	------	0.0233	------
	(10.853)		(0.028)	

Table A7.3 Estimates of Equipment and Technical/Professional Intensity Functions, Computer-Electronics Companies (Con.)

Variable	Equipment		Technical/Professional	
	Equat. 1	Equat. 2	Equat. 1	Equat. 2
BUSSVC88	-5.2158	------	-0.0254	------
	(9.123)		(0.023)	
AMUSE88	-1.7821	------	0.0189	------
	(12.112)		(0.031)	
HEALTH88	-21.1190	------	-0.0533	------
	(39.553)		(0.103)	
EDUCAT88	-2.0801	------	-0.0157	------
	(6.435)		(0.016)	
SCLSVC88	1.3836	------	-0.0011	------
	(1.995)		(0.005)	
R&DTSVC88	-1.3572	------	0.0007	------
	(3.920)		(0.010)	
HOSPIT88	5820.9703	------	-0.3008	------
	(5496.68)		(14.383)	
Adj. R-sq.	0.0518	0.1064	0.2385	0.2819

Note: 1. Standard errors are in parentheses.
2. * and ** indicate statistically significant at 0.90 and 0.95 levels respectively.

the wage rates largely reflect workers' wage in this industry group. Urban population percentage has a positive estimate in technical and professional input intensity function--companies located in highly urbanized areas take advantage of high skilled labor pool, using proportionally more technical and professional labor input.

R & D input intensity appears independent from most company attribute and regional variables, although companies that are certified suppliers are likely to have intensive R & D input and companies in areas with large social services sectors have less intensive R & D. A certified company must deliver quality products in a timely fashion. As a result, the company tend to do more in R & D to meet the requirement. On the other hand, intensive R & D input may lead to certification of its products by many industrial users. The causal direction in this relation can go either way. The significant negative estimate of social services sector indicates that companies in the areas with large social services devote proportionally less resources to R & D activities. Because areas with large social services sectors are likely to have social difficulties, these areas are not considered by business developers as good choices for R & D activities.

Table A7.4 Estimates of Intensity Functions of R & D Input and Other Technological Inputs, Computer-Electronics Companies

Variable	R & D		Inputs in Adoption	
	Equat. 1	Equat. 2	Equat. 1	Equat. 2
INTERCEPT	-12.8337	-14.4475*	19.6147	------
	(15.034)	(8.291)	(21.366)	
PUBLIC	0.4376	------	1.2658	------
	(2.167)		(3.079)	
HQ-US	4.1615	3.3137	-1.6115	------
	(2.726)	(2.311)	(3.874)	
AGE-CMPNY	-0.0752	------	-0.0743	------
	(0.062)		(0.088)	
STANDARD	0.7518	------	2.1922	------
	(2.150)		(3.056)	
R&DCRDT	2.7213	------	4.1005	------
	(2.637)		(3.747)	
BUYCRTF	-2.3950	------	-1.3010	------
	(2.176)		(3.093)	
SALECRTF	2.4680	------	2.3269	------
	(2.211)		(3.143)	
VALUE90	0.0149	------	-0.0024	------
	(0.015)		(0.022)	
P-EDUC90	0.0741	------	-1.0101	------
	(0.712)		(1.012)	
P-EXP90	-0.2791*	-0.2687*	-0.2982	------
	(0.159)	(0.150)	(0.226)	
METRO	-13.1417**	-11.1697**	1.3600	------
	(4.298)	(3.445)	(6.108)	
URBANPOP	0.2321*	0.1551**	0.0178	------
	(0.119)	(0.063)	(0.169)	
COLLEGE	0.1585	0.1815*	0.1550	------
	(0.138)	(0.108)	(0.196)	
PCMINC85	0.00004	------	0.0000246	------
	(0.001)		(0.001)	
CMPTRW88	0.5157*	0.4937*	-0.1751	------
	(0.304)	(0.261)	(0.432)	
ELECW88	0.6353*	0.5883*	-0.1715	------
	(0.378)	(0.318)	(0.537)	
CMPTRE88	-39.5776*	-19.8719*	-31.6263	------
	(23.661)	(10.568)	(33.626)	
ELECE88	11.9801	------	17.9638	------
	(12.629)		(17.947)	
TRNSVC88	0.7126	------	0.4044	------
	(0.676)		(0.961)	
CMMNCT88	-0.3032	------	1.7566	------
	(1.632)		(2.320)	
UTILIT88	-1.1466	------	-3.0330	------
	(1.809)		(2.572)	
FIRE88	-3.2703	-2.4145	-1.6268	------
	(2.327)	(1.728)	(3.307)	

Table A7.4 Estimates of Intensity Functions of R & D Input and Other Tech. Inputs, Computer-Electronics Companies (Con.)

	R & D		Inputs in Adoption	
Variable	Equat. 1	Equat. 2	Equat. 1	Equat. 2
BUSSVC88	-2.2251	------	-3.4526	------
	(1.956)		(2.779)	
AMUSE88	2.5804	------	-0.2807	------
	(2.597)		(3.690)	
HEALTH88	-6.7505	------	-1.9854	------
	(8.480)		(12.052)	
EDUCAT88	-0.1904	------	-0.1173	------
	(1.379)		(1.960)	
SCLSVC88	0.0265	------	0.0917	------
	(0.427)		(0.608)	
R&DTSVC88	0.2090	------	-1.3000	------
	(0.840)		(1.194)	
HOSPIT88	-1756.119	------	-613.6758	------
	(1178.5)		(1674.85)	
Adj. R-sq.	0.0473	0.0834	-0.0629	

Note: 1. Standard errors are in parentheses.
          2. * and ** indicate statistically significant at 0.90 and 0.95 levels respectively.

Intensity of input in adoption of technologies is positively influenced by ownership, certified intermediate input, local textile wage rate, and area hospital services; the intensity is also negatively related to social services. Public corporations generally devote proportionally more inputs in adoption of advanced technologies than do partnership or private corporations. Companies that buy intermediate inputs from certified producers spend proportionally more on adoption of technologies, suggesting that quality inputs provided by certified suppliers in a timely manner lead industrial users to adopt advanced product and process technologies to better use the certified inputs.
The negative estimate of social services sector is consistent with earlier discussion.

A7.2.2. Computer-Electronics Industry Group

Intensities of technology related input of computer-electronics companies are related to a different set of variables. The estimates of equipment intensity function show that computer-electronics companies in the areas with state and local R & D credit policies, higher per capita personal income, and a large computer industry are more capital intensive. A state and local R & D credit policy not only induces R & D investment but also leads to intensive production capital outlay. The estimate of area personal money income indicates that computer-electronics industries compare favorably with textile-apparel companies in well developed, high income areas in competing for capital input. The size of area computer industry measured as number of establishments is an important surrogate of technological externalities, which is expected to have positive influence on production capital input.

Intensity of technical and professional input is positively related to (1) public ownership of companies, (2) urban population percentage, and (3) size of area computer industry measured as number of establishment. It is not immediately apparent why public corporations employ proportionally more technical and professional employees. Of many possible reasons, management style and economies of scale of public corporations can be two important explanations because public corporations are managed by professional personnel and these corporations are larger than private corporations and sole partnerships; therefore, not only are they willing to be engaged in technological innovation and improvement but also they can afford to hire proportionally more technical and professional people. Urban population percentage and size of the industry are all proxy measures of technological externalities and competition, but it is not clear without additional investigation which factor as a complemental input makes computer companies hire more technical and professional people.

On the other hand, the intensity of technical and professional input is negatively related to (1) the mode of standardized production, (2) certified suppliers of intermediate products, (3) college degree holders as percent of area population, and (4) area wage rate of the electronics industry. Standardized production is obviously less demanding for technical modification and professional management. Thus, proportionally less technical and professional labor input is needed. Certified suppliers hire proportionally fewer technical and professional employees probably because the majority of certified suppliers produces less sophisticated intermediate products which need less intensive input of highly skilled labor than do final products. Unexpectedly, percentage of college degree holders in area population is negatively related to technical and professional input intensity. Because proportionally more college degree holders in an area means more knowledge, skills, and information available at lower or no cost, a large number of college degree holders outside companies can either substitute for internal technical labor input or discourage producer internal technical and professional activities. Although not fully credible, a reasonable interpretation may address both as underlying causes of the negative estimate. Finally, the negative estimate of area wage rate of electronics industry confirms the classic notion of inverse relationship between price and amount of an input.

Intensity of R & D input is estimated to be positively dependent on (1) urban population percentage, (2) college degree holders as percent of area population, and (3) area wage rates of the computer and electronics industries. Urbanization is not only related to proportionally more technical and professional input but also associated with more R & D intensity. Evidently, urbanization may induce intensities of companies' technological activities. The positive estimate of college degree holder percentage appears to support earlier interpretation. To realize the benefit of technological externalities from large amount college degree holders, computer-electronics companies tend to input more in R & D capital, although they hire proportionally fewer technical and professional people. The positive estimates of wage rates, again, echo the classic concept of the cross substitution of a less expensive factor input for a more expensive one.

The R & D input intensity is estimated to have been negatively dependent on (1) experience of technical and professional employees and (2) size of area computer industry measured as number of establishment. The more experienced the technical and professional crew, the less input in R & D the company makes. Nevertheless, any causal relationship is hard to be justified. Localization measured as number of computer establishments within each area appears to have substitution impact on internal R & D input.

Intensity of inputs in adoption of advanced technologies is independent from all company attribute variables and regional factors included. This finding implies that computer-electronics companies almost always invest in adoption of existing technologies proportionally similar to labor input.

Notes

1. OLS estimates of simultaneous equations are biased and inconsistent. Instrument variable methods, including two stage least square and three stage least square, can generate consistent estimates-- the estimates are asymptotically unbiased as the sample size approaches infinity. However, the finite sample property, unbiasedness, does not hold in general, even using the advanced technique.

2. Because the capital stock is the carrier of the embodied technology, the demand for new equipment can be considered as a demand for new technology. In this research, the demand for capital is measured by the demand for capital in equipment.

3. In Griliches' 1984 article four factor input variables are used. The collinearity and unstable estimates may be a less serious problem, but still he uses a C-D production function. As he states, 'One could, of course, also consider more complicated functional forms, such as the CES or Translog functions. We felt, based on past experience and also on some exploratory computations, that this will not matter as far as our main purpose of estimating the output elasticities of R & D and physical capital, or at least their relative importance, is concerned.' (Griliches, Zvi and Mairesse, Jacques 1984, *Productivity and R & D at Firm Level*, in Z. Griliches, eds., *R & D, Patents, and Productivity*, p338)

4. Because such regional variables as size and the wage rates of an industry are industry-specific, also because these variables only affect the observations belonging to the relevant industry, significant parameters of this kind are used to compute the overall impact of regional factors only for the relevant industries. As a result, two industries in each group can have different estimates.

8 Production Function and Nature of Technological Change

Many producer characteristics such as ownership, mode of production, and headquarters location, are constant over time. Therefore, these variables cannot be included in growth equations. Moreover, many regional contextual factors may not evolve fast enough to affect production and productivity growth. Yet the level of production at any time can be partly determined by these producer characteristics and regional contextual factors. Earlier research (e.g., Griliches and Lichtenberg 1984) also suggests that although the deterministic versions of growth equation and production function may be equivalent and parameter estimates have the same meaning (i.e., output elasticities of inputs), the empirical estimates are generally different due to different stochastic structures. To investigate the technological relationship between any inputs and output, a researcher needs also to estimate production function. Given data for two different periods, a production function approach can generate two sets of estimates. This allows the researcher to evaluate technological change over time.

In this chapter, the researcher will estimate the empirical production functions for textile-apparel and computer-electronics producers for 1985 and 1990 and examine the impacts of technological inputs, producer characteristics, and regional factors on output level. The researcher will also investigate the nature of technological change over the five-year period and assess the difference between the two industry groups in the technological change. Section 8.1 reviews earlier studies. The findings in these earlier studies can be compared to the current study. Section 8.2 justifies an appropriate model used to estimate the production functions. Section 8.3 presents and discusses empirical findings. Section 8.4 concludes this chapter.

8.1. EARLIER RESEARCH

Collectively, researchers in different areas have made a significant effort to estimate industrial production functions, returns to technological inputs, and technological change. The difficulty to collect input-output data from individual companies forced most earlier studies to use 2-digit or larger industry aggregate data to estimate industrial production functions. To investigate the variation in production technology across regions, earlier studies either employed cross sectional analyses with specific regional factors as additional independent variables in production functions, or several time series models for different regions to reveal regional difference of production functions.

Using state level cross sectional manufacturing sectors data, Besen (1968) estimated a general Cobb-Douglas production function with educational attainment as an additional explanatory variable for eighteen 2-digit industries. He found that the output elasticity of capital was in the range from under 0.1 to over 0.3 and the output elasticity of labor varied from about 0.4 to 1.36, implying a substantial inter-industry variation in production technology. Production in most industries could not be characterized by constant return to scale. Educational attainment of labor force emerged to be a significant contributor to output in more than half of the industries. As references of the current study, Besen's parameter estimates of capital were 0.070 and 0.256 for apparel and machinery industries respectively and insignificant for textile and electrical machinery; the estimates of labor were 0.865, 0.854, 0.786, and 1.215 for textile, apparel, machinery, and electrical machinery respectively; and the estimates of educational attainment were positive and significant for all the four industries. In Besen's study, variation in the input-output technological relationship across areas or over time was not investigated.

Williams (1985) used state level aggregate data to estimate a labor-share equation, which was a partial derivative of a Translog production function. The author further employed the estimates to compute the growth rates of efficiency factors of capital and labor for each state. Adopting Hicks' classification of technological change, Williams analyzed technological change for 48 states and concluded that 'technical change across states within census regions over the period (1972-1977) tend to be capital-using'. Although this conclusion is consistent with literature, his labor-share equation is doubtful[1]. Since the author did not measure and control any change in capital-labor ratio over time or across regions when he was assessing the nature of technological change, he implicitly assumed a constant capital-labor ratio across the states and over the period of 1972-77. No attempt was made to identify the sources of technological progress.

Sazaki (1985) applied a factor-augmenting sectoral production function of Translog type to Japanese regional data. The author used three factor inputs -- labor, capital, and material -- and three regional factor-augmenting variables -- number of firms, average size of each firm, and potential index (i.e., accessibility) -- to estimate the production function for fifteen industries separately. His findings suggested that, among the fifteen industrial sectors, the textile industry had no technological variation across the forty one regions investigated, while electronics machinery had non-neutral technological variations across the regions. In his study, however, no significant individual parameter estimate showed a direction of the technological bias. His findings also suggested that, on the average, economies of scale could explain about one half of the regional technological difference, while agglomeration (the number of firms) and accessibility (the potential index) could each account for one quarter of the regional technological variation. Sazaki's study is of a static type which cannot reveal the nature of technological change over time. The test for Hicks' neutral technological difference was conducted without controlling for the change in inputs ratios. Furthermore, his estimates may have a technical problem of 'overfitting' because his study used a data set with 41 or fewer observations to estimate several equations with 20 variables each.

Uno (1986) investigated Japanese regional Translog production function with capital and labor inputs differentiated by educational attainment. The author used cross sectional aggregate data for all Japanese industries on output, capital, and the two types of labor (well educated and less educated) to estimate a production function for developed and less developed regions separately. The author estimated production functions for four different years to examine the change in technological substitutability between inputs over time. Using Allen partial elasticities of substitution, Uno found that production technology was capital- educated workers complemental to each other and both capital and educated workers substitutive for less educated workers. The evidence was much stronger in developed areas than in less developed areas. Unskilled labor was in a disadvantaged position, especially in developed areas. Uno's estimates also showed that the technological bias decreased over time. In Uno's study, however, all different industries were assumed to have the same production function, and no spatial factors were included to examine the sources of the technological difference between the developed and less developed areas.

Luger and Evans (1988) adopted a Translog cost function to estimate 2-digit manufacturing sector production function for two different metro areas, Philadelphia and Las Angeles. Comparing two sets of parameter estimates for the two metro areas, the authors found a spatial variation in production parameters for the same industries. However, as the authors noted, they could not tell whether the coefficient estimates were statistically different because they did not perform statistical test to assess the significance of the spatial variation. Since the authors used time series data to establish empirical production functions, they implicitly assumed a neutral technological change over time for all the industries in both study areas.

Applying a generalized C-D cost function -- Truncated Translog without quadratic terms -- and related labor and capital demand functions to nine major Canadian manufacturing sectors 20-year's time series data, Bernstein (1989) estimated that the gross rate of return on R & D capital was 2.5 to 4 times those on physical capital in the nine industries. He also estimated that the social return due to spillovers effect was about twice the private return. Because the author estimated one set of coefficients for each industry, he could assess inter-industrial variation of the rate of return. However, the author could not examine technological change over time. The author was not concerned about regional variation of technology. From a technical point of view, his estimates may not be very reliable given the 20 observations and more than 15 variables for each equation.

A set of Griliches' (1980, 1984, 1986) research is so far the most significant studies using firm level data to estimate production function and return to technological inputs. He started with a general C-D production function to develop alternative operational equations. To explore and eliminate the fixed effect of company attributes on input-output relationship, the author employed both production function and growth equation equivalent to the fixed effect regression[2]. The parameter estimate of R & D input was largely consistent: the elasticity of output with respect to R & D capital was from 0.08 to 0.13, regardless of sample size, which varied from 133 firms to over 900 in different studies. Parameter estimates of conventional inputs, which are not Griliches' primary concern in these studies, usually implied a decreasing return to scale. In his 1986 study, output elasticity of labor was about 0.6 and the output elasticity of capital was around 0.2-0.3. However, Griliches' studies only included large R & D intensive firms and implicitly assumed all the firms having the same production function.

In short, earlier research employed either C-D or Translog production functions to estimate parameters of production technology. The estimated return on R & D were usually significant and greater than that on production capital. Technological change, if estimated, was labor-saving. Regional factors, if included, emerged to have some influence on technological change. Further evidence is yet to be discovered to understand the nature of technological change over time and the impact on production of companies' characteristics and regional factors.

8.2. MODEL AND METHODOLOGY

As discussed in chapter 2 and 7, application of Translog production function has some advantages and disadvantages in an empirical research. The disadvantage turns out to be obvious if the number of inputs under investigation is large. Based on the general argument and results of a pretest (see section 7.2), this study uses a general C-D form to estimate the empirical production function.

The general C-D production function (7.1) is rewritten as (8.1)

(8.1)
$$Q = A \prod_{i=1}^{k_1} X_i^{\beta_i} \prod_{j=1}^{k_2} R_j^{\alpha_j},$$

where all the variables and parameters are the same as in equation (7.1), namely, Q is the output level, A the neutral technological efficiency, X_i the ith producer input, R_j the jth pure exogenous variable, β_i and α_j are the output elasticities of input X_i and variable R_j respectively. Simply taking logarithm of both sides yields a log linear function, numbered as (8.2),

$$(8.2) \qquad LnQ = LnA + \sum_{i=1}^{k_1} \beta_i LnX_i + \sum_{j=1}^{k_2} \alpha_j LnR_j \ .$$

Most earlier studies employed functions similar to (8.2) but without regional factors, R_j, $j = 1, 2, \dots k_2$.

To investigate the impact of embodied technology on production, the expressions of capital jelly and efficiency labor input are substituted for conventional capital and labor respectively. The corresponding terms in equation (8.2) become

$$(8.3) \qquad \begin{aligned} & \beta_J LnJ_t = \beta_J (Lna_0 + \lambda_k t) - \beta_J \alpha_k LnA_t + \beta_J LnK_t \ , \\ & \beta_M LnM_t = \beta_M (Ln\gamma_0 + \lambda_L t) + \beta_M \alpha_s LnE_{st} + \beta_M \alpha_e LnE_{et} + \beta_M LnL_t. \end{aligned}$$

Applying the proposed production function to the data for 1985 and 1990 separately allows the researcher to go farther than many earlier studies to evaluate the influences on production and their changes over time of the embodied technology and knowledge/skills, technological inputs, and regional factors. A straightforward method to evaluate the technological change is to follow the pattern of earlier research and directly compare one set of estimates with another. A more rigorous approach is to impose a statistical test of the difference between the two sets of estimates. The joint F test (i.e., Chow test) could be performed to test whether the two sets of sample data could be considered from the same population, implying no change in production technology over time. The current study, however, is interested in the nature of technological change in terms of the bias toward intensive use of individual inputs. It is desirable to test those input factors individually.

Hicks' classification of technological change requires that the marginal rate of substitution of one input for another be evaluated at a fixed inputs ratio. To identify a neutral or a biased technological change with respect to capital or labor, the change in the capital-labor ratio should be statistically controlled. Assessment of technological change can be accomplished by comparing the marginal rate of technical substitution in an earlier period with the new rate in a later period while controlling for the change in capital-labor ratio. Let MP_L,

MP_K, and dK/dL be the marginal product of labor, the marginal product of capital, and the rate of technical substitution respectively, and the subscript t indicates time period, then the evaluation of the bias of technological change can be based on the following formula:

(8.4)
$$-\left(\frac{dK}{dL}\right)_t \; \underset{<}{\overset{>}{=}} \; -\left(\frac{dK}{dL}\right)_{t-1},$$

or

(8.4')
$$\left(\frac{MP_L}{MP_K}\right)_t \; \underset{<}{\overset{>}{=}} \; \left(\frac{MP_L}{MP_K}\right)_{t-1},$$

The technological change is capital-using or, equivalently, labor-saving if the left hand side is less than the right hand side because the marginal product of capital relative to labor is higher at time t than at time $t-1$ and the derived demand for capital has increased relative to the demand for labor. Consequently, proportionally more capital will be used as time passes. Conversely, the technological change is capital-saving or, equivalently, labor-using if the left hand side is greater than the right hand side. The technological change is said neutral if the equation holds. In the meantime, factor price ratios are assumed constant or statistically controlled.

To test the direction of biased technological change, the researcher elaborates the production function to control the impact of change in the capital-labor ratio. First, a dummy variable for the year 1990 is created. The dummy equals 1 if an observation is for 1990, zero for 1985. Second, all input variables are multiplied by this dummy, resulting in the second set of input variables. Third, a new data set combining the data for 1985 and 1990 is created. The new data set includes a capital-labor ratio variable, which is the 1990 capital-labor ratio divided by the 1985 capital-labor ratio if an observation is for 1990, 1 if an observation is for 1985. Fourth, a single production function including the second set of input variables (i.e., the dummy-input interactive terms) and the capital-labor ratio variable is estimated. The estimates of the new input variables indicate the direction of the bias of technological change in Hicks' sense. The statistical test for the nature of technological change boils down to the t-test for the parameter estimates of the second set of input variables (i.e., dummy-input interactive terms). Mathematically, the expression is

$$
\begin{aligned}
(8.5) \quad LnQ_t &= LnA_t + DUM_{90} + \beta_{KL} RATIO_{KL} + \sum_{i=1}^{k_1} (\beta_i LnX_i + \gamma_i (DUM_{90} L \\
&\quad + \sum_{j=1}^{k_2} (\alpha_j LnR_j + \delta_j (DUM_{90} LnR_j)) \ ,
\end{aligned}
$$

where DUM_{90} is the dummy variable for 1990, $RATIO_{KL}$ is the change in capital-labor ratio over 1985-90 period, and $DUM_{90}LnX_i$ is the ith dummy-input interactive term. Expectedly, a significant positive coefficient, γ_K (or γ_L) will be observed, if technological change over 1985-90 period is biased toward capital-using or labor-saving (or labor-using or capital-saving). Otherwise, technological change, if any, is neutral.

Following the same logic, the ratio of R & D capital to production capital and the ratio of professional to production workers are included to test the direction of technological change toward more intensive use of R & D capital relative to production capital and more intensive use of technical and professional employees relative to production workers. It is expected that in the computer-electronics industries, technology advances toward more R & D intensity and technical/professional intensity, while in the textile-apparel industries, technological change is likely to be more capital intensive over time. An equation the same as (8.5) is used in the empirical study. A set of regional variables discussed in the preceding chapters is included in the equations.

Depending on assumptions, the level of a producer input may be treated exogenously or endogenously. One might argue that firms make hiring and investment decisions based on their production plans. Therefore, if actual output level is close to planned output level, input and output variables should be determined simultaneously. On the other hand, one can argue that actual output level normally is different from planned level and the factor inputs are predetermined relative to the actual output. Because an empirical production function represents an *ex post* technological relationship between factor inputs and output, only the actual output level is relevant. Also due to the uncertainty of return to R & D or other technological inputs, it is very unlikely that a firm makes a technological input based on its current production plan. In an empirical study, it is not necessary to treat all producer inputs as endogenous. In this chapter, most inputs are treated exogenously and a single production function is estimated.

8.3. ESTIMATES AND DISCUSSION

Production function (8.2) with embodied technologies, company characteristics, and regional factors are estimated for textile-apparel companies and computer-electronics companies for 1985 and 1990 separately. County Business Patterns (CBP) data for 1983 are merged with 1985 sample company data and CBP data for 1988 are merged with 1990 sample company data, then the two data sets are used to estimate 1985 and 1990 equations respectively. After a direct comparison of the estimates for 1985 and 1990, a rigorous test for the technological change is performed applying equation (8.5) to a combined data set. The study provides evidence of different input-output technological relationships and different technological change in the two industry groups over the 1985-90 period.

8.3.1. Estimates of Production Function for Each Period
The production function includes producer input variables, producer attributes, and regional contextual factors. As mentioned earlier, inclusion of producer internal inputs is justified by economic theory, while inclusion of company characteristics and regional factors is primarily based on experience and intuition. Therefore, examination of company characteristics and regional variables is exploratory in nature. Company characteristics and regional variables which lower adjusted R^2 are excluded after a comprehensive test with all company attributes and regional variables included. The estimates of production function with all company attributes and regional factors included are documented in Appendix 8. The final set of parameter estimates for the textile-apparel and the computer-electronics producers are shown in Table 8.1 and Table 8.2. Variables and definitions of producer inputs, company attributes, and regional factors are shown in Table 3.5, Table 4.1, and Table 5.1 respectively, except that the variables are measured for two different years to estimate two equations respectively.

Table 8.1 OLS Estimates of Production Function
Textile-Apparel Companies
(Dependent Variable: Value Added, Observation: 279)

Variable	(1985) Estimate	(1985) Std Err	(1990) Estimate	(1990) Std Err
INTERCEPT	3.8240**	(1.051)	5.2031**	(1.585)
W-EMP	0.4716**	(0.052)	0.4930**	(0.047)
P-EMP	0.1210**	(0.047)	0.1347**	(0.045)
K-BD	0.1235**	(0.021)	0.1192**	(0.019)
K-UTLZ	0.1089**	(0.024)	0.1045**	(0.023)
K-R&D	0.0144**	(0.006)	0.0108**	(0.004)
PATENT	0.0499*	(0.029)	0.0341*	(0.021)
K-CC	0.0000	(0.018)	-0.0089	(0.016)
K-MCN	0.0379**	(0.013)	0.0169	(0.013)
K-MNG	-0.0323	(0.020)	0.0250	(0.019)
K-TRN	0.0247	(0.019)	0.0009	(0.017)
K-AGE	-0.0353**	(0.010)	-0.0482**	(0.009)
W-EDUC	-0.1787	(0.279)	-0.2425	(0.392)
W-EXP	0.0573	(0.065)	0.0819	(0.060)
P-EDUC	0.2151	(0.330)	-0.2044	(0.464)
P-EXP	-0.0210	(0.062)	-0.0417	(0.063)
HQ-CNTY	-0.2349**	(0.108)	-0.1407*	(0.076)
HQ-STATE	------		------	
HQ-US	-0.2235*	(0.123)	------	
AGE-CMPNY	------		------	
BUYCRTF	------		------	
SALECRTF	------		------	
R&DCRDT	0.2659**	(0.125)	0.2759**	(0.117)
COLLEGE	------		------	
PCMINC	------		------	
POP	------		------	
TXTLEE	------		------	
TXTLEW	------		------	
APPLE	------		------	
APPLW	------		------	
AIR	------		------	
TRNSVC	------		------	
CMMNCT	------		------	
UTILIT	------		0.0765**	(0.033)
FIRE	------		------	
BUSSVC	------		------	
AMUSE	-0.0829**	(0.034)	------	
HEALTH	------		------	
EDUCT	------		------	
SCLSVC	------		------	
ENGNRG	0.0606**	(0.029)	0.0565**	(0.026)
Adj. R-Sq.	0.8092		0.8285	

Note: * and ** indicate statistically significant at 90% and 95% levels respectively.

**Table 8.2 OLS Estimates of Production Function
Computer-Electronics Companies**
(Dependent Variable: Value Added, Observation: 210)

Variable	(1985) Estimate	Std Err	(1990) Estimate	Std Err
INTERCEPT	3.2612**	(1.118)	4.1862**	(1.956)
W-EMP	0.1678**	(0.066)	0.2404**	(0.070)
P-EMP	0.4939**	(0.056)	0.4883**	(0.061)
K-BD	0.0910*	(0.046)	0.1706**	(0.049)
K-UTLZ	0.1036**	(0.032)	0.0214	(0.045)
K-R&D	0.0487*	(0.026)	0.0834*	(0.045)
PATENT	0.0122	(0.027)	0.0239	(0.023)
K-CC	0.0133	(0.024)	0.0045	(0.023)
K-MCN	0.0141	(0.018)	0.0163	(0.020)
K-MNG	0.0118	(0.025)	-0.0072	(0.030)
K-TRN	0.0209	(0.029)	-0.0125	(0.031)
K-AGE	-0.0320**	(0.012)	-0.0513**	(0.016)
W-EDUC	-0.0158	(0.392)	-0.1148	(0.617)
W-EXP	0.0668	(0.092)	0.1113	(0.103)
P-EDUC	0.1046	(0.211)	-0.0228	(0.415)
P-EXP	-0.0513	(0.094)	-0.0485	(0.108)
HQ-CNTY	-0.2437**	(0.107)	-0.2328*	(0.118)
HQ-STATE	------		------	
STANDARD	------		------	
AGE-CMPNY	0.1701**	(0.082)	------	
BUYCRTF	------		------	
SALECRTF	------		------	
R&DCRDT	------		------	
COLLEGE	------		------	
PCMINC	------		------	
POP	0.0958*	(0.059)	0.1939*	(0.102)
CMPTRE	------		------	
CMPTRW	------		------	
ELECE	------		------	
ELECW	------		------	
AIR	0.1084**	(0.039)	0.0565	(0.042)
TRNSVC	------		-0.1737**	(0.069)
CMMNCT	-0.1896**	(0.084)	------	
UTILIT	------		------	
FIRE	------		------	
BUSSVC	------		------	
AMUSE	------		0.1648	(0.099)
HEALTH	------		-0.3851**	(0.163)
EDUCAT	------		0.1439**	(0.056)
SCLSVC	------		------	
ENGNRG	------		------	
Adj. R-Sq.	0.8240		0.7912	

Note: * and ** indicate statistically significant at 90% and 95% levels respectively.

8.3.1.1. Outline of Input-Output Relation of Production

The estimated equations all show very high explanatory power
with adjusted R^2 around 0.8. As expected, the most significant variables
are producer inputs. Several producer characteristics and regional
factors also have significant influence on the output level. Evidently,
the levels of production in both industry groups are primarily
determined by producer internal inputs and partly influenced by
external factors. Unlike many earlier studies that examines influence of
external factors on production without controlling for producer internal
inputs, the current study provides less biased estimates of external
factors.

In both industry groups and for both 1985 and 1990 periods,
producer physical inputs, including production capital, R & D capital,
and labor input, are all significant determinants of output level.
Technology embodied in capital also emerges as a contributor to output
in both industry groups in the two periods. The influence is estimated
to have increased over time. Knowledge or skills of technical and
professional labor input, which is significant in the growth equations,
is insignificant, showing the difference between growth equations and
production functions in stochastical structure. The impacts of producer
characteristics and regional variables on production vary from factor to
factor, from industry to industry, and occasionally from period to
period. Estimated neutral technological change (the intercept) is a
significant contributor to output for both industry groups and in both
1985 and 1990 periods.

Adding up output elasticities of producer physical inputs, one
arrives at a decreasing return to scale with respect to the inputs for both
industry groups. The estimated economies of scale measured by the
sum of output elasticities of producer physical inputs are about 0.825
in 1985 and 0.851 in 1990 for textile-apparel companies. The
corresponding figures for computer-electronics companies are 0.856
and 0.921. Treating embodied technologies as producer inputs, return
to scale is 0.962 in 1985 and 0.945 in 1990 for textile-apparel, while
the figures for computer-electronics are 0.937 and 1.055. The findings
confirm earlier studies (Griliches 1984, 1986) where it is estimated that
(1) return to scale with respect to capital and labor inputs using
different sample firm data is almost always about 0.9 and (2) return to
scale appears to increase over time[3]. The estimates appear to be
greater than those shown in chapter 5 and chapter 6 where economies

of scale were derived from growth equation and were also below unity for both industry groups. Considering the estimated increase in economies of scale over time of computer-electronics production and the result from the estimate of growth equations, one can infer that the producers have adjusted their production over time toward constant return or producer equilibrium in the computer-electronics industries.

8.3.1.2. Technological Change

To examine technological change, parameter estimates of production for 1985 are compared with those for 1990. In either industry group the output elasticity of labor increased, while the output elasticity of capital was constant over 1985-90 period. The estimated elasticity of labor including production workers and technical and professionals increased from 0.592 in 1985 to 0.627 in 1990 in textile-apparel companies. The comparable figures for computer-electronics are 0.661 and 0.729. The estimated output elasticity of capital including structure and equipment is 0.232 for 1985 and 0.224 for 1990 in textile-apparel group, 0.194 for 1985 and 0.192 for 1990 in computer-electronics. However, it is not clear why the estimate for equipment in 1990 for computer-electronics is insignificant. According to the estimates, non-neutral technological change, if any, is labor-using (or capital-saving) in both industry groups, a finding contradicting normal expectations.

Impact on production of technology embodied in capital is estimated to have increased for both industry groups: from 0.0353 to 0.0482 in the textile-apparel industries and 0.032 to 0.0513 in the computer-electronics industries. The estimates imply that the technology embodied in the new machines becomes more and more important to the users over time. Because production equipments are made by machine tools manufacturers, the increasing return to new capital, indicated by negative estimate of average age of production capital, implies that machine tools manufacturers have increasingly incorporated advanced technology in new equipment. Adoption of new equipment in production emerges as an important avenue to raise output level.

The estimates also show that output elasticity of R & D capital falls by 25% from 0.0144 to 0.0108 in textile-apparel group and increases by 71% from 0.0487 to 0.0834 in computer-electronics. The estimates signify the increasing importance of R & D input in computer-electronics as opposed to that in textile-apparel. The findings are consistent with estimates and interpretations in earlier chapters. Computer-electronics manufacturers either enjoy higher return to R & D input or, as Anderla and Dunning (1987) found, are trapped by intensive competition in R & D activities. In contrast, R & D input in textile-apparel seems to have lower return in 1990 than in 1985.

Neutral technological change is an important part of technological progress. The estimate measured by intercept is significant in 1985 and 1990 for both industry groups. The magnitude increased from 3.824 to 5.203 for textile-apparel and from 3.261 to 4.186 for computer-electronics over 1985-90 period. Both industry groups appear to have experienced accelerating progress in their input-output technological relation due to improvement of social organization, resources allocation, and external factors not included in the research. However, as in the case of biased technological change, the results are subjected to a more rigorous test.

8.3.1.3. Marginal Products of Producer Inputs

Because output elasticity of an input is determined by marginal product of the input and the level of the input, and because marginal product is also a crucial indicator of technology in production, logically, a researcher needs to estimate the rates of marginal products of inputs. Marginal product of a significant physical input can be computed using the estimated output elasticity multiplied by sample mean of value added and then divided by sample mean of the input. The estimates are reported in Table 8.3. Since the deflator of manufacturing goods in the second half of 1980s is almost constant (*Statistical Abstract of the United States*), the estimates of the value of marginal products for 1985 and 1990 are directly comparable.

Table 8.3 shows that the marginal products of production workers and technical and professional employees all increased over the 1985-90 period for the both industry groups, while average level of inputs of production workers and technical and professionals actually fell over the same period. Coupled with the increased capital input in both industry groups, the findings indicate that higher output elasticities of labor is attributable to higher labor productivity rather than higher labor-capital ratio. The paradox here is that higher marginal product of labor is supposed to result in intensive use of labor, i.e., technological change should be labor-using or capital-saving, but the levels of inputs in capital and labor in 1985-90 period actually varied in the opposite

Table 8.3 Estimates of Average Value
of Marginal Products (VMP)

Textile-Apparel

VALUE ADDED	(1985) ($12,698)			(1990) ($14,277)		
Variable	Output Elasticity	Average Input	Average VMP	Output Elasticity	Average Input	Average VMP
W-EMP	0.4716	306	19.569	0.4930	296	23.770
P-EMP	0.1210	41	37.474	0.1347	41	46.905
K-BD	0.1235	3929	0.399	0.1192	4361	0.390
K-UTLZ	0.1089	4313	0.321	0.1045	4657	0.320
K-R&D	0.0144	134	1.365	0.0108	155	0.995
PATENT	0.0499	127	4.989	0.0341	178	2.735
K-MCN	0.0379	1485	0.324	0.0169	2543	0.095

Computer-Electronics

VALUE ADDED	(1985) ($15,144K)			(1990) ($16,184K)		
Variable	Output Elasticity	Average Input	Average VMP	Output Elasticity	Average Input	Average VMP
W-EMP	0.1678	147	17.287	0.2404	123	31.631
P-EMP	0.4939	65	115.071	0.4883	61	129.552
K-BD	0.0910	4170	0.330	0.1706	4470	0.618
K-UTLZ	0.1036	3335	0.470	0.0214	3350	0.103
K-R&D	0.0487	729	1.012	0.0834	864	1.562

direction. Reasons for the reduced use of labor input may be an increasing cost of labor and the limitation of the products markets. On the other hand, gross return to capital input is basically constant in 1985-90 period for textile-apparel and similar to buildings and equipment. The return to capital appears quite erratic to computer-electronics: in 1985 the return to equipment was higher than that to buildings, in 1990 the return to equipment dropped sharply while the return to buildings almost doubled. It is very unlikely that gross rate of return to input in structure could be as high as 0.618. Probably, the estimate for capital in buildings absorbed the effect of capital in equipment on output level, but it is unknown how this could happen.

Using Accelerated Cost Recovery System, net return to capital on the average is about 0.2 with return to capital in computer-electronics slightly higher than that in textile-apparel. The estimates are lower than those from growth equations in chapter 5, but seem closer to common knowledge. On the other hand, the estimated values of marginal products of labor from the production functions are higher than from growth equations or from published sources (CBP) by a significant margin[4]. This suggests that either the production functions overestimate the output elasticities of labor inputs or the values of marginal products are indeed much higher than the market wage rates. The real marginal productivity is very likely to be in between.

The return to technological inputs, R & D capital, patent purchase, and machine upgrading, are all estimated to have decreased over the study period for the textile-apparel industries. The rates of the returns in 1990, however, were still much higher than conventional capital inputs. For example, marginal product of R & D capital is as high as 0.99 (i.e., 0.0108*14276/155, where 14276 is sample mean of value added and 155 is sample mean of R & D input of textile-apparel companies, with both measured by $1,000) in 1990. The decrease in return to technological inputs of textile-apparel companies suggest that producers in this group react to the technological opportunities and profitability positively towards producer equilibrium.

In contrast, return to R & D input of computer-electronics producers increased over the study period. The higher level of R & D input in 1990 indicates that the computer-electronics industries responded actively to technological opportunity and higher profit. It is interesting to observe that the marginal product of R & D input in the computer-electronics industries appears to grow faster than that of R & D input itself. This implies that technological change in the industry group is faster than is producer equilibrium process. To investors in the computer-electronics industries, the findings appear to be better news than Anderla and Dunning's earlier findings that suggest that computer producers are trapped in intensive R & D competition without a gain.

As indicated earlier, although the estimates in the production functions have the same meanings as those in growth equations, the estimates can be quantitatively different because of the unequal stochastical specifications. Nevertheless, the estimates for production functions are qualitatively consistent with the estimates in growth equation or with experience. For instance, marginal product of technical and professional labor input is much higher than that of production worker labor input, return to R & D capital is greater than those to conventional capital inputs, returns to labor and the return to R & D in the computer-electronics industries are higher than those in the textile-apparel industries and so on.

8.3.1.4. Company Characteristics

A few company characteristics are likely to be influential factors to production. Of four types of headquarters locations, two types of location have significant negative impact on production. Other things being equal, companies with headquarters located in the same county (most of these companies are single plant firms) tend to have lower level of output in 1985 and 1990 for both industry groups. The estimates suggest that local or single establishment firms are generally smaller and probably less efficient, because smaller single establishment firms ussually lack the economies of scale. In 1985, textile-apparel companies with headquarters in different states also appear to have lower output level, implying that out-of-state owned branch companies tend to be smaller. The reason may reside in the way that resources are allocated and managed: compared with the branch companies in owners' states, the branch companies of textile-apparel firms in other states may be given lower priority by their headquarters in improving management and upgrading production technology. The difference, however, disappeared in 1990. It is estimated that older computer-electronics companies seem to have higher output level and/or higher productivity than younger ones in 1985. The difference between older and younger companies suggests that older computer-electronics companies are likely to be technologically well established after competition for a longer period. However, the difference statistically disappeared in 1990. No other company attribute variables are statistically significant in the estimates. In general, company attributes appear to affect production only marginally.

8.3.1.5. Regional Factors

To some extent, producer output level is also affected by regional contextual factors. State and local R & D investment credit policy is estimated to lead to a higher level of textile-apparel production. From local policy makers' point of view, R & D credit policies or programs are successful because the policies or programs not only induced R & D input as estimated in the preceding chapter, but also directly resulted in higher output level.

Two producer services variables, utilities services and engineering and management services, appear to have contributed to a higher level of textile-apparel production. The parameter estimate for utilities services is significant only for 1990, signifying the increasing importance of this services sector over time. Recreation and amusement services are negatively associated with output level. It is likely that areas with large recreation and amusement services sector host many other social economic activities. As a result, labor, land, and all other local owned resources tend to be expensive. This makes textile-apparel companies worse off. Notably, the negative influence becomes weaker as time passed: the estimate became insignificant in 1990.

Computer-electronics production are affected by very different regional factors. Agglomeration measured by population is positively related to output level. The estimates are consistent with earlier findings (Sveikauskas 1975, Moomaw 1980, 1986, and Beeson 1987).

Three producer services sectors, transportation by air, other transportation services, and the communication services, are estimated to have influences on computer-electronics production level. As expected, transportation by air is positively associated with output because air transportation allows computer-electronics producers to access large market in a just-in-time fashion. The positive influence seems to be less important over time--the estimate is insignificant for 1990. Unexpectedly, communication services and other transportation services have negative estimates in the production functions for 1985 and 1990 respectively. The negative estimates cannot be explained by any theory or intuition and it is not clear if the peculiar estimates happen to result from the particular sample areas. Estimates also show that health services is negatively related to production, and education services is positively associated with production in 1990. The positive estimate of the education services means a spillover effect in absorbing, developing, and diffusing knowledge, in addition to improving labor quality. However, the negative estimate of health services is unexpected. The estimate indicates that larger computer-electronics companies are mostly located in the areas with smaller health services sector, a peculiar location pattern and no explanation readily available.

In short, regional producer services have moderate influence on production. Textile-apparel and computer-electronics productions are affected by very different regional factors. The mechanism by which some regional factors affect production requires further investigation.

8.3.2. Statistical Test for Biased Technological Change

It is straightforward to compare one set of estimates with another to assess the technological change over time. Nevertheless, two important conditions, constant relative factor prices and constant ratio of factor inputs, must be met to adequately evaluate technological change. In Equation (8.5), the relative wage rates are controlled using 1983 and 1988 wage rate variables, while the ratio of capital to labor, the ratio of technical and professional employees to production workers, and the ratio of R & D capital to production capital are controlled using three input ratio variables. Base measures (in 1985) of producer input variables and regional factors (in 1983) are applied to all observations, while additional measures of producer input variables (1990 dummy multiplied by producer inputs in 1990) and regional factors (1990 dummy multiplied by regional factors in 1988) are only applied to observations for 1990. As a result of the arrangement, a significant parameter estimate of an additional measure indicates a change of input-output technical relation between that internal input (or regional factor) and output level. This allows the researcher to use a t-statistic to test any biased technological change. For example, a significant positive parameter estimate of K-UTLZ90 coupled with a significant parameter estimate of base measure of K-UTLZ implies a change in production technology toward capital-using from 1985 to 1990, while a significant negative parameter estimate of K-UTLZ90 implies a change in production technology toward capital-saving from 1985 to 1990, other things being equal. The estimates of the equation (8.5) are presented in Table 8.4.

The estimates in Table 8.4 show that after introducing statistical controls and imposing a statistical test, most of the technological change observed in the preceding section become insignificant. Specifically, in the textile-apparel industries only input in R & D and input in management system have significant excess impact on the production in 1990, and the influences on the production of all other producer inputs and regional factors are mostly constant over 1985-90 period. In computer-electronics production, there is no statistically significant change in any input-output relationship over the five-year period, suggested by the insignificant estimates of all additional measures of producer input variables and regional variables. The expected nature of technological change (i.e., in the computer-electronics industries technological advance is biased toward R & D using relative to production capital and professional using relative to production workers, while in the textile-apparel industries technological

Table 8.4 Estimates of Parameter Shift over 1985-90 Period
(Dependent Variable: Value Added)

Textile-Apparel (558 obs.)   **Computer-Electronics** (420 obs)

Variable	Estimate	Std Err	Variable	Estimate	Std Err
INTERCEPT	3.2922*	1.7750	INTERCEPT	0.7076	2.5380
Base Measures of Conventional Input (1985)					
W-EMP	0.4753**	0.0533	W-EMP	0.2078**	0.0731
P-EMP	0.1126**	0.0487	P-EMP	0.4767**	0.0621
K-BD	0.1255**	0.0214	K-BD	0.0789	0.0524
K-UTLZ	0.1016**	0.0252	K-UTLZ	0.1029**	0.0351
Base Measures of Technological Inputs (1988)					
K-R&D	0.0149**	0.0055	K-RD	0.0487**	0.0173
PATENT	0.0468	0.0301	PATENT	0.0015	0.0305
K-CC	0.0035	0.0190	K-CC	0.0227	0.0277
K-MCN	0.0362**	0.0134	K-MCN	0.0255	0.0203
K-MNG	-0.0327	0.0200	K-MNG	0.0137	0.0283
K-TRN	0.0295	0.0193	K-TRN	0.0059	0.0326
Base Measures of Embodied Technology/Knowledge/Skills (1988)					
K-AGE	-0.0368**	0.0103	K-AGE	-0.0233	0.0142
W-EDUC	-0.1042	0.2852	W-EDUC	0.0601	0.4302
W-EXP	0.0597	0.0678	W-EXP	0.0619	0.1027
P-EDUC	0.1466	0.3331	P-EDUC	0.1250	0.2301
P-EXP	-0.0365	0.0626	P-EXP	-0.0083	0.1081
Input Ratios					
K-E-RATIO	-0.0849	0.0680	K-E-RATIO	0.0681	0.1092
P-W-RATIO	0.0450	0.0971	P-W-RATIO	-0.1584	0.1030
RD-K-RATIO	-0.2642*	0.1359	RD-K-RATIO	-0.0055	0.1141
Additional Input Variables for 1990 Observations					
DUMMY90	2.4645	2.2078	DUMMY90	1.4702	2.7371
W-EMP90	0.0378	0.0727	W-EMP90	-0.0131	0.1048
P-EMP90	-0.0072	0.0683	P-EMP90	0.0232	0.0900
K-BD90	-0.0039	0.0303	K-BD90	0.1106	0.0725
K-UTLZ90	-0.0230	0.0375	K-UTLZ90	-0.0814	0.0583
K-R&D90	-0.0041*	0.0021	K-R&D90	0.0412	0.0478
PATENT90	-0.0447	0.0377	PATENT90	0.0177	0.0382
K-CC90	-0.0114	0.0258	K-CC90	-0.0189	0.0366
K-MCN90	-0.0163	0.0194	K-MCN90	-0.0157	0.0291
K-MNG90	0.0639**	0.0287	K-MNG90	-0.0036	0.0424
K-TRN90	-0.0249	0.0272	K-TRN90	-0.0207	0.0453
K-AGE90	-0.0114	0.0148	K-AGE90	-0.0285	0.0223
W-EDUC90	-0.0627	0.5126	W-EDUC90	-0.2529	0.7628
W-EXP90	0.0325	0.0929	W-EXP90	0.0192	0.1500
P-EDUC90	-0.5831	0.6036	P-EDUC90	-0.1678	0.4840
P-EXP90	-0.0138	0.0919	P-EXP90	-0.0290	0.1537

Note: * and ** indicate statistically significance at 90% and 95% levels respectively.

Table 8.4 Estimates of Parameter Shift over 1985-90 Period (Con.)
Textile-Apparel (558 obs.)   **Computer-Electronics** (420 obs)

Variable	Estimate	Std Err	Variable	Estimate	Std Err
Company Attributes					
HQ-CNTY	-0.3008*	0.1802	HQ-CNTY	-0.2049**	0.0952
HQ-STATE	-0.0746	0.1990	HQ-STATE	0.1305	0.1731
HQ-US	-0.2326	0.1871	STANDARD	0.0482	0.0983
AGE-CMPNY	0.0357	0.0373	AGE-CMPNY	0.0596	0.0662
BUYCRTF	0.0002	0.0628	BUYCRTF	-0.0212	0.0706
SALECRTF	-0.0078	0.0482	SALECRTF	-0.0404	0.0532
Base Measures of Regional Factors (1983)					
R&DCRDT	0.2664**	0.0914	R&DCRDT	-0.0113	0.1212
COLLEGE	0.0296	0.0669	COLLEGE	0.1231	0.1111
PCMINC	0.0142	0.0466	PCMINC	0.0378	0.0608
POP	-0.1136	0.1154	POP	0.3488	0.2190
TXTLE	0.0383	0.0358	COMPTE	-0.0932	0.0684
TXTLW	0.2580	0.3528	COMPTW	0.4470	0.4376
APPLE	0.0251	0.0336	ELECTE	-0.0668	0.0511
APPLW	-0.0631	0.2405	ELECTW	0.1864	0.2959
AIR	0.0477*	0.0279	AIR	0.1292**	0.0546
TRNSVC	-0.0548*	0.0325	TRNSVC	-0.0475	0.0699
CMMNCT	-0.0424	0.0532	CMMNCT	-0.3052*	0.1653
UTILIT	-0.0238	0.0394	UTILIT	-0.0327	0.0938
FIRE	-0.0126	0.1058	FIRE	-0.0088	0.2354
BUSSVC	-0.0487	0.0566	BUSSVC	0.1274	0.1999
AMUSE	-0.0611	0.0501	AMUSE	0.1041	0.1383
HEALTH	0.0933	0.0854	HEALTH	-0.3069*	0.1801
EDUCAT	0.0064	0.0304	EDUCAT	0.0614	0.0687
SCLSVC	0.0517	0.0611	SCLSVC	0.1074	0.1857
ENGNRG	0.1041**	0.0518	ENGNRG	-0.1213	0.1299
Additional Measures of Regional Factors (1988)					
TXTLE88	-0.0020	0.0469	CMPTRE88	0.0670	0.0887
TXTLW88	-0.0762	0.2945	CMPTRW88	-0.3285	0.5338
APPLE88	0.0148	0.0476	ELECE88	0.0192	0.0701
APPLW88	-0.2170	0.3292	ELECW88	-0.0263	0.3581
AIR88	-0.0345	0.0382	AIR88	-0.0659	0.0730
TRNSVC88	0.0735	0.0493	TRNSVC88	-0.1365	0.1046
CMMNCT88	0.0058	0.0723	CMMNCT88	0.1860	0.2082
UTILIT88	-0.0458	0.0577	UTILIT88	0.0965	0.1370
FIRE88	0.0062	0.1353	FIRE88	0.0226	0.3223
BUSSVC88	0.0240	0.0697	BUSSVC88	-0.2260	0.2609
AMUSE88	0.0290	0.0692	AMUSE88	0.1034	0.1930
HEALTH88	0.0537	0.1142	HEALTH88	-0.0536	0.2412
EDUCAT88	0.0124	0.0425	EDUCAT88	0.0695	0.0915
SCLSVC88	-0.0847	0.0858	SCLSVC88	-0.0866	0.2484
ENGNRG88	-0.0324	0.0820	ENGNRG88	0.0917	0.2098
Adj R-sq	0.7904		Adj R-sq	0.7649	

Note: * and ** indicate significance at 90% and 95% levels respectively.

change tends to be more capital-using/labor-saving) are not supported by any statistically significant evidence.

The significant negative excess influence of R & D capital on textile-apparel production in 1990 could suggest a technological change biased toward R & D saving or, equivalently, production capital-using. Given the average input and output levels listed in Table 8.3, the marginal products of production capital and R & D capital are computed to be 0.299 and 1.412 for 1985 and 0.311 and 0.995 for 1990 respectively. Thus, the marginal rate of substitution of R & D capital for production capital for 1985 and 1990 are 4.722 and 3.006 respectively. Applying the criterion (8.4) to the figures, since -$(dK/dR\&D)_{90}=3.006$ < -$(dK/dR\&D)_{85}=4.733$, the textile-apparel industries are likely to have experienced technological change toward using more production capital relative to R & D capital.

No control variables are used for the ratios of several inputs in adoption of advanced technologies to any other producer inputs. Nevertheless, coupled with sample means[5], the insignificant estimate for the input for 1985 and the significant excessive estimate for 1990 indicate that many textile-apparel companies made substantial effort to adopt new or better technology in management during the five-year period and the effort shows a systematical influence on production by 1990.

The estimates are also used to test the change in neutral technological progress and the changes in the influences of regional factors over time. The parameter for the 1990 dummy is not statistically significant for textile-apparel and the computer-electronics industries. No statistically significant change in regional influences is found -- the estimates of additional measures of regional factors for 1990 are all insignificant.

The results of the stringent test suggest that over the 5-year period technological change in both textile-apparel and the computer-electronics industries is not significantly biased toward either capital-using (equivalently, labor-saving) or technical and professional labor-using (equivalently, production labor-saving). The results also show that the impacts of regional factors tend to be constant over this period. There are three alternative interpretations behind the findings of the unbiased technological change: (1) the five-year period is not long enough to observe a statistically significant change of technology, (2) the statistical test at 90% or 95% significance level is too stringent to confirm a technological change toward intensive use of one input relative to others even if the hypothesis is supported by apparent evidence in the separate production functions, (3) the technological change is indeed not biased. Given the 5-year study period and the method of statistical test used, the researcher would propose that the interpretation (1) and (2) are more likely to be the case. This implies that in this study the probability of making Type II error of the statistical test is likely to be high[6].

8.4. SUMMARY AND CONCLUSION

This chapter reviews earlier works of estimating production function and technological change. A general C-D production function with embodied technology, technology related inputs, company characteristics, and regional factors is applied to 1985 and 1990 survey data for textile-apparel and computer-electronics manufacturers.

The direct comparison of parameter estimates for 1985 and those for 1990 suggests that there exist some technological changes: (1) labor input becomes more productive as time passes on, (2) productivity of production capital is constant, (3) technology embodied in new equipment is increasingly more important to production and productivity, (4) although return to R & D capital is always much higher than that to production capital for both industry groups, productivity of R & D capital in the textile-apparel industries appears to fall over time, while the productivity of R & D in computer-electronics increases, (5) contribution of neutral technological change to production level increases over time, and (6) company characteristics and regional variables have moderate influences on production and the influences are constant over the five-year period.

A very stringent test is imposed on the estimates of technological change. Most of the technological variation over the period is not statistically significant. The only significant evidence is the technological change biased against R & D capital relative to production capital in the textile-apparel industries. Input in improving or adopting advanced management system becomes more important to production in textile-apparel.

From the research technique used and the statistical estimates obtained, the researcher concludes that direct comparison and stringent test can yield very different results. In most earlier research, only the direct comparison method is used, resulting in conclusion which may not be very convincing. Applying the rigorous test, however, researchers are very likely to end up with a conclusion of unbiased technological change, rejecting a hypothesis of biased technological progress when the hypothesis is actually true. Some compromise may have to be made when assessing the nature of technological change.

Appendix 8: OLS Estimates of Production Functions with Additional Variables

Table A8.1 Estimates for Textile-Apparel Companies

Variable	Equation 1 (1985) Estimate	Std Err	Equation 2 (1990) Estimate	Std Err
INTERCEPT	3.3898	(2.200)	4.8999**	(2.316)
W-EMP	0.4749**	(0.057)	0.4945**	(0.051)
P-EMP	0.1107**	(0.052)	0.1280**	(0.050)
K-BD	0.1244**	(0.022)	0.1190**	(0.021)
K-UTLZ	0.1031**	(0.026)	0.0972**	(0.026)
K-R&D	0.0149**	(0.006)	0.0110**	(0.005)
PATENT	0.0453	(0.031)	0.0324	(0.023)
K-CC	0.0035	(0.020)	-0.0085	(0.017)
K-MCN	0.0355**	(0.014)	0.0200	(0.013)
K-MNG	-0.0325	(0.020)	0.0242	(0.020)
K-TRN	0.0302	(0.020)	0.0029	(0.019)
K-AGE	-0.0372**	(0.010)	-0.0491**	(0.010)
W-EDUC	-0.1108	(0.298)	-0.1537	(0.423)
W-EXP	0.0550	(0.071)	0.0966	(0.065)
P-EDUC	0.1240	(0.350)	-0.2202	(0.506)
P-EXP	-0.0390	(0.065)	-0.0517	(0.067)
HQ-CNTY	-0.3277	(0.261)	-0.2783	(0.253)
HQ-STATE	-0.0924	(0.287)	-0.0269	(0.281)
HQ-US	-0.2931	(0.272)	-0.1761	(0.262)
AGE-CMPNY	0.0620	(0.054)	-0.0032	(0.051)
BUYCRTF	-0.0185	(0.091)	0.0230	(0.087)
SALECRTF	0.0033	(0.070)	-0.0084	(0.067)
R&DCRDT	0.2576*	(0.134)	0.2806**	(0.126)
COLLEGE	0.0302	(0.093)	0.0328	(0.097)
PCMINC	0.0240	(0.068)	0.0049	(0.065)
POP	-0.1114	(0.163)	-0.1204	(0.166)
TXTLE	0.0383	(0.039)	0.0442	(0.034)
TXTLW	0.2388	(0.475)	0.2377	(0.395)
APPRLE	0.0286	(0.035)	0.0330	(0.036)
APPRLW	-0.0953	(0.258)	-0.1939	(0.241)
AIR	0.0478	(0.029)	0.0170	(0.026)
TRNSVC	-0.0534	(0.034)	0.0088	(0.036)
CMMNCT	-0.0482	(0.055)	-0.0271	(0.049)
UTILIT	0.0237	(0.041)	0.0730*	(0.042)
FIRE	-0.0135	(0.115)	-0.0099	(0.106)
BUSSVC	-0.0542	(0.060)	-0.0197	(0.040)
ANUSE	-0.0596	(0.052)	-0.0360	(0.047)
HEALTH	0.0922	(0.096)	0.1328	(0.092)
EDUCAT	0.0054	(0.032)	0.0119	(0.030)
SCLSVC	0.0514	(0.064)	-0.0195	(0.060)
ENGNRG	0.1096**	(0.054)	0.0848	(0.065)
Adj. R-Sq.	0.8072		0.8250	

Note: * and ** indicate statistically significant at 90% and 95% levels respectively.

Table A8.2 Estimates for Computer-Electronics Companies

Variable	Equation 1 (1985) Estimate	Std Err	Equation 2 (1990) Estimate	Std Err
INTERCEPT	-0.5885	(3.047)	3.5459	(3.689)
W-EMP	0.2090**	(0.072)	0.2435**	(0.077)
P-EMP	0.4787**	(0.061)	0.4717**	(0.068)
K-BD	0.0637	(0.051)	0.1878**	(0.053)
K-UTLZ	0.1024**	(0.034)	0.0198	(0.048)
K-R&D	0.0517*	(0.027)	0.0942*	(0.050)
PATENT	0.0025	(0.030)	0.0215	(0.024)
K-CC	0.0296	(0.027)	0.0053	(0.026)
K-MCN	0.0223	(0.019)	0.0180	(0.022)
K-MNG	0.0094	(0.028)	0.0011	(0.033)
K-TRN	-0.0004	(0.032)	-0.0118	(0.033)
K-AGE	-0.0283**	(0.013)	-0.0542**	(0.018)
W-EDUC	0.0225	(0.418)	-0.1709	(0.657)
W-EXP	0.0657	(0.100)	0.0768	(0.112)
P-EDUC	0.1080	(0.224)	0.0885	(0.453)
P-EXP	-0.0292	(0.105)	-0.0380	(0.116)
HQ-CNTY	-0.2273*	(0.130)	-0.1679	(0.139)
HQ-STATE	-0.0236	(0.241)	0.2666	(0.249)
STANDARD	0.0286	(0.116)	0.0628	(0.176)
AGE-CMPNY	0.1598*	(0.090)	-0.0563	(0.097)
BUYCRTF	-0.0130	(0.095)	-0.0267	(0.105)
SALECRTF	-0.0925	(0.074)	-0.0019	(0.076)
R&DCRDT	0.1154	(0.166)	-0.1303	(0.176)
COLLEGE	0.1809	(0.147)	0.0907	(0.169)
PCMINC	0.0295	(0.086)	0.0554	(0.086)
POP	0.3864	(0.288)	0.3943	(0.338)
CMPTRE	-0.0912	(0.067)	-0.0244	(0.060)
CMPTRW	0.5690	(0.454)	-0.1707	(0.415)
ELECE	-0.0623	(0.051)	-0.0498	(0.055)
ELECW	0.3620	(0.327)	-0.1401	(0.372)
AIR	0.1288**	(0.053)	0.0568	(0.052)
TRNSVC	-0.0538	(0.068)	-0.1724**	(0.083)
CMMNCT	-0.2912*	(0.163)	-0.1079	(0.141)
UTILIT	-0.0481	(0.093)	0.0770	(0.108)
FIRE	0.0055	(0.238)	-0.0165	(0.259)
BUSSVC	0.1082	(0.202)	-0.0598	(0.198)
AMUSE	0.1013	(0.140)	0.1804	(0.154)
HEALTH	-0.2864	(0.188)	-0.3970*	(0.231)
EDUCAT	0.0650	(0.067)	0.1346**	(0.064)
SCLSVC	0.0851	(0.184)	0.0133	(0.177)
ENGNRG	-0.1325	(0.126)	-0.0412	(0.178)
Adj. R-Sq.	0.8257		0.7892	

Note: * and ** indicate statistically significant at 90% and 95% levels respectively.

Notes

1. Equation (21) in his article should be $\beta_3=\beta_4=\beta_5$, not $\beta_3=\beta_4=-\beta_5$. Correspondingly, the labor share equation (23) should be $\partial LnY/\partial LnL = \beta = \beta_1 + \beta_3(LnL + LnK)$ rather than $\partial LnY/\partial LnL=\beta=\beta_1+\beta_3Ln(L/K)$. If he used his specification to estimate the equation, the whole results are wrong.

2. Elimination of the effect of company attributes on input-output relationship in fixed effect model, when the company attribute variables are missing, can be justified as follows: equation $Y_t= \sum \alpha_i D_i + \sum \beta_j X_{jt}$ minus $Y_t^{bar}= \sum \alpha_i D_i^{bar} + \sum \beta_j X_{jt}^{bar}$ results in an equation without fixed company attributes D_i's, $y_t= \sum \beta_j x_{jt}$, where uppercase Y and X represent the original measures and lowcase y and x are the deviations from means. The estimation of equation $y_t= \sum \beta_j x_{jt}$ can provide unbiased estimates of β_j while excluding the fixed company attributes.

3. Griliches (1986) estimates a general C-D production function using 1967, 1972, and 1977 company level data. The estimates show that return to scale with respect to labor and capital is 0.828, 0.822, and 0.902 for basically the same companies in 1967, 1972, and 1977 respectively (see Table 2, Griliches 1986).

4. Using CBP data, this author computed that in 1988 average annual wage rates in textile, apparel, computer, telecommunication equipment, electronics components industries are $17,720, $13,628, $31,701, $29,313, and $24,622 respectively. No separate figures for production workers and technical/ professional employees are available. But it is known that professionals in textile and apparel industries are about five percent of total employment as opposed to over twenty percent of total employment in computer and electronics industries (refer to sample means in this study and Smith 1989).

5. The sample means of accumulated value of the input in improving management system in 1985 is $76,000 as opposed to $194,000 in 1990.

6. One makes a Type II error by accepting a null hypothesis when the hypothesis is in fact false. In the statistical test performed, the null hypothesis is that there is no biased technological change. The null hypothesis test is translated into the test of significance level of interactive terms of 1990 dummy and the producer inputs.

9 Conclusion

This research consolidated the relevant theories and methods in economics, regional science, and economic geography, and developed an analytical framework and a set of operational equations to examine company production and productivity growth. Applying the analytical framework and the operational equations to a unique data set from a nationwide survey, this research systematically investigated the direct and indirect contributions of technology and regional factors to production and productivity growth. This chapter concludes the research findings and briefly addresses theoretical and policy implications of the study.

9.1. CONTRIBUTION OF TECHNOLOGY TO PRODUCTION AND PRODUCTIVITY GROWTH

The theoretical justification and the empirical estimation both suggest that technological progress and technology related physical inputs give rise directly to production and labor productivity growth. They also suggest that technological progress and technological inputs indirectly contribute to production and labor productivity growth by raising technological efficiency and inducing high-return producer internal inputs.

9.1.1. Direct Contribution

The empirical evidence arising from this study shows that embodied technology and knowledge/skills account for a significant part of production and labor productivity growth. First, technology embodied in capital contributes positively to growth. The traditional measure, average age of capital stock, is a useful but conservative proxy of embodied technology. Reduction in the weighted average age of capital stock of computer-electronics companies stimulates production and productivity growth, while aging of capital stock of textile-apparel companies hinders production and productivity from growth. This study clearly demonstrates that an even larger part of the contribution of embodied technology to production and productivity growth is absorbed by the intercept in an empirical study. This part of contribution can only be estimated using an indirect method. The estimated rate of technological progress embodied in new capital, $\lambda_k \approx 4$ percent per year, appears to be consistent and stable for the technologically very different industries. Embodied technological progress is responsible for a production and labor productivity growth of about 0.8 percent per year, even if the average age of capital remains unchanged over time.

Second, knowledge and skills embodied in labor inputs can amount to an important part of production and productivity growth, but the importance is strikingly different between different labor inputs and across different industries. The most disturbing divergence is that knowledge or skills in technical/ professional/ managerial personnel apparently has positive influence on production and production growth, but knowledge or skills of production workers makes no direct contribution to production and productivity growth. The findings suggest that technological change in modern production tends to place workers in a disadvantaged position. The empirical findings also reveal a subtle difference between the two industry groups, implying a technological difference between the two groups. Specifically, accumulated professional experience, but not advanced fundamental knowledge, is a treasure in the technologically stable textile-apparel industries. Conversely, advanced fundamental knowledge, but not technical and professional experience, is a key factor in the technologically very dynamic computer-electronics industries. Also notable, these estimates are conservative, since a part of the contribution of the embodied knowledge and skills cannot be explicitly estimated. Estimated returns to labor inputs indicate that after controlling for the embodied knowledge and skill, the marginal product of technical and professional labor input is 1.5 times as high as that of production worker input of textile-apparel companies ($26,800 vs. $17,900) and 2.5 times that of computer-electronics companies ($57,400 vs. $22,000). Therefore, production and productivity growth in computer-electronics industries are more crucially dependent on technical and professional labor input than on production worker input. If these estimates reflect a general trend of dependence of technologically advanced industries on sophisticated human capital input, the U.S. major industrial sectors will experience structural reform in labor inputs and labor market as technology advances and diffuses throughout most sectors of the national economy.

Third, the contribution of neutral technological change to production and productivity growth is negligible when the estimation incorporates important technology related internal inputs and regional contextual factors. The empirical results support the justification that neutral technological change is actually not 'fallen from heaven like manna'; instead, there are a set of specific factors responsible for the 'unexplained residual' of growth. These specific sources of production and productivity growth are embodied technology, technology related physical inputs, and regional contextual factors.

Fourth, R & D input directly leads to production and productivity growth for both industry groups. In textile-apparel industries, investments in patent purchase/license and employee training make an additional contribution to production and productivity growth. These technology related physical inputs account for a production and labor productivity growth of about 0.66 percent per year for textile-apparel companies, and about 0.30 percent per year for computer-electronics companies. Considering the small amounts of these technological inputs relative to production capital, one may infer that investment in these technological inputs are particularly effective to production and labor productivity growth.

Evidently, embodied technological progress (including the estimate of the part absorbed into the intercept) and growth in technological physical inputs give rise directly to a similar amount of annual production and labor productivity growth for textile-apparel and computer-electronics companies: 1.8% vs. 1.6% annually. The direct contribution of technology to production and labor productivity growth for textile-apparel producers is not less than that for computer-electronics companies.

9.1.2. Indirect Contribution

This research adopts two sets of measures to examine the indirect contribution of technology to production and productivity growth. One set of the measures is the influence of technological progress and technological inputs on the efficiency of production. The other is the induced producer internal inputs attributable to technological progress and technological inputs.

Technological efficiency in this study is measured by total factor productivity (TFP) and its component measures: neutral technological progress and economies of scale. Evidently, TFP is a better empirical indicator than economies of scale to measure technological efficiency, although the two measures are inversely related to each other. On the other hand, TFP and neutral technological change are two similar measures both conceptually and empirically. The estimates suggest that TFP and neutral technological progress are more suitable than economies of scale to measure technological efficiency in empirical studies. Educational attainment and experience of employees, technology embodied in new equipment, and other technology related inputs are important contributors to companies' production efficiency. Technology related physical inputs contribute more to efficiency growth in computer-electronics than in textile-apparel.

The second part of the indirect contribution of technology to production and productivity growth is estimated using factor demand functions for technology related producer inputs. The estimates show that embodied technology has an inducement effect on the technological inputs, and that the technological inputs can affect each other, although the inducement effect and the mutual influence have complex patterns. All types of technology-related activities, R & D or adoption of existing technologies, are complementary to each other. Once a company makes one technological input (technical and professional input, R & D, or adoption of advanced technologies), the company will almost certainly explore the potential of all other technological inputs, especially in textile-apparel industries. This relatively consistent pattern of technological inputs clearly divides all producers into two distinct groups. One group actively promotes technological progress by making a variety of technological inputs and occupies a technologically advanced position. The other merely conducts routine production without pursuing a technological edge. The outcome of the race between the two groups in competitive markets is predictable: unless factor cost remains as a critical variable, there is no room for those technologically stagnant firms to survive.

9.2. CONTRIBUTION OF REGIONAL FACTORS TO PRODUCTION AND PRODUCTIVITY GROWTH

This study conceptually elaborates the notion of restricted input in production theory. The study also empirically proves the relevance and importance of regional factors to production and productivity growth. The empirical estimates of the growth equations indicate that within a production theoretical framework, regional contextual factors can influence production and productivity growth directly. Regional factors also raise technological efficiency and induce producer technological inputs as well, indirectly contributing to production and productivity growth. However, compared with many producer internal inputs, the regional contextual factors play a more complex role in companies' production. Therefore, empirical research findings should be interpreted with caution, and further research on the impact of regional factors on production and productivity growth are required. Interpretation presented is tentative and, to some extent, speculative.

9.2.1. Direct Contribution

As proposed earlier, industries rely on regional factors differently due to their different input combination. Technologically advanced industries are influenced by a wide array of regional services and technological externalities, whereas technologically stable and standardized sectors depend on low factor costs more than sophisticated regional services and other contextual factors.

The empirical findings are consistent with the conceptual justification. The influence on production and productivity growth of regional factors, including regional services, is very limited for textile-apparel. The influence is stronger for computer-electronics, no matter what standard (e.g., the significance level of estimates, the number of significant regional factors, or the absolute and relative contribution of regional factors to production growth) is adopted. The empirical study shows that apparel producers grow faster in metro areas than in non-metro areas and computer-electronics companies benefit from regional consumer services and amenities, such as recreation and amusement services, and health services. Textile producers rely less on regional externalities and all services sectors. In general, the direct contribution of regional factors to production and productivity growth in computer-electronics is greater than that in textile-apparel.

9.2.2. Indirect Contribution

This study also examines indirect contribution of regional contextual factors to production and productivity growth using technological efficiency equations (i.e., TFP, neutral technological change, and economics of scale equations) and factor input functions. The research generates two sets of significant estimates.

The regional factors contribute to the technological efficiency of production of both industry groups. Regional impact on productivity growth is stronger for computer-electronics industries than for textile-apparel. In particular, regional communication services, R & D and testing services, utilities services, health services, recreation and amusement services, and localization economies significantly influence TFP, neutral technological change, or economies of scale of computer-electronics companies, while utilities services and education services can change the economies of scale and total factor productivity of textile-apparel industries respectively. The impacts of regional factors are more complex than technology related variables, with some factors facilitating firms' technological efficiency growth and some others adversely influencing the growth.

The second part of the indirect contribution of regional factors to production and productivity growth is evidenced by the significant estimates of factor demand functions. All technology related inputs except technical and professional labor input are more or less affected by broadly defined producer services and consumer services. Technical and professional labor input is related to consumer services more than producer services in both industry groups. Since each individual regional factor can be substitutable for one input while complementary to others, a proportionate growth of regional services cannot lead to a universal growth (or decline) of producer outlay in all technology-related activities. The effect needs to be examined case by case. Besides complementarity and substitutability between internal inputs and external factors, another force with regional influence may be the competition between manufacturing sectors and other sectors for limited local resources.

Combining the estimates of the several sets of different equations, the study apparently shows that regional contextual factors can contribute to production and productivity growth indirectly. Moreover, the indirect contribution is greater for computer-electronics industries than for textile-apparel.

9.3. THEORETICAL IMPLICATIONS

This study develops an analytical framework which examines the direct and indirect contributions of technology and regional factors to production and productivity growth from various angles. The results of the empirical study imply that regional external factors can be incorporated into traditional production functions, although these free or near-free external factors present difficulties to modeling input-output relationship. Further research is warranted to integrate regional factors into traditional economic theory. This study attempts to clarify how the free inputs can serve as direct inputs to production and also act as external forces to induce internal inputs, although operational difficulties have not yet been fully worked out (e.g., ambiguity of meanings of insignificant regional factors).

The research findings cast a doubt on the possibility for producers to achieve an equilibrium position. The question is not about the existence of the equilibrium position or the tendency for an economic agent to move toward this equilibrium. Instead, given the classic definition of producer equilibrium -- productions are optimized and the rates of return to all inputs for all producers are the same, the question is whether or not the producers can react to the disequilibrium forces fast enough to approach an equilibrium. Therefore, the related question is whether or not the equilibrium assumption is appropriate in empirical studies. There may exist a negative relationship between technological progress and producer equilibrium. If the estimated relationship is common to other technologically advanced sectors, economic equilibrium, which economic researches (especially cross sectional analyses) have so heavily relied on, may become a less meaningful proposition or assumption. Some significant modification or new theory may be called for in a technologically dynamic era.

Apparently, even if this study controls for knowledge and skills of different labor inputs, the rate of return to technical and professional labor input is persistently higher than that to production labor input, and the rate of return to the same labor input in computer-electronics is persistently higher than that in textile-apparel. This research findings imply that sectoral and factorial income distributions may move in an opposite direction of what neoclassic theory has long suggested. This evidence needs a different income distribution theory to interpret.

9.4. POLICY IMPLICATIONS

The empirical findings of this study have practical bearings on industrial development policies and production location decisions. Investment in R & D is a viable strategy to facilitate technological progress, stimulate production and productivity growth, and obtain high return on investment. Earlier research (e.g., Bernsten 1989) estimates that due to the spillover effect, the gross social return is twice as much as the private return. Therefore, private R & D is usually underinvested from a social standpoint. Estimates of this study depict a positive relationship between the use of R & D credit, the level of R & D investment, and production and productivity growth. R & D credit policies can be considered important and should be expanded, provided the social cost for the credit policy is smaller than net social gain. It is unlikely that the social cost of the policy can be as high as the net social return, which is the gross social return less the private return, estimated in the earlier research. To fill the gap between the existence of a R & D credit policy and the actual use of the credit, the R & D policy should be made easy to implement and the cost of using the credit should be lower. This can be a key factor for the policy to be effective.

The research findings provide companies with an encouraging message. All the companies ought to be actively engaged in R & D activities, regardless of the existence of R & D credit policies, because return on R & D is higher than that on conventional capital input and the competition between companies for a technologically advantaged position always exists. As an earlier study concluded, the firms that constantly introduce successful new technologies earlier than other firms earn higher-than-average profits all the time; firms that innovate somewhat later break even; and those that never innovate fall behind and leave the industry. (Dewar 1988).

Spending on patent purchase/license and investment in employee training are appropriate avenues to raise production and productivity growth rates in textile-apparel industries. The practical implication for individual textile-apparel companies is obvious. The research findings have similar implications for other technologically stable industries. Unlike R & D activities, returns to patent purchase and employee training can be effectively appropriated. Therefore, underinvestment should not occur in this case and any favorable public policy is theoretically unnecessary. On the other hand, reallocation of resources for the most efficient use can benefit the whole economy. It is desirable to inform the relevant economic agents of the opportunity to better use their resources if public agencies have reliable information concerning the benefit of making these inputs.

The estimated significant contribution of embodied technology to production and productivity growth has practical meanings both to public policy makers and private investors. To exploit the technology embodied in capital, private sectors should introduce new equipment in a timely manner. Because investment in production capital is a major part of total investment in private sectors, any public policy to affect this investment is likely to be very expensive and is likely to be biased in favor of one group of population and against other. Probably, the only feasible approach to facilitate progress and exploitation of the embodied technology is to show private investors the importance of embodied technology to production growth.

In contrast, it is easier to translate the significant estimates of professional education into a policy proposition. Individuals pay for their advanced professional education, at least in part. Investment in public higher education is highly rewarding, particularly in technologically dynamic fields. Higher education also has a strong spillover effect on the whole economy. Public expenditure in higher education is not an investment without social return, although the precise social cost-benefit is yet to be known. In the long run, investment in higher education is crucial to a country's competitive position in the world economy. Since an educated labor force can move from place to place, a policy of enhancing higher education is more relevant at the federal level than at any local level. Nevertheless, it is profitable for computer-electronics companies and probably other technologically advanced producers to invest more in professional training, including on-the-job and off-the-job formal education to update their technological capability. In contrast, it is desirable for textile-apparel companies to maintain a stable technical and professional crew and enrich employees' professional experience.

Regional factors contribute to production and productivity growth in a complex manner. No decisive conclusion has been reached. It may be important for regional developers and policy makers to build their strength in several selected producer and consumer services sectors in order to attract technologically advanced industries and foster growth. Because most regional factors have no or modest influence on production and productivity growth in textile-apparel industries, regional or local developers or policy makers cannot rely on the improvement of the regional business environment to attract and retain the technologically stable and standardized industries. As long as factor cost is the most important location factor, these industries will continue to migrate from high cost areas or countries to low cost areas or countries. The estimate of reliance of apparel producers on metro area markets suggests that a viable strategy for helping U.S. apparel companies to thrive is to hold and expand the upper segment of the product market by accessing affluent metro areas and focusing on the quality and fashion of their products.

9.5. RECOMMENDATION FOR FUTURE RESEARCH

This study assessed the contributions of technology and regional factors to production and productivity growth and the nature of technological change in two very different industry groups. Many new questions emerged from this study. Further research is called for to answer the questions.

Further research may better explore the influence of each regional factor on productivity growth if the research design is modified and different variables and data are employed. First, a stratified sampling method should be employed to collect more cases from non-metro areas (in the current study only 27 computer-electronics companies are located in non-metro areas) in order to increase the variation of regional factors. Second, there is a good deal of room for improvement of measurement of regional variables. For example, most regional services sectors are measured by employment and its growth rate. In the real world, the level and quality of services are not equal to the level of employment. Instead of using employment data, future study may use number of commercial flights to measure air transportation service, and use different communication technologies in place to measure communication services, and so on. Third, due to the unavailability of data at the time the analysis was done, many important regional factors such as educational attainment of regional population, local tax rate, accessibility, and interregional interaction (e.g., various potential indices) are not included. These omitted regional variables can be important factors to explain the regional variation of production and productivity growth. Moreover, omission of these relevant variables may have biased the estimates.

Research on the nature of technological change should be further advanced to reveal the impact of technological change on resource allocation. This study has developed an operational form to statistically test the usually hypothesized bias of technological change over time. However, the data for a 5-year time span may not be sufficient to detect the real change in production technology. A new data set covering a longer period needs to be developed to examine the nature of technological change.

The contributions of various labor inputs to production and productivity growth are very different. If production workers are doomed to be insignificant contributors to production and productivity growth and if production and productivity growth is determined by sophisticated technical and professional labor input, policy considerations of facilitating the transition and mitigating the pain of low skilled production workers should be justified and relevant action should be taken. Because of the significant bearings on policy consideration in an advanced society, further study on the contributions of different labor inputs to production and productivity growth are required.

References

Adams, J.D., 1990, 'Fundamental Stocks of Knowledge and Productivity Growth', *Journal of Political Economy*, Vol. 98, No. 4

Allen, R.G.D., 1967, 'Macroeconomic Theory', St. Martin's Press, New York

Anderla, G. and Dunning, A. 1987, 'Computer Strategies 1990-9, Technologies-Costs-Markets', John Wiley & Sons, New York

Antonelli, C., 1990, 'Induced Adoption and Externalities in the Regional Diffusion of Information Technology', *Regional Studies*, Vol 24, pp31-39

Barro, R.J., 1990 'Government spending in a Simple Model of Endogenous Growth', *Journal of Political Economy*, Vol. 98

Becker, G.S., Murphy, K.M., and Tamura, R., 1990, 'Human Capiral, Fertility, and Economic Growth', *Journal of Political Economy*, Vol. 98, No. 4

Beeson, P., 1987, 'Total Factor Productivity Growth and Agglomeration Economies in Manufacturing, 1959-73', *Journal of Regional Science*, Vol. 27, No.2

Bereau of Census, 1991, 'Manufacturing Technology: 1988', Bereau of Census, Washington D.C.

Bernsten, J.I., 1989, 'The Structure of Canadian Inter-Industry R&D Spillovers, and the Rates of Return to R&D', *The Journal of Industrial Economics*, Vol. XXXVII, pp315-28

Besen, S.M., 1968, 'Education and Productivity in U.S. Manufacturing: Some Cross-Section Evidence', *Journal of Plitical Economy*, Vol. 76

Bohrnstedt, G.W., 1983,'Measurement', in P.H.Rossi, J.D.Wright, and A.B.Anderson, ed., Handbook of Survey Research, Academic Press, New York

Branson, W.H., 1980, 'Macroeconomic Theory and Policy', Harper & Row, Publishers, New York

Christensen, L.R., Jorgenson,D.W., and Lau,L.J., 1971, 'Duality in the Theory of Production', *Econometrica*, Vol. 39, No. 4

Christensen, L.R., Jorgenson,D.W., and Lau,L.J., 1973, 'Transcendental Logarithmic Production Frontiers', *American Economic Review*, Vol. 63, Feb., 1973

Cline, W.R., 1987, 'The Future of world Trade in Textile and Apparel', Institute of International Economics, Washington, D.C.

De Long, J.B. and Summers, L., 1990, 'Equipment Investment and Economic Growth', NBER Working Paper No. 3515

Denison, E.F., 1962, 'The Sources of Economic Growth in the United States and Alternatives Before Us'

Denison, E.F., 1964, 'The Unimportance of the Embodied Question', *American Economic Review*, Vol 54, March 1964

------ , 1980, 'The Contribution of Capital to Economic Growth', *American Economic Review*, Vol. 70, May 1980

------ , 1985, 'The Trends in American Economic Growth, 1927-1982', Washington: The Brookings Institute

Dewar, M.E., 1988, 'Adopting New Manufacturing Technology: Can It Help Declining Manufacturing Industries?', *Economic Development Quarterly*, Vol. 2, No. 3.

Dickie, M. and Gerking, S., 1987, 'Interregional Wage Differentials: An Equilibrium Perspective', *Journal of Regional Science*, Vol. 27, No. 4

Dillman, D.A., 1977, 'Mail and Telephone Surveys: The Total Design Method', A Wiley-Interscience Publication, New York

Farber, S. C. and Newman, R.J., 1989, 'Regional Wage Differentials and The Spatial Convergence of Worker Characteristic Prices', *The Review of Economics and Statistics*, May 1989

Glasmeier, A., Hall, P., and Markusen, A., 1983, 'Recent Evidence on High Technology Industries Spatial Tendencies: A Preliminary Investigation', Working Paper No. 417, Institute of Urban and Regional Development, University of California, Berkeley

Gorden, R.J., 1989, 'The Postwar Evolution of Computer Prices', in D.W. Jorgenson and R. Landau (ed.), Technology and Capital Formation, The MIT Press, Cambridge, Massachusetts

Goto, A. and Suzuki, K., 1989, 'R&D Capital, Rate of Return on R&D Investment and Spillover of R&D in Japanese Manufacturing Industries', *The Review of Economics and Statistics*, Vol LXXI, Nov. 1989

Griliches, Z., 1963, 'The sources of Measured Productivity Growths, U.S. Agriculture 1940-1960,' *Journal of Political Economy*, Vol. 71, Aug. 1963

Griliches, Z., 1980, 'Return to Research and Development Expenditures in the Private Sector,' in J. W. Kendrick and B. Vaccara, eds., New Developments in Productivity Measurement, NBER Studies in Income and Wealth No. 44, Chicago: University of Chicago Press, 1980, 419-54.

------, 1980, 'R&D and the Productivity Slowdown', *American Economic Review*, Vol. 70, May 1980

------, 1984, 'Productivity and R & D at the Firm Level', in Z. Griliches, eds., R & D, Patents, and Productivity, Chicago, The University of Chicago 1984

------, 1986, 'Productivity, R&D, and Basic Research at the Firm Level in the 1970's', *American Economic Review*, Vol. 76, March 1986

Griliches, Z. and Lichtenberg,F., 1984, 'R&D and Productivity Growth at the Industry Level: Is There Still a Relationship?', in Zvi Griliches, eds., R&D, Patents, and Productivity, The University of Chicago Press, Chicago, 1984

Harrington, James W, Jr., 1986, 'Learning and Locational Change in the American Semiconductor Industry', in John Rees, eds., Technology, Regions, and Policy, Rowman & Littlefield, Publishers, Totowa, New Jersey

Harrod,R.F., 1956, 'Towards a Dynamic Economics', London

Heertje, A., 1977, 'Economics and Technology Change', Halsted Press, John Wiley & Sons, New York

Hicks, J., 1963, 'The Theory of Wages' Macmillan, London

Hulten, C.R., 1975, 'Technical Change and the Reproducibility of Capital', *American Economic Review*, Vol. 65, Dec 1975

------, 1979, 'On the Importantce of Productivity Change', *American Economic Review*, Vol. 69, March 1979

Hulten, C.R. and Wykoff, F.C., 1984, 'The Measurement of Economic Depreciation', in Charles R. Hulten, eds., Depreciation, Inflation, Taxation of Income from Capital, 1984

Hulten, C.R. and Schwab, M., 1984, 'Regional Productivity Growth in U.S. Manufacturing: 1951-78', *American Economic Review*, Vol. 74

Jaffe, A.B., 1986, 'Technological Opportunity and Spillovers of R&D: Evidence from Firms' Patents, Profits, and Market Value', *American Economic Review*, Vol. 76

Jorgenson, D.W., and Griliches, Z., 1967, 'The Explanation of Productivity Change', *Review of Economic Studies*, July 1967

Jorgenson, D.W., 1989, 'Capital as a Factor of Production', in Jorgenson, D.W., and Landau, R., ed. Technology and Capital Formation, The MIT Press

Katz, L.F., 1986, 'Efficiency Wage Theories: A partial Evaluation', NBER Macroeconomics Annual 1986

Kuznets, S., 1955, 'Economic Growth and Income Inequality', *American Economic Review*, Vol. 45, March 1955

Landau, R., 1989, 'Technology and Capital Formation', in D.W.Jorgenson and R.Landau ed. Technology and Capital Formation, The MIT Press

Levin, R.C., 1988, 'Appropriability, R&D Spending, and Technological Performance', *American Economic Review*, Vol. 78, May 1988

Lösch, A., 1940, 'The Economics of Location', Translated by Woglan, W.H., from Dieräumliche Ordnung der Wirtschaft, Yale University Press, New haven, Conn., 1940

Luger, M.I. 1986, 'Depreciation Profiles and Depresiation Policy in a Spatial Context', *Journal of Regional Science*, Vol. 26, No. 1

Luger, M.I. and Evans, W.N., 1988, 'Geographic Differences in Production Technology', *Regional Science and Urban Economics*, Vol. 18, pp399-424

Mchugh, R., and Lane, J., 1983, 'The Embodied Hypothesis: An Interregional Test', *The Review of Economics and Statistics*, 1983, pp323-27

Mchugh, R., and Lane, J., 1987, 'The Age of Capital, The Age of Utilized Capital, and Tests of The Embodiment Hypothesis', *The Review of Economics and Statistics*, 1987, pp362-67

Mansfield, E., 1968, 'Industrial Research and Technological Innovation: An Econometric Analysis' New York: Norton for the Cowles Foundation for Research in Economics, Yale University

Mansfield, E., 1980, 'Basic Research and Productivity Increase in Manufacturing', *American Economic Review*, Vol. 70, Dec. 1980

Mansfield, E., 1980, 'Comment on Productivity and R & D at the Firm Level' in Kendrick and Vaccara eds., New Development in Productivity Measurement and Analysis, The University of Chicago Press, Chicago

Mansfield, E., Rapoport, J., Romeo, A., Villani, E., Wabner, S., and Husic, F., 1977, 'The Production and Application of New Industrial Technology', New York, W.W. Norton

Markusen, A., 1986, 'Defense Spending and the Geography of High-Tech Industries' in John Rees, eds., Technology, Regions, and Policy, Rowman & Littlefield, Publishers, Totowa, New Jersey

Markusen, A., Hall,P., and Glasmeier,A., 1983, 'Recent Evidence on High Technology Industries Spatial Tendencies', Working Paper No. 417, Institute of Urban and Regional Development, University of Califonia, Berkeley

Markusen, A., P. Hall, and A. Glasmeier, 1986, 'High-Tech America: The What, How, and Why of the Sunrise Industries', Boston, MA: Allen and Irwin

Mitchell, R.C., and Carson, R.T., 1989, 'Using Surveys to Value Public Goods: The Contingent Valuation Method', Resources for the Future, Washington, D.C. 1989

Moomaw, R.L., 1987, 'Agglomeration Economies: Localization or Urbanization?', Urban Studies, 1987

Moomaw, R.L., 1986, 'Have Change in Localization Economies Been Responsible for Declining Productivity Advantages in Large Cities?', *Journal of Regional Science*, Vol. 26, No.1

Moomaw, R.L., and M. Williams, 1991, 'Total Factor Productivity Growth in Manufacturing: Further Evidence From the States', *Journal of Regional Science*, Vol. 31, No. 1

Nelson, R.R. 1964, 'Aggregate Production Function and Medium-Range Growth Projections', *American Economic Review*, Vol. 54, September 1964

Nelson, R.R., and Phelps, E.S., 1966, 'Investment in Humans, Technological Diffusion, and Economic Growth', *American Economic Review*, Vol. 56, March-June 1966

Office of Technology Assessment, 1984, 'Technology, Innovation, and Regional Development', Washinton, DC: U.S. Government Printing Office

Pack, H., 1987, 'Productivity, Technology and Industrial Development, A Case Study in Textiles' Oxford University Press

Pakes, A. and Schankerman, M. 1984, 'The Rate of Obsolescence of Patents, Research Gestation Lags, and the Private Rate of Return to Research Resources', in Zvi Griliches, eds., the University of Chicago Press, Chicago

Perroux, F. 1950, 'Economic Space, Theory, and Applications', *Quarterly Journal of Economics*, Vol. 64, pp90-92

------, 1955, 'Notes sur la notion de 'Pole de croissance'. Écomonie appliquée 7, pp307-20

Rees, J., Stafford, H.A., 1983, 'A Review of Regional Growth and Industrial Location Theory: Towards Understanding the Development of High-Technology Complexes in the U.S.', Paper prepared by the U.S. Congress Office of Technology Assessment

Rees, J., Briggs, R., and Oakey, R., 1986, 'Adoption of New Technology in the American Machinery Industry', in John Rees, eds., Technology, Regions, and Policy, Rowman & Littlefield, Publishers, Totowa, New Jersey

Rees, J., 1991, 'State Technolopgy Programs and Industry Experience in the United States', *Review of Urban and Regional Development Studies*, Vol. 3, 39-59

Romer,P.M., 1990, 'Endogenous Technological Change', *Journal of Political Economy*, Vol. 98, No. 5

Rosenberg, N., 1972, 'Technology and American Economic Growth', New York, Harper and Row

Rosenzweig, M.R., 1990, 'Population Growth and Human Capital Investments: Theory and Evidence', *Journal of Political Economy*, 1990, Vol. 98, No. 5

Sasaki, K., 1985, 'Regional Difference in Total Factor Productivity and Spatial Features, Empirical Analysis on the Basis of a Sectoral Translog Production Function', *Regional Science and Urban Economics*, Vol. 15, pp489-516

Scott, A.J. and Drayse, M.H., 1991, 'The Electronics Industry in Southern California: Growth and Spatial Development from 1945 to 1989', *The Review of Regional Studies*, Vol. 20, Spring 1991

Smith, E.D., 1989, 'Reflections on Human Resources in the Strategy of Rural Economic Development', *The Review of Regional Studies*, Vol. 19

Solow, R.M., 1956, 'A Contribution to the Theory of Economic Growth', *Quarterly Journal of economics*, Feb. 1956

Solow, R.M., 1957, 'Technical Change and the Aggregate Production Function', *Review of Economics and Statistics*, Aug. 1957, pp312-320

------, 1960, 'Investment and Technical Progress', in K.J.Arrow, S.Karlin and P.Suppes, eds., Mathematical Methods in Social Sciences, Stanford Univ. Press

------, 1962, 'Technical Progress, Capital Formation, and Economic Growth', *American Economic Review*, Vol. 52, May 1962

------, 1988, 'Growth Theory and After', *American Economic Review*, Vol. 78, June 1988

Sveikauskas, L., 1975, 'The Productivity of Cities', *Quarterly Journal of Economics*, pp393-413

Terleckyj, N.E., 1982, 'R & D and U.S. Industrial Productivity in the 1970s' in D.Sahal (ed.), The transfer and Utilization of Technical Knowledge, Lexington: Lexington Books

Terleckyj, N.E., 1984, 'Comment on R&D and Productivity Growth at the Industry Level', in Zvi Griliches, eds., R&D, Patents, and Productivity, The University of Chicago Press, Chicago

Thünen, H.Von, 1826, 'Isolated State', 1st edn, Hamburg

Toyne, B., Arpn,J.S., Barnett,A.H., Ricks,D.A., Shimp,T.A., 1984, 'The Global Textile Industry', George Allen & Unwin (Publishers) Ltd, London

Uno, Kimiko, 1986, 'Regional Translog Production Functions with Capital and Labor Inputs Differentiated by Educational Attainment', *Regional Science and Urban Economics*, Vol. 16

Varian, H.R., 1986, 'Microeconomic Analysis', W. W. Norton & Company, New York, 1986

Vernon, R., 1966, 'International Investment and International Trade in the Product Life Cycle', *Quarterly Journal of Economics*, Vol. 80, pp190-207

Weber, A., 1909, 'Theory of the Location of Industry', University of Chicago Press, Chicago, 1929, Translated by Friedrich, C.J., from Über den Standort der Industrien

Williams, M., 1985, 'Technical Efficiency and Region - The U.S. Manufacturing Sector 1972-1977', *Regional Science and Urban Economics*, Vol. 15

You, J.K., 1976, 'Embodied and Disembodied Technical Progress in the United States, 1929-1968', *The Review of Economics and Statistics*, pp123-27

Index